Parliament Great Britain.

The Beauties of the British Senate

Vol. 1

Parliament Great Britain.

The Beauties of the British Senate
Vol. 1

ISBN/EAN: 9783744715607

Printed in Europe, USA, Canada, Australia, Japan

Cover: Foto ©Suzi / pixelio.de

More available books at **www.hansebooks.com**

THE

BEAUTIES

OF THE

BRITISH SENATE:

TAKEN FROM THE

DEBATES OF THE LORDS AND COMMONS,

FROM THE

BEGINNING OF THE ADMINISTRATION
OF SIR ROBERT WALPOLE,

TO THE

END OF THE SECOND SESSION OF THE
ADMINISTRATION OF THE RIGHT HON.
WILLIAM PITT:

BEING

AN IMPARTIAL SELECTION OF, OR FAITHFUL EXTRACTS
FROM, THE MOST EMINENT SPEECHES, DELIVERED IN THE
COURSE OF A MOST IMPORTANT AND TRULY INTERESTING
PERIOD, OF MORE THAN FIFTY YEARS; SEVERALLY AR-
RANGED UNDER THEIR RESPECTIVE HEADS, WITH THE
NAMES OF THE MEMBERS, TO WHOM THEY ARE ASCRIBED,
ANNEXED THERETO.

TO WHICH IS PREFIXED,

THE LIFE OF SIR ROBERT WALPOLE.

VOL. I.

LONDON,

PRINTED FOR JOHN STOCKDALE, OPPOSITE BURLING-
TON-HOUSE, PICCADILLY.

M DCC LXXXVI.

ADVERTISEMENT.

THE extreme utility, as well as intrinfic merit of the following Work, is fo obvious, that the Editor has little more to obferve, than that it will be found equally candid and impartial.

While, however, he experiences every fatisfaction in the confidence he has, that it will have its admirers for fome of the fineft reading to be met with, he fuffers much in the fear he has, of being expofed to the cenfure of others, who may probably think he has either neglected them, or failed in the attempt he has made to do them juftice.

In his defence, he thinks it neceffary to reprefent, that the Debates of Parliament, for the laft fifty years, were found to produce fo many beauties, that it would have been altogether impracticable, however defirous he might have been of doing it, to have felected them all, at leaft, without running into a very expenfive and voluminous work indeed. He was, therefore, under the painful neceffity of paffing by a number of beauties deferving notice, and could only make choice of thofe that were the moft ftriking; determining, at the fame time, to give as much variety, and to include as many fpeakers as poffible.

Notwithftanding thefe difficulties in the way of rendering that complete and general fatisfaction he wifhed to afford, he trufts the Work will, neverthelefs, be found worthy univerfal patronage and fupport.

To the Public in general it will furnifh much ufeful and entertaining matter, while the Politician, and

Member of Parliament in particular, will find it a fource of the moft neceffary information and inftruction. It will be found to contain the Speeches of the firft Speakers that ever ornamented the Britifh Senate, and their opinions on the moft important and interefting topics.

The whole is fo arranged, as to exhibit, in one point of view, all the Eloquence, the Wit, or Satire, &c. that has been in the Lords and Commons, from the Adminiftration of SIR ROBERT WALPOLE, down to the prefent time, with the name of each Member annexed to the Beauty afcribed to him.

Thofe Beauties that would, from the nature of them, admit of it, will be found fhort and concife; others more at large, either as meriting it from their excellence, or to prevent their being disjointed or unintelligible; whilft fome are felected entirely from the vaft mafs of matter they contain, or the great fund of knowledge they poffefs.

Upon the whole—the Editor flatters himfelf, that the BEAUTIES of the BRITISH SENATE will prove particularly acceptable to thofe who have not the Debates of Parliament, and ferve as a valuable companion to thofe who have; nor be thought unworthy, either as an elegant or ufeful work, a place in the LIBRARY of every GENTLEMAN in the Britifh Empire.

January 26, 1786.

INDEX

INDEX

TO

VOLUME THE FIRST.

INDEX.

LIFE

L I F E

O F

Sir ROBERT WALPOLE.

THE commencement of the Adminiftration of Sir Robert
Walpole, having been judged a proper period for beginning the Beauties of the Britifh Senate, it may naturally be expected that the work fhould be preceded by fome account of
his life.

Sir Robert Walpole, whofe political hiftory forms as important an æra as any to be met with in the annals of the Britifh empire, was born on the 6th of September, 1674, at
Houghton, in Norfolk, and appears to have been educated on
the foundation of Eton School. He was elected to King's Col-
lege, in Cambridge, and admitted in the year 1681; but fucceeding to the family eftate by the death of his elder brother,
he refigned his Fellowfhip.

This great political character firft took his feat in the Houfe
of Commons in the year 1700, for King's Lynn, which Borough he reprefented in feveral fucceeding Parliaments; and in
the year 1705 he had the honour of being nominated one of the
Council to Prince George of Denmark, Lord High Admiral of
England. In 1707 he was appointed Secretary at War, and in
1709 was made Treafurer to the Navy. In the year following,
however, upon a change of the Miniftry, he was removed from
all his pofts, and continued out of office during the whole of
the Queen's reign.

In the year 1711, he was voted by the Houfe of Commons
guilty of an high breach of truft, and notorious corruption in
his

his office of Secretary at War; and it was refolved, that he fhould be committed to the Tower, and expelled the Houfe. Upon a cool and difpaffionate review of this affair, it has not been thought that there was fufficient proof to juftify the feverity ufed towards him; and, perhaps, his attachment to the Marlborough Miniftry, and his great influence in the Houfe, owing to his popular eloquence, were the true caufes of his cenfure and imprifonment, as they had been before of his advancement. All the Whigs, however, on this occafion, confidered him as a kind of martyr in their caufe.

He was re-elected for the borough of Lynn, and though the Houfe declared his election void, yet they perfifted in the choice. On the death of the Queen a revolution of politics took place, and the Whig Party prevailed both at Court and in the Senate, and in a few days Sir Robert Walpole was appointed Receiver and Paymafter General of all the Guards and Garrifons, and likewife a Privy Counfellor. Thefe promotions, it is probable, he owed to his having recommended himfelf to the Houfe of Hanover, by his zeal for its caufe, when the Commons confidered the ftate of the nation with regard to the Proteftant fucceffion, and the affurance he procured of the Houfe to the new King, upon its Addrefs of condolence and congratulation, " *That the Commons would make good all Parliamentary funds.*"

On the opening of a new Parliament, a Committee of Secrefy was chofen, to enquire into the conduct of the late Miniftry, of which Sir Robert Walpole was the Chairman; and, by his management, articles of impeachment were read againft the Earl of Oxford, Lord Bolingbroke, the Duke of Ormond, and the Earl of Strafford. The eminent fervice he was thought to have done the Crown and the nation, by the vigorous profecution of thofe Minifters, who were deemed the chief inftruments of the Peace, was foon rewarded by the extraordinary promotions of Firft Commiffioner of the Treafury, and Chancellor and Under Treafurer of the Exchequer.

In

In two years time, a mifunderftanding appeared amongft his Majefty's fervants, and it became evident, that the intereft of Secretary Stanhope and his adherents, began to outweigh that of the Exchequer, and that Sir Robert Walpole's power was vifibly on the decline.   King George had purchafed of the King of Denmark the duchies of Bremen and Verden, which his Danifh Majefty had gained by conqueft from Charles XII. of Sweden.   The Swedifh Hero, enraged to fee his dominions publicly fet to fale, conceived a refentment againft the purchafer, and formed a defign to gratify his revenge on the electorate of Hanover.   Upon a meffage, fent to the Houfe of Commons by the King, Secretary Stanhope moved for a fupply, to enable his Majefty to concert fuch meafures with foreign Princes and States, as might prevent any change or apprehenfions from the defigns of Sweden for the future.   This occafioned a warm debate, in which it is to be remarked, that Walpole kept a profound filence.   The Country-party infifted, that fuch a proceeding was contrary to the Act of Settlement.   They infinuated, that the peace of the empire was only a pretence, but that the fecurity of the new acquifitions was the real object of this unprecedented fupply; and they took occafion to obferve too, that his Majefty's own Minifters feemed to be divided. But Walpole thought proper on this furmife to fpeak in favour of the fupply, which was carried by a majority of four voices only.

In a day or two he refigned all his places to the King.   Various have been the motives faid to have induced Sir Robert Walpole to take this ftep.   If the true caufe, however, of his defection from the Court had been his difapprobation of the meafures then purfuing, his conduct muft be acknowledged to have been, in this inftance, truly noble and praife-worthy.   But they who confider the intrigues of party, and that he fpoke in favour of thofe meafures, will find little room to fuppofe, that his refignation proceeded from any attachment to liberty or love of his country.   He refigned, moft probably, with a view of being reftored with greater power; and the number of his friends,

who

who accompanied him in his refignation, prove it to have been, or at leaft to have very much the appearance, of its having been a mere factious movement.

On the day of his refignation he brought in the Sinking Fund Bill, which he prefented as a country Gentleman, and which, he faid, he hoped would not fare the worfe for having two fathers, and that his fucceffor (Mr. Stanhope) would bring it to perfection. His being called the father of a project, which hath fince been employed fo often to other purpofes than were at firft declared, gave his enemies frequent opportunities for fatire and ridicule; and it hath been farcaftically obferved, that the father of this fund appeared in a very bad light, when viewed in the capacity of a nurfe.

In the courfe of the debates on this Bill, a very fharp conteft took place between Walpole and Stanhope. On fome fevere reflections thrown upon him, the former loft his ufual ferenity of temper, and replied with great warmth and impetuofity. The acrimony on both fides produced very unbecoming expreffions, the betraying of private converfation, and the revealing a piece of fecret hiftory, viz. " *The fcandalous practice of felling places and reverfions,*" which occafioned a Member to fay on the occafion—" I am forry to fee thefe two great men fall foul of one " another: however, in my opinion, we muft ftill look on " them as patriots and fathers of their country: and fince they " have by mifchance difcovered their nakednefs, we ought, ac- " cording to the cuftom, to cover it, by turning our backs " upon it."

Sir Robert Walpole, in the next Seffion of Parliament, oppofed the Miniftry in every thing, and even exceeded Wyndham or Shippen in patriotifm. Upon a motion in the Houfe for continuing the army, he made a fpeech of above an hour long, and pointed out the danger of a ftanding army in a free country, with all the powers of eloquence. Early in 1720, the rigour of the Patriot began to foften, and the complaifance of the Courtier to appear, and he was again appointed Paymafter

of

of the Forces, and feveral of his friends were found foon after in the lift of promotions. No doubt now remained of his entire converfion to Court meafures; for before the end of the year, we find him pleading as ftrongly for the forces required by the War-office, as he had before declared againft them, even though at this time the fame pretences for keeping them on foot did not exift.

He was foon after again appointed Firft Lord of the Treafury, and Chancellor of the Exchequer; and when the King went abroad in 1723, he was nominated one of the Lords Juftices for the Adminiftration of Government, and was fworn fole Secretary of State. About this time he received another diftinguifhed mark of the Royal favour; his eldeft fon, then on his travels, being created a Peer, by the title of Baron Walpole, of Walpole. In 1725 he was made Knight of the Bath, and the year after Knight of the Garter.

Sir Robert Walpole, however, refigned all his places on the 18th of February, in the year 1741, after having been Firft Lord of the Treafury, and Under Treafurer of the Exchequer, ever fince the 4th of April, 1721, a courfe of nearly twenty years. He had fucceeded the Earl of Sunderland in the former fituation, and Mr. Aiflabie in the latter. Three days after his refignation, his Majefty was pleafed to create him Earl of Orford, Vifcount Walpole, and Baron of Houghton, and to allow him a penfion of 4000 l. though upon his removal, and the alterations made in the Miniftry, there were public rejoicings in London and Weftminfter; but pofterity will be the beft Judges of the advantages the nation derived from the change.

The meafures of his Adminiftration, during the long time he remained *prime*, or rather *fole* Minifter, have been often canvaffed with all the feverity of critical inquiry. It is difficult to difcern the truth through the exaggerations and mifreprefentations of party; and it muft be left to the impartial Hiftorian to fet it in a proper light. The Reader need not be informed, that he was long called " *The Father of Corruption*," though, perhaps,

2

perhaps, he had only been an improver of it ; but notwithstanding this, and that he boasted that he knew every man's price,
he found himself, at length, unable any longer to procure a majority in the House of Commons.

There is an instinctive propensity in mankind to think reve-
rently of the mysteries of Government; and a person who is
able, in whatever manner, to preside over the affairs of a nation
for a considerable period, is infallibly exalted into a great man.
In pursuance of this propensity, we have heard much of the abilities of Sir Robert Walpole. He had a great fluency and rea-
diness of language ; and though what he uttered was neither
nervous nor elegant, yet it had its weight with those, who
estimate the value of a speech by its length, and think him the
best Orator, who can harangue upon all occasions without hesi-
tation. He was well skilled in parliamentary business, and pos-
sessed a certain easiness of foul, and calloufness of sensation,
which made him proof against all attacks, and raised him superior to every embarrassment. By an unwearied attention to
figures and calculations, he had acquired a knowledge of the
subject of finance, which his system of Government did not
always allow him to turn to the greatest advantage. That system was founded on the narrowest and most detestable principles. As he had never known what it was to be concerned in
a popular Administration, he was acquainted with no means of
preserving his power but that of corruption. The maxim which
he pursued and avowed is well known. He ridiculed the very
ideas of patriotism and public spirit, thought self-interest the
wisest principle by which a man could be actuated, and bribery
the most elevated and comprehensive system that ever entered
into the human mind.

After this, it is but fair to add, that in the well-known debate
relating to *Steele*, for publishing the " *Crisis*," he greatly distin-
guished himself in behalf of liberty ; and the *Schism Bill* soon
after gave him a fine opportunity of exerting his powers, and
appearing

appearing in the character of the champion of civil and religious liberty.

But whatever objections his minifterial conduct may be liable to, in his *private* character, he is univerfally allowed to have poffeffed very amiable and benevolent qualities. That he was a tender parent, a kind mafter, a beneficent patron, a firm friend, an agreeable companion, are points that have feldom been difputed him; and Pope, who was no friend to Courts and Courtiers, hath paid him *gratis*, an handfomer compliment on the laft of thefe heads, than any liberality could ever purchafe. In anfwer to his friend, who perfuades him to go and fee Sir Robert, he fays——

" Seen him I have, but in his happier hour,
" Of focial pleafure ill-exchang'd for power;
" Seen him, uncumber'd with the venal tribe,
" Smile without art, and win without a bribe."

No Minifter, perhaps, ever diftinguifhed himfelf more by his writing than Sir Robert Walpole. About the end of Queen Anne's reign, and the beginning of George the Firft, he wrote the following pamphlets.—1. " The Sovereign's Anfwer to the Gloucefterfhire Addrefs." The Sovereign meant Charles Duke of Somerfet, fo nick-named by the Whigs. 2. " Anfwer to the Reprefentation of the Lords on the State of the Navy." 3. " The Debts of the Nation ftated and confidered in four pages, 1710." 4. " The thirty-five millions accounted for, 1710." 5. " A Letter from a Foreign Minifter in England to Mofieur Pittecum, 1710." 6. " Four Letters to a Friend in Scotland upon Sacheverell's Trial." 7. " A Short Hiftory of the Parliament." 8. " The South-Sea Scheme confidered." 9. " A Pamphlet againft the Peerage Bill, 1719." 10. " The Report of the Secret Committee, June 9, 1715."

Upon the whole, the firft remarkable concuffion that the Government of Walpole occafioned in the minds of the governed,

was

was owing to a fcheme he had formed for extending the Laws of Excife, by which, under fpecious pretences, he hoped to fwell the number of dependents, and add to the means of corruption. But what filled up the meafure of his unpopularity, was his inglorious fyftem with relation to foreign affairs. As he was the Minifter of the King, and not the Man of the People, he had long facrificed the interefts, and lavifhed the treafures of Great-Britain, in fubferviency to a fyftem of continental meafures, to which his Mafter was invincibly attached.

After his refignation, Sir Robert Walpole fpent the remainder of his life in tranquillity and retirement, and died in the year 1745, in the 71ft year of his age.

B E A U-

BEAUTIES

OF THE

BRITISH SENATE.

I Rife not only to offer my fentiments againft the terms of the Addrefs propofed, but likewife to make a Motion. It has, Sir, upon fuch an occafion, been the ancient cuftom of this Houfe, to prefent an Addrefs of Thanks to his Majefty, for his moft gracious Speech from the Throne, but fuch Addreffes were in former days always in general terms; there were in them no flattering paragraphs, no long compliments made to the Throne, for tranfactions and fucceffes which had never been laid before the Houfe, and of which, by a neceffary con-fequence, the Houfe muft have been fuppofed to have been en-tirely ignorant : it is true, Sir, we have of late years, fallen into a cuftom of complimenting the Throne upon every fuch occafion with long Addreffes ; and this cuftom has been followed fo long, that I am afraid it may at laft become a Vote of courfe, to vote an Addrefs to his Majefty, in fuch terms as fhall be concerted by thofe very men, whofe meafures are approved of by the compliment made to the Throne. I confefs, Sir, that I am fo little of a courtier, that I cannot return thanks for what I know nothing of; nor can I applaud before I know a

Vol. I.   B   reafon

reafon for fuch applaufe. I am not at all againft an Addrefs of
Thanks in the ancient ufual ftyle : but tho' I fhould happen to
be fingle and alone in my oppofition, which I hope I fhall not,
yet I am refolved to oppofe addreffing in thofe terms ; for, if it
were for no other reafon than this, that fuch a Motion may not
ftand upon the Journals of the Houfe, as agreed to *nem. con.*
for if not taken notice of in time, fuch humble Addreffes to
the Throne may at laft come to pafs as matters of courfe, and
be as little regarded or oppofed, as fome affairs now are, which
at firft ftood a long conteft before they could be introduced.

It is no new thing in me to oppofe fuch Addreffes ; I always
have oppofed them ; and though I do not thereby appear to be
a good courtier, yet it fhews that I have fome refpect for the
honour and dignity of this Houfe : befides, when fuch Addreffes
have been propofed, it has been promifed, and we have been
affured, that no advantage fhould afterwards be taken of any
words contained in any complimentary part of fuch Addrefs :
but every Member in this Houfe knows, that when the Houfe
had an opportunity of examining things more particularly, and
Debates enfued thereupon, they have been told, that they could
not cenfure any of the paft tranfactions, becaufe they had approved of them all by their Addrefs of Thanks to his Majefty
for his moft gracious Speech from the Throne. I hope, for
the fake of my country, that all things are well ; that our affairs
both at home and abroad are in that profperous condition in
which they have been reprefented to us ; but as we cannot yet
judge from the effects, and as the treaties, from which this great
profperity and lafting tranquillity is to arife, have not yet been
laid before us, I cannot but look upon it as an anticipation of
the Refolutions of this Houfe, to thank his Majefty for thofe
Treaties, which we have not as yet had an opportunity either
to perufe or confider ; and therefore I move, that the firft part
only of the Motion already made fhould ftand, and that all the
other complimentary paragraphs fhould be left out.

Mr. Shippen, Jan. 13, 1732.

I can-

·I CANNOT agree to the terms for addreffing his Majefty, becaufe though every thing may now be well fettled upon a folid
and lafting foundation, yet I cannot think that our conduct has
in every refpect been right; or that the intereft of this nation
has been, by his Majefty's Minifters, principally and fteadily
purfued. At one time we were frightened out of our wits with
apprehenfions that the Pretender was to be put upon us, and
that without any reafon, for all that I have yet feen or heard
upon the fubject. Then Don Carlos was made fuch a giant of,
that he, that Infant, was to fwallow up and deftroy all the
powers of Europe; and at that time we fued to France for an
alliance, and befought their affiftance, by which we put it in
their power to commence a war whenever they pleafed: and
if they had not been more taken up with whims and difputes
about religion, than any wife nation ought to be, they would
certainly have involved us in a war, in conjunction with them,
and thereby would have made us affift them in recovering all
that they had loft in the two laft wars, the taking of which
from them had caft us fo much blood and treafure. Some time
after we fhook off all fears of the Pretender, Don Carlos was
again diminifhed to an ordinary fize, and then we began to
bully France as much as we had courted it before: fuch
conduct cannot appear to me to be right, at leaft it does
not appear to be fteady and uniform., Upon the other
hand, it muft be faid of the Imperial Court, that they have
acted with fteadinefs and prudence; they have properly adhered
to the natural interefts of their native country, and have fteadily
purfued the plan they had in view, through all the different.
fhapes in which the affairs of Europe have been put within
thefe few years; and by this firmnefs and refolution they have
at laft brought us to their own terms, and have accomplifhed
their defigns, notwithftanding the conjunction and alliance of
fo many formidable powers againft them: whereas we have been
obliged, in fome manner, to comply with the demands of almoft
every power we have treated with; and if by fuch means we

have

have at laſt got off by any tolerable conditions, it muſt be ſaid, that we have been like a man in a room, who wants to get out, and though the door be open, and a clear way to it, yet he ſtalks round the room, breaks his ſhins over a ſtool, tumbles over a chair, and at laſt, rumbling over every thing in his way, by chance finds the door and gets out, after abundance of needleſs trouble and unneceſſary danger.

Sir William Wyndham, Jan. 13, 1732.

I HAVE always been againſt long Addreſſes ; I am ready enough to agree to an Addreſs of Thanks to his Majeſty for his moſt gracious ſpeech from the Throne ; but ſuch Addreſs ought to be in the moſt conciſe terms, and the moſt general words : this was the antient uſage of Parliament, and I find but few of our old cuſtoms that are altered for the better : however, if we muſt go on with the cuſtom of making long-winded Addreſſes, I think we ought to take ſome notice of the ſpirit that is at preſent amongſt the people. It is very certain, that there are great fears, jealouſies, and ſuſpicions, out doors ; that ſomething is to be attempted this Seſſion of Parliament, which is generally thought to be deſtructive to the liberties, and to the trade of this nation. There is at preſent a moſt general and remarkable ſpirit amongſt the people, for protecting and defending their liberties and their trade, in oppoſition to thoſe attempts which they expect are to be made againſt both.

Mr. Shippen, Jan. 16, 1733.

As this is a new Parliament, I hope we ſhall begin with ſhewing a little more regard to the ancient cuſtom and dignity of Parliaments, than has been ſhewn of late years. In former times, the Addreſſes of this Houſe, in return to his Majeſty's Speech from the Throne, were always conceived in the moſt general terms. Our anceſtors would never condeſcend upon that occaſion, to enter into the particulars of his Majeſty's Speech : when they were to approach the King, and to declare

2   their

their affection and their fidelity to him, they thought it was inconfiftent with that fidelity they were to declare, to approve, upon that occafion, of any minifterial meafures, and much more fo, to declare their fatisfaction with meafures they knew, nothing about. This Houfe is the grand inqueft of the nation, appointed to inquire diligently, and to reprefent faithfully to the King, all the grievances of his people, and all the crimes and mifmanagement of his fervants; and therefore it muft always be a breach of our fidelity to our Sovereign, as well as a breach of our duty to the people, to approve blindly the conduct of his fervants. When we have examined diligently, and confidered deliberately the conduct of any Minifter, and are at laft fully convinced that he has acted prudently and wifely for the public good, it is then our duty to return him the thanks of the public, and to reprefent him as a faithful Minifter to his Mafter; but to make panegyrics upon the conduct of any of the King's fervants, before we have examined into it, is more like the language of flaves and fycophants to a Prime Minifter, than that of loyal and faithful fubjects to their Sovereign.

I muft acknowledge, Sir, that the Motion now made for addreffing his Majefty is more general, and more adapted to the ancient cuftom of Parliament, than moft I have heard fince I have had the honour to be a Member of this Houfe. I hope we fhall not find that this extraordinary modefty proceeds from a confcioufnefs of mifconduct. For the fake of the public, I heartily wifh we may find that it proceeds from fuperior merit; which is, indeed, generally attended with fuperior modefty: but as I have always been, upon fuch occafions, againft general encomiums upon Minifters, and as the propofition now before us, or at leaft a great part of it, implies a general approbation of all our late meafures, particularly thofe relating to the prefent war, which the majority of this Houfe are, in my opinion, entirely ignorant of, I cannot agree to it; becaufe I have not yet learned complaifance enough to approve of what I know

B 3 nothing

nothing about, much lefs to approve of what I fufpect to be violently wrong.

I had the honour, Sir, to be a Member of this Houfe, in the laft Parliament, and I remember feveral Motions were then made, for getting fome infight into the ftate of our foreign affairs, and our late tranfactions : Motions which appeared to me highly reafonable, and even abfolutely neceffary to be complied with, before the Houfe could reafonably comply with the demands that were then made upon them : but every one of thefe Motions had a negative put upon them. I have always had a fufpicion of the works of darkuefs; I do not like any conduct that cannot ftand the light at noon-day ; and therefore I am afraid, fome of our late tranfactions are fuch as no man could approve of, if they were expofed to public view. We have long been amufed, with hopes of fome extraordinary bene-fits that were to accrue to the nation from our many tedious and expenfive negotiations : we have been long in expectation ; but when one negotiation was over, we have been always told, to have patience, the next was to accomplifh all our defires ; we accordingly have had a great deal of patience, but, fo far, as I apprehend, I can obferve no benefits that have accrued, or are like to accrue ; but on the contrary, many dangers and dif-advantages : fo that the whole train of our late negotiations really feem to me, to be calculated for no other end, but to ex-tricate a fet of puzzled, perplexed negotiators, from fome former blunder, by which they have generally been led into a fecond of worfe confequence than the firft : every fubfequent negoti-ation feems to me to have had no other view or defign, but to get rid of fome dilemma we were thrown into by the former ; and happy have we thought ourfelves, after a great deal of money fpent, if we could but recover our former condition. In fhort, Sir, if any Gentleman will rife up and fhew me any addition, or any new advantage, with refpect either to our trade or our poffeffions, that this nation has acquired by any of our late tranfactions, I fhall agree to the Motion : but con-

                                                                    fidering

fidering the great expence the nation has been put to, and the great losses many of our merchants have, without any redress or fatisfaction fuftained, I cannot agree to pass compliments upon, or declare my fatisfaction with, our late management in general, till it be made appear to me, that thefe public and private loffes, have been fome way balanced by national advantages.

The fecond paragraph of the Motion I am, indeed, furprifed at upon another account, to make our acknowledgments to his Majefty, for not involving the nation too precipitately in a bloody war, is, in my opinion, very far from being a compliment to his Majefty; it is impoffible, it is not to be prefumed that his Majefty can do any fuch thing: but if it were poffible, and if any fuch thing had been done, to be fure it would have been doing the nation a very notable mifchief; and according to the idiom of our language, at leaft in private life, to thank a man, or to make our acknowledgments to a man, for his not doing us a notable mifchief, is a contemptuous way of expreffing ourfelves, and is always an infinuation, that from fuch a man's malice, or his weaknefs, or imprudence, we expected fome notable mifchief; and therefore when we are difappointed, when the mifchief is not fo great as we expected, we fay, by way of contempt, that we are obliged to him. If none but Minifters were concerned in this part of the Motion, I fhould have let it pafs without any remark, nay, I fhould readily have agreed to it; but as his Majefty is concerned, I hope the Gentlemen who made the Motion will take care to have it fome way altered, if they are refolved to have it ftand part of the Addrefs. This fhews, Sir, how apt people are to fall into blunders, when they attempt to make extravagant or forced compliments; and therefore I wifh we would avoid fuch dangers, by confining our Addrefs to a general acknowledgment of Thanks to his Majefty, for his moft gracious Speech from the Throne, and a declaration of our affections towards him, of our attachment to his family, and our zeal for his fervice.

However,

However, Sir, as it has been granted on all hands, that nothing contained in our Addrefs can prevent the future inquiries
of this Houfe, or can be a bar to our cenfuring what we fhall,
upon inquiry, find to be amifs, therefore I'fhall propofe no
Amendment to the former part of the Motion : but I muft take
notice of one thing which is apparent, without any inquiry, to
every man in this Houfe, to every man who knows any thing of
public affairs, and that is, the great charge this nation has already
been put to on account of the war, while the other powers of
Europe, not yet engaged in the war, have not put themfelves
to one fhilling expence : nay, even our allies, the Dutch, who,
as his Majefty has been pleafed to tell us, are under the fame
engagements with us, have not put themfelves to the leaft
charge on account of the prefent war. Now, Sir, as his
Majefty has told us, that we had no concern with the
caufes or motives of the war, we cannot, therefore, be involved in it, unlefs it be for the prefervation of the balance of
power : and as all our allies are as much interefted in this
refpeét as we are, it is reafonable they fhould bear their proportionable fhare of the expence : and as they have yet done
nothing like it, I think it is become neceffary for us to take
fome notice of this matter in our Addrefs to his Majefty ; for
which reafon, I fhall move this Amendment to the latter part
of the Addrefs, viz. " That this Houfe will cheerfully and
" effeétually raife fuch fupplies, as fhall be neceffary for the
" honour and fecurity of his Majefty and his kingdoms ; *and* ·
" *in proportion to the expenzes to be incurred by the other powers*
" who were under the fame *engagements with this nation, and*
" *not then involved in the war :* and whatever fhall be the fuccefs
" of his Majefty's gracious endeavours to procure the bleffings
" of peace and general tranquillity, will enable his Majefty to
" aét that part, which honour and juftice, and the true intereft
" of his people fhall call upon him to undertake."

Mr. William Pulteney, *Jan.* 27, 1735.

IT

IT has always been the cuftom of this Houfe, at the beginning of every Seffion of Parliament, to return his Majefty our Thanks for his Speech from the Throne; but the fevere ftroke, which not only his Majefty and the Royal Family, but all the nation have received fince our laft meeting, in the death of the Queen, requires, that on this occafion our Thanks to his Majefty, for his moft gracious affurances, fhould be attended with our condolence for his inexpreffible lofs. A lofs, Sir, which, I flatter myfelf, I read in the eyes of every Gentleman who hears me, and which muft be regretted by every fubject in the kingdom, who retains in his breaft one fpark of loyalty and gratitude.

Gentlemen cannot mifs to obferve, that if his Majefty has expreffed himfelf with more brevity than ufual, it is owing to the remembrance of a Princefs *, who endeared herfelf in every relation of life, either as a confort, a mother, or a Queen. And though her death, Sir, is an afflicting difpenfation to all the nation, yet we cannot fuppofe, that any of us can feel it fo deeply as the royal breaft; which, while fhe was alive, fhe fo much eafed of the toils of government by her counfels, which never had any other tendency than to promote his honour, by promoting the happinefs of the people. Of this, Sir, we had many late inftances, efpecially when the fovereign power, in the abfence of her royal confort, was delegated into her hands. On that occafion, Sir, we may all remember with what moderation fhe governed, with what cheerfulnefs fhe rewarded, and with what reluctance fhe punifhed; though the prudence of her meafures rendered the exercife of this laft and moft ungrateful branch of the royal prerogative but feldom neceffary. Therefore, Sir, however fome amongft us may differ in particular views and interefts, I hope we fhall unite in paying a debt of gratitude to the memory of the beft of Princeffes, as well as of duty to the beft of Kings.

Henry Fox, Efq; Jan. 24, 1738.

* The confort of George the Second.

As

As speeches from the Throne have been taken for the sense of the Ministry, too lavish Addresses from this House have been regarded rather as incense to the Minister, than a just acknowledgment to the Sovereign. But, Sir, I hope we shall always look upon ourselves as the trustees of the people, and endeavour to speak their sense in our Addresses, as well as act for their interests in our proceedings. Though the expression, Sir, proposed to be inserted in this Addrefs, *that we will carefully avoid all heats and animofities*, is, to be sure, a very proper part of a Resolution of this nature, and what I am persuaded every Gentleman will willingly agree to; yet there have been instances, Sir, when from as well-guarded expressions Ministers have taken occasion to attempt the subversion of that liberty of debate, and freedom of speech, which ought to distinguish the Representatives of a free people. Amongst such a people, Sir, an opposition always must, and, perhaps, it is their happiness that it does exist. And, Sir, though it is to be wished that heats and animofities were banished from all opposition, yet, I am afraid, while men have different passions, different interests, and different views, this can scarcely be effected.

The granting necessary supplies for the current year, Sir, is what seems very reasonable and indispensible in a House of Commons: but, Sir, I believe there are instances when, in former reigns, the Commons have refused to grant a shilling for the services of the current year, till they were sure the money granted for the services of the preceding had been properly applied. Besides, Sir, the true old parliamentary method of proceeding, was not immediately to grant a Vote of Addrefs for every thing the Minister had done during the intermediate time, right or wrong, but to appoint a day for examining the grievances of the nation; and redrefs of these, was always insisted on before any supplies were granted.

No House of Commons ever had greater reason than we have to be frugal of the public money, and to inquire in what manner it has been applied. We have already granted to his

Majesty

Majefty fums fufficient to have enabled his Majefty to have put the nation in fuch a fituation, that fhe might have nothing to fear from any enemies, either at home or abroad; and, confequently, to have diminifhed the taxes, and eafed the people of fome part of the unfupportable load of debt they now lie under. If, upon inquiry, it fhall appear that they have acted in this manner; if it fhall appear that the people have fo much as a profpect of relief from their prefent preffures, I fhall think the fums we have already granted, not only well beftowed, but fhall concur in any Motion that may be made, for our granting the like in time to come: but, Sir, notwithftanding the fums we have already granted, if the public debt, inftead of being diminifhed, is daily increafing; if it fhall appear that any part of it has been applied in promoting the arts of corruption and betraying the nation, I think it is our duty to put a ftop to any fuch grants in future. In the mean time, Sir, I am as forward as any Gentleman here, that we fhould condole on the irreparable lofs of our late Queen; and that we teftify our refolution of lofing no opportunity of fhowing our zeal for the fupport of his government, and the prefervation of our excellent conftitution; nay, of our going the greateft lengths in fecuring the Crown to his Majefty's perfon and family. But, Sir, give me leave to fay, that the readieft way to make thefe engagements good, is by referving to ourfelves a right for inquiry into any application that may have been made of the public money and credit; and, by determining, let the world fee, that we are refolved to do as much as lies in our power for making his Majefty the Sovereign of a great, a happy, and an uncorrupted people.

Watkin Williams-Wynne, Jan. 24, 1738.

I KNOW, my Lords, it has been of late years a cuftom, to make the Addrefs of this Houfe a fort of *echo* to his Majefty's Speech from the Throne; and as *echoes* never fail to repeat the laft words of a fentence, fo, it feems, we muft never fail *echoing*

back

back the laft paragraph of his Majefty's Speech. This, I fay, has been a cuftom of this Houfe for fome years paft; but I cannot think, that a religious obfervance of this cuftom is either confiftent with the character we ought to preferve, or neceffary for our fhewing our refpect to our Sovereign.

Earl of Chefterfield, Oct. 23, 1739.

My Lords, I have a Motion to make to your Lordfhips, which, as a friend to our prefent happy eftablifhment, as a friend to his moft gracious Majefty now upon the Throne, as a friend to my country, and as a Member of this Houfe, I think I am in duty bound to make; but as it is a Motion of an extraordinary, though not an unprecedented nature, I muft firft beg leave to fhow you my reafons for making it; and I hope to fhow fuch reafons, as will induce every Lord of this Houfe to think, that it is now abfolutely neceffary to comply with it.

My Lords, it is the duty of Parliament, and efpecially of this Houfe, to give our Sovereign the moft fincere advice, not only when it is afked, but often when it is not defired by the Crown. As Members of this Houfe, we are in duty bound to have a watchful eye over the public meafures his Majefty is advifed to purfue, and over the chief Minifters he is pleafed to employ in the adminiftration of public affairs; and when we are of opinion, that the meafures he is advifed to purfue are wrong, or that the Minifters he is pleafed to employ are weak or wicked, it is our duty and our bufinefs, while we fit here, to warn our Sovereign of his danger, and to remove weak or wicked Counfellors from about his Throne. As to the parliamentary methods of removing a Minifter, I need not acquaint your Lordfhips that they are of feveral kinds, and that all but one tend to punifh as well as remove. When we proceed by impeachment, by bill of attainder, or bill of pains and penalties, the defign is to punifh as well as remove: but there is another way of proceeding in parliament, which tends only to remove the Minifter from the King's Councils, without inflicting any

real

real punifhment upon him; and that is, by an humble Addrefs
to our Sovereign, that he would be gracioufly pleafed to remove
fuch a one from his Councils. I therefore move your Lordfhips, " Whether an humble Addrefs fhould be prefented to
his Majefty, that he would be gracioufly pleafed to remove *the
Right Honourable Sir Robert Walpole*, Knight of the Moft Noble
Order of the Garter, Firft Commiffioner for executing the office
of Treafurer of the Exchequer, Chancellor and Under-Trea-
furer of the Exchequer, and one of his Majefty's Moft Honourable Privy Council, from his Majefty's prefence and councils for ever ? "

I believe, my Lords, it will not be queftioned, that either
Houfe of Parliament may offer fuch advice to the Crown, by
way of humble Addrefs; I believe it will not be faid, that it is
unufual, or unprecedented; and therefore I fhall not trouble
your Lordfhips with calling to your remembrance, any of the
precedents that may be found in the Journals of Parliament. I
fhall only take notice of the difference between the methods of
proceeding by Impeachment, by Bill of Attainder, or Bill of
Pains and Penalties; and this method of proceeding, by way of
humble Addrefs to the Crown. When we proceed by way of
Impeachment, by Bill of Attainder, or by Bill of Pains and Penalties, fome particular criminal tefts muft be alledged, and
there muft be fome fort of proofs of thefe facts. But when we
proceed by way of Addrefs to the King, that he would be gracioufly pleafed to remove fuch a Minifter from his Councils, a
general view of that Minifter's conduct, a general view of public affairs, may afford juft caufe for fuch an Addrefs, and common fame is a fufficient proof; for when no particular fact is
infifted on, it is impoffible to bring any particular proof. This,
my Lords, is the difference; and the reafon of this difference is
very plain. When a man is to be punifhed, either in his perfon,
his freedom, or eflate, fome crime or criminal neglect, ought
to be not only alledged, but proved by a legal proof, or by ftrong
prefumptions: but as his not being employed in the King's

Councils

Councils neither affects his perfon, his freedom, nor his eftate, therefore weaknefs alone, or a general bad character, may be a good caufe for removing him. A weak man is certainly, in any country, very unfit for being in the King's Councils; and, in a popular government, a man who has incurred the general ôdium of the people, ought not to be continued in the King's Councils; becaufe the unpopularity of the Minifter may, at leaft, affect the Throne itfelf, and render the people difaffected to their Sovereign.

I muft, therefore, defire your Lordfhips to take particular care to diftinguifh between the method of proceeding againft a Minifter by Impeachment, by Bill of Attainder, a Bill of Pains and Penalties, and the method of proceeding againft a Minifter by Addrefs only; becaufe, if you do not take care to fix this diftinction in your minds, you may expect from me what I do not intend to give, and what the nature of the motion I have made, renders it not only unneceffary, but unfit for me to give. I am to move only for an humble Addrefs to his Majefty, that he would be gracioufly pleafed to remove a Minifter, I may fay, the Minifter, from his Councils; and therefore, it is both un-neceffary and unfit for me, to charge that Minifter with any particular crime, or to acquaint your Lordfhips that I have, or I am ready to produce particular proofs againft him : if this were my intention, I fhould think it below my dignity, as a Member of this Houfe, to content myfelf with moving for an humble Addrefs; I fhould think it incumbent upon me directly to impeach, let the confequence be what it would. Therefore your Lordfhips are not to expect, that I am to accufe any Mini-fter of a particular crime, or that I am to tell you, that I am ready to bring proofs of what I alledge againft him. If I can fhew, that the affairs of Europe have been brought into the unlucky fituation in which they are at prefent, by the conduct of this nation; or if I can fhew, that the diftreffed condition in which our people now are, is wholly owing to our own conduct; either of thefe will be an argument that muft, that ought at

1   leaft,

leaft, to prevail with every Lord who is convinced, that this Minifter has been the principal, if not the fole advifer of that conduct. If the people be generally diffatisfied with the conduct of our public affairs, and if that general diffatisfaction be wholly directed againft any one man now in adminiftration, as our government is ftill, I hope, a popular government, it is a fufficient caufe for this Houfe to let his Majefty know the character of his Minifter, by an Addrefs to remove him from his Councils. If there be any one of his Majefty's Minifters that has ufurped, or that even is generally thought to have ufurped the fole power of directing all public affairs, and recommending to all public pofts, honours, and employments, it is our duty, at leaft, to addrefs his Majefty to remove fuch a Minifter, becaufe fuch a one is inconfiftent with the conftitution of our government.

Upon this queftion, my Lords, it fignifies nothing whether the general character the Minifter has gained, or the mifconduct he has been guilty of, has been owing to his weaknefs or his wickednefs; for either is a fufficient caufe for having him removed. But I muft obferve, that till he is removed, it cannot be made manifeft by proper proofs, whether his mifconduct, or his general bad character, be owing to his weaknefs or wickednefs; for artful Minifters always act by tools, and under agents, who, whilft their patron is in power, will never reveal the flagitious fecrets committed by him to their charge: but as fuch men are feldom faithful any longer than it is their intereft to be fo, remove the Minifter once from the King's Councils, put it out of his power to reward the wicked fidelity of his affociates and tools, and the fecret hiftory of his dirty jobs will then begin to unfold itfelf, and may be made manifeft by a legal proof. Suppofe the King fhould be advifed, by a favourite Minifter, to keep up a conftant friendfhip and alliance with the greateft rivals and moft inveterate enemies of his country; and that he fhould, for this purpofe, facrifice the intereft, and forfeit the friendfhip of the moft natural allies; whilft the Minifter is in power, this may feem to proceed from his weaknefs, or from the ignorance he

has

has of the true intereft of his country: but remove him from the perfon and councils of his Sovereign, and then it may appear to have proceeded from his wickednefs: it may appear that he was corrupted by the enemies of his country, or that he knowingly and wickedly facrificed the intereft of his country to fome private view of his own. If he employed any one in tranfacting or receiving the bribe, if he was ever fo free in converfation with his friends as to unfold the motives of his mifconduct, or the reafons why he gave fuch wicked advice to his Sovereign, fome of them, either from confcience or intereft, may be induced to difcover the fecret, when it is fafe for them to do fo; but whilft he continues folely to enjoy the ear of the Sovereign, it can never be any man's intereft to accufe him, it will always be unfafe for a private man to do fo; becaufe the power of the Crown will be employed in blafting the credit, or preventing the effect of his evidence; and probably in making the punifhment fall, not upon the guilty Minifter, but upon the brave and honeft accufer.

Earl of Carteret, Feb. 13, 1740.

I can by no means think that the complicated queftion now before us, is the proper, is the direct manner of taking the fenfe of the Committee. We have here the foft name of an humble Addrefs to the Crown propofed, and for no other end but to lead Gentlemen into an approbation of the convention. But is this that full deliberate examination, which we were with defiances called upon to give? Is this curfory blended difquifition of matters of fuch variety and extent, all we owe to ourfelves and our country? When trade is at ftake, it is your laft intrenchment; you muft defend it or perifh: and whatever is to decide, that deferves the moft diftinct confideration, and the moft direct and undifguifed fenfe of Parliament. But how are we now proceeding? Upon an artificial minifterial queftion? Here is all the confidence, here is the confcious fenfe of the greateft fervice that ever was done to this country; to be

complicating

complicating queftions, to be lumping fanction and approbation, like a Commiffary's account, to be covering and taking
fanctuary in the royal Name, inftead of meeting openly, and
ftanding fairly the direct judgment and fentence of Parliament
upon the feveral articles of this Convention.

Sir, you have been moved to vote an humble Addrefs of
Thanks to his Majefty for a meafure, which (I will appeal to
Gentlemen's converfation in the world) is odious throughout
the kingdom : Such Thanks are only due to the fatal influence
that framed it, as are due for that low, unallied condition
abroad, which is now made a plea for this Convention. To
what are Gentlemen reduced in fupport of it ? Firft try a little
to defend it upon its own merits ; if that is not tenable, throw
out general terrors; the Houfe of Bourbon 'is united, who
knows the confequence of a war ? Sir, Spain knows the confequence of a war in America ; whoever gains, it muft prove
fatal to her : She knows it, and muft therefore avoid it ; but
fhe knows England does not dare to make it. And what is a
delay, which is all this magnified Convention is fometimes
called to produce ? Can it produce fuch conjunctures as thofe
you loft, while you were giving kingdoms to Spain, and all
to bring her back again to that great branch of the Houfe of
Bourbon, which is now thrown out to you with fo much
terror ? If this union be formidable, are we to delay only till.it
becomes more formidable, by being carried farther into execution, and more ftrongly cemented ? But be it what it will, is
this any longer a nation, or what is an Englifh Parliament, if
with more fhips in your harbours than in all the navies of
Europe, with above two millions of people in your American
colonies, you will bear to hear of the expediency of receiving
from Spain, an infecure, unfatisfactory, difhonorable Convention ? Sir, I call it no more than it has been proved in this
Debate ; it carries fallacy or downright fubjection in almoft
every line : It has been laid open and expofed in fo many ftrong

VOL. I. • C and

and glaring lights, that I can pretend to add nothing to the conviction and indignation it has raifed.

Sir, as to the great national objection, the fearching your fhips, that favorite word, as it is called, is not omitted, indeed, in the Preamble to the Convention, but it ftands there as the reproach of the whole, as the ftrongeft evidence of the fatal fubmiffion that follows : On the part of Spain, an ufurpation, an inhuman tyranny. claimed and exercifed over the American feas ; on the part of England, an undoubted right by Treaties and from God and Nature, declared and afferted in the Refolutions of Parliament, are referred to the difcuffion of Plenipotentiaries upon one and the fame equal foot. Sir, I fay this undoubted right is to be difcuffed, and to be regulated, and if to regulate be to prefcribe rules (as in all conftructions it is) this right is, by the exprefs words of this Convention, to be given up and facrificed ; for it muft ceafe to be any thing, from the moment it is fubmitted to limits.

The Court of Spain has plainly told you, (as appears by papers laid on the table) you fhall fteer a due courfe, you fhall navigate by a line to and from your plantations in America ; if you draw near to her coafts (though from the circumftances of that navigation you are under a neceffity of doing it) you fhall be feized and confifcated : if then upon thefe terms only, fhe has confented to refer, what becomes at once of all the fecurity we are flattered with in confequence of this reference ? Plenipotentiaries are to regulate finally the refpective pretenfions of the two Crowns, with regard to trade and navigation in America ; but does a man in Spain reafon, that thefe pretenfions muft be regulated to the fatisfaction and honor of England ? No, Sir ; they conclude, and with reafon, from the high fpirit of their Adminiftration, from the fuperiority with which they have fo long trufted you, that this reference muft end, as it has begun, to their honor and advantage.

But Gentlemen fay, the Treaties fubfifting are to be the meafure cf this regulation. Sir, as to Treaties, I will take part of the words of *Sir William Temple*, quoted by the Honorable Gentleman near me, *It is in vain to negotiate and make Treaties*, if there is not dignity and rigor to enforce the obfervance of them; for under the mifconftruction and mifinterpretation of thefe very Treaties fubfifting, this intolerable grievance has arifen; it has been growing upon you Treaty after Treaty, through twenty years of negotiation, and even under the difcuffion of Commiffaries to whom it was referred. You have heard from Captain Vaughan at your bar, at what time thefe injuries and indignities were continued; as a kind of explanatory comment upon the Convention Spain has thought fit to grant you, as another infolent proteft, under the validity and force of which fhe has fuffered this Convention to be proceeded on. We will treat with you, but we will fearch and take your fhips; we will fign a Convention, but we will keep your fubjects prifoners, prifoners in Old Spain; the Weft-Indies are remote, Europe fhall be witnefs how we ufe you.

Sir, as to the interference of an admiffion of our right not to be fearched, drawn from a reparation made for fhips unduly feized and confifcated, I think that argument is very inconclufive. The right claimed by Spain, to fearch our fhips, is one thing, and the exceffes admitted to have been committed, in confequence of this pretended right, is another: but furely, Sir, reafoning from inferences and implication only, is below the dignity of your proceedings, upon a right of this vaft importance. What this reparation is, what fort of compofition for your loffes, forced upon you by Spain in an inftance that has come to light, where your own Commiffaries could not in confcience decide againft your claim, has fully appeared upon examination; and as for the payment of the fum ftipulated, (all but feven and twenty thoufand pounds) it is evidently a fallacious, nominal payment only. I will not attempt to enter into a detail of a dark, confufed, and fcarcely intelligible account; I will only beg leave to conclude with one word upon it in the light of a fubmiffion, as well as of an adequate reparation.

Spain

Spain stipulates to pay to the Crown of England, 95,000l. by
a preliminary protest of the King of Spain, the South Sea Company is at once to pay 68,000 l. of it: If they refuse, Spain, I
admit, is still to pay the 95,000l. but how does it stand then?
The Affiento Contract is to be suspended : you are to purchase
this sum at the price of an exclusive trade, pursuant to a national treaty, and at an immense debt of God knows how many
hundred thousand pounds, due from Spain to the South Sea
Company. Here, Sir, is the submission of Spain by the payment of a stipulated sum ; a tax laid upon subjects of England,
under the severest penalties, with the reciprocal accord of an
English Minister, as a preliminary that the Convention may
be signed : a condition imposed by Spain in the most absolute
imperious manner, and received by the Ministers of England
in the most tame and abject. Can any verbal distinctions, any
evasions whatever, possibly explain away this public infamy?
To whom would we disguise it? To ourselves and to the nation : I wish we could hide it from the eyes of every Court in
Europe : They see Spain has talked to you like your Master,
they see this arbitrary fundamental condition, and it must stand
with distinction, with a pre-eminence of shame, as a part even
of this Convention.

   This Convention, Sir, I think from my soul is nothing but
a stipulation for national ignominy, an illusory expedient to
baffle the resentment of the nation ; a truce without a suspension
of hostilities, on the part of Spain ; on the part of England, a
suspension ; as to Georgia, of the first law of nature, self-pre-
servation and self-defence ; a surrender of the trade and rights
of England to the mercy of Plenipotentiaries, and in this infinitely highest and sacred point, future security, not only inadequate, but directly repugnant to the Resolutions of Parliament, and the gracious Promise from the Throne. The complaints of your despairing Merchants, the voice of England has
condemned it ; be the guilt of it upon the head of the ad-
viser ;

viser; God forbid that this Committee should share the guilt by approving it !

William Pitt, Efq; March 6, 1739.

AMONG the many advantages arifing from our happy Conftitution, there is one that is reciprocal to King and People, which is a legal and regular method by which the People may lay their grievances, complaints, and opinions, before their Sovereign; not only with regard to the meafures he purfues, but alfo with regard to the perfons he employs. In abfolute monarchies, the People may fuffer, they may complain; but though their fufferings be public, their complaints muft be private; they muft not fo much as murmur againft their King's Meafures or Minifters; if they do, it is certain perdition to the few that are guilty of fo much indifcretion. This is a moft terrible misfortune to the People in all abfolute monarchies, and occafions thofe fevere punifhments and cruel tortures, which are fo frequent in all fuch; but it is a misfortune to the abfolute Monarch, as well as to the people under his defpotic fway, for as he has no way of coming at the knowledge of the unpopularity of his Minifters or Meafures, he often goes on purfuing the fame Meafures, or employing the fame Minifters, till the difcontents of his People become quite univerfal and furious; and then by a general infurrection, he and his Minifters are involved in one common ruin. However upright his intentions may have been, however much he may have been impofed on by his Minifters, an impetuous domineering mob can feldom make any difference: The defpotic Monarch himfelf, and fometimes his whole family, are borne down by the impetuofity of the torrent, and become a facrifice to the refentment of an injured populace.

In this kingdom, Sir, it can never be fo, as long as the King allows-Parliaments to fit regularly and freely, and the Members of this Houfe perform faithfully the duty they owe to their King, their Conftituents, and their Country. As

C 3

Members

Members of this Houfe, Sir, we are obliged to reprefent to
his Majefty, not only the grievances, but the fentiments of the
People, with regard to the meafures he purfues, and the perfons he advifes with or employs in the executive part of our
Government ; and therefore whilft we fit here and do our duty,
no general difcontent can arife, without his Majefty's being
informed of its caufes, and of the methods for allaying it: If we
negleft to do fo, or from felfifh motives abftain, or delay
giving his Majefty a proper information and advice upon
any fuch occafion, we neglect or betray, not only our duty
to our Country and Conftituents, but alfo our duty to our
Sovereign.

This, Sir, is my opinion ; this muft be the opinion of every
man who has a true notion of our Conftitution ; and therefore,
I can no longer delay making you the Motion, with which
I fhall conclude what I have to fay upon this occafion. I believe there is not a Gentleman of this Houfe, who is not fenfible, that both the foreign and domeftic meafures of our Government, for feveral years paft, have been diffatisfactory to a
great majority of the nation ; I may fay to almoft every man
in the nation, who has not been concerned in advifing or carrying them on. I believe there is not a Gentleman in this
Houfe, if he will freely declare his fentiments, who is not
fenfible, that one fingle perfon in Adminiftration has not only
been thought to be, but has actually been the chief, if not the
fole advifer and promoter of all thofe meafures. This is known
without doors, as well as it is within ; and therefore the difcontents, the reproaches, and even the curfes of the people,
are all directed againft that fingle perfon. They complain of
our prefent meafures ; they have fuffered by paft meafures ;
they expect no-redrefs ; they expect no alteration, or amendment, whilft he has a fhare in advifing or directing our
future. Thefe, Sir, are the fentiments of the People with regard to that Minifter : Thefe fentiments we are in honor and
duty bound to reprefent to his Majefty, and the proper method

for

for doing this, as eftablifhed by the Conftitution, is to addrefs his Majefty to remove him from his councils.

Sir, if the general difcontent which hath arifen againft the Minifter, were but of yefterday, or without any juft or folid foundation, I fhould expeft it would foon blow over, and therefore fhould not think it worthy the notice of Parliament; but it has lafted for fo many years, was at firft fo well founded, and has every year fince been gathering, from his conduft, fo much additional ftrength, that I have for feveral Seffions expefted fuch a Motion, as I am now to make, from fome other Gentleman, more capable than I am to enforce what he propofes : but as no Gentleman has hitherto attempted it, and as this is the laft Seffion of this Parliament, I was unwilling it fhould expire without anfwering the People's expeftations, which in this refpeft are fo juft, fo well founded, and fo agreeable to our Conftitution; therefore I hope I fhall be excufed for attempting what I think my duty, as a Member of this Houfe, and as a friend to our prefent happy Eftablifhment.

After what I have faid, Sir, I believe no Gentleman can miftake the perfon I mean : I am convinced every one fuppofes I mean the Honorable Gentleman, who fits upon the floor, over againft me ; and the whole Houfe may fee, he takes it to himfelf. Againft him, there is, I believe, as general a popular difcontent, as ever was againft any Minifter in this kingdom ; and this difcontent has lafted fo long, that I muft fay, his having withftood it for fo many years, is no great fign of the freedom of our Government; for a free People neither will, nor can be governed by a Minifter they hate and defpife, As I am only to propofe an Addrefs to remove him from his Majefty's Councils, I have no occafion to accufe him of any crime : The People's being generally diffatisfied with him, and fufpicious of his conduft, is a fufficient foundation for fuch an Addrefs, and a fufficient caufe for his Majefty's removing him from his councils ; becaufe, no Sovereign of thefe kingdoms ought to employ a Minifter, who is become difagreeable to the

C 4

generality of the People ; and when any Minister happens to
become fo, it is our duty to inform his Majesty of it, that he
may give fatisfaction to his People, by the removal of fuch a
Minister.

However, Sir, though I shall not at present charge this
Minister with any particular crime, I must beg leave to examine
a little into his conduct, in order to shew, that the difcontents
of the People are not without foundation ; and if it be true,
what was, and is still generally fuppofed, it must be allowed,
that the methods by which he first advanced himfelf to the high
offices he has ever since enjoyed, were fuch as could not but be
offenfive to every honeft man in the nation.   The making and
unmaking the famous Bank contract ; the fcreening from condign punifhment thofe who, by their wicked and avaricious
execution of the truft repofed in them by the South-Sea fcheme,
which had ruined many thoufands ; the lumping of public
juftice, and the fubjecting the lefs guilty to a punifhment too
fevere, in order that the moft henious offenders might efcape
the punifhment they deferved ; and the giving up to the South-
Sea Company the fum of feven millions fterling, which they
had obliged themfelves to pay to the Public, a great part of
which fum was given to old ftockholders, and confequently to
thofe who had never fuffered by the fcheme, were the fteps by
which he was fuppofed to have rifen to power, and fuch fteps
could not but raife a general diftafte at his advancement, and a
dread of his adminiftration.

Thus, Sir, he entered into adminiftration with the general
difapprobation of the People ; and I am fure, his meafures fince
have been far from reftoring him to their love or efteem.   As
he began, fo has he gone on, oppreffing the innocent, impofing
upon the credulous, fcreening the guilty, wafting the public
treafure, and endangering the liberties of the People.   All this
I could evince from every ftep of his adminiftration, from the
beginning to this very day, but I shall confine myfelf to fome of
the moft remarkable inftances.   In general, I shall obferve,
that

that by his advice and influence, a much greater army has all along been kept up than was neceffary for the fupport of our Government, or confiftent with our Conftitution, and even that army often augmented without any real caufe; that many fquadrons have been fitted out, to the great expence of the nation, and general difturbance of our trade, without any juft caufe, and, I believe, without fo much as a defign to employ them effectually, either againft our enemies, or for the affiftance of our allies; that every method propofed of late years, for fecuring our Conftitution againft our moft dangerous enemy, Corruption, has been, by his means, rejected, or rendered ineffectual; whilft, on the other hand, many penal laws have been paffed, which have reduced a great number of his Majefty's fubjects under the arbitrary power of a Minifter and his creatures.

That almoft every article of public expence has been increafed by the addition of new and ufelefs Officers; and all enquiries into the management of any public money, either prevented or defeated; that votes of credit at the end of a Seffion of Parliament, which always have been thought of dangerous confequences to our Conftitution, have by him been made fo frequent, that few Seffions have paffed without one; that the expence of the Civil Lift has been vaftly increafed fince the beginning of his Adminiftration, though it was then much greater than it had ever amounted to in former times; to thefe, Sir, which are all of a domeftic nature, I fhall add, with regard to our foreign affairs, that ever fince his advice began to be prevalent in our foreign affairs, the trade and particular intereft of this nation, have in all treaties and negociations been neglected, the confidence of our moft natural allies difregarded, and the favour of our moft dangerous enemies courted; and that to this moft unaccountable conduct, the prefent melancholy fituation of the affairs of Europe is principally to be afcribed.

I know, Sir, it will be objected, that as every material ftep in the late conduct of our public affairs, either at home or abroad,

abroad, has been authorized or approved of by Parliament, what I have faid muft be looked on as a general charge againft his Majefty's Councils and our Parliament, rather than a perfonal charge againft any one Minifter; but this, upon a due confideration, becomes the moft heavy, and the moft evident charge againft the Minifter I aim at. According to our Conftitution, we can have no fole and prime Minifter; we ought always to have feveral prime Minifters or Officers of State; every fuch Officer has his own proper department, and no Officer ought to meddle in the affairs belonging to the department of another: but it is publicly known, that this Minifter, having obtained a fole influence over all our public councils, has not only affumed the fole direction of all public affairs, but has got every Officer of State removed that would not follow his directions, even in the affairs belonging to his own proper department. By this means he hath monopolized all the favours of the Crown, and engroffed the fole difpofal of all Places, Penfions, Titles, and Ribbons, as well as of all Preferments, Civil, Military, or Ecclefiaftical.

This, Sir, is of itfelf a moft heinous offence againft our Conftitution; but he has greatly aggravated the heinoufnefs of his crime; for, having thus monopolized all the favours of the Crown, he has made a blind fubmiffion to his direction at elections and in Parliament, the only ground to hope for any honours or Preferment, and the only tenure by which any Gentleman would preferve what he had. This is fo notorioufly known, that it can ftand in need of no proof. Have not many deferving Gentlemen been difappointed in the preferment they had a juft title to, upon the bare fufpicion of not being blindly devoted to his perfonal intereft? Have not fome perfons of the higheft rank and moft illuftrious characters been difplaced, for no other reafon, than becaufe they difdained to facrifice their honour and confcience to his direction in Parliament? As no crime, no neglect, no mifbehaviour could ever be objected to them, as no other reafons could ever be affigned for depriving

the

/

the Crown of their fervice, this only could be the reafon. Nay, has not this Minifter himfelf not only confeffed it, but boafted of it? Has he not faid, and in this Houfe too, that he would be a pitiful fellow of a Minifter, who did not difplace any Officer that oppofed his meafures in Parliament?

: Can any Gentleman who heard this declaration defire a proof of the Minifter's mifconduct, or of his crimes? Was not this openly avowing one of the moft heinous crimes that can be committed by a Minifter in this kingdom? Was it not avowing, that he had made ufe of the favours of the Crown for obtaining a corrupt Majority in both Houfes of Parliament, and keeping that Majority in a flavifh dependance upon himfelf alone? Do not we all know, that even the King himfelf is not, by our Conftitution, to take notice of any man's behaviour in Parliament, far lefs to make that behaviour a means by which he is to obtain, or a tenure by which he is to hold, the favour of the Crown? And fhall we allow a Minifter not only to do, but openly to avow, what he ought to be hanged for, fhould he advife his Sovereign to do fo? It is by means of this crime, Sir, that the Minifter I am fpeaking of has obtained the authority or approbation of Parliament in every ftep of his conduct, and therefore that authority or approbation is fo far from being an alleviation, that it is a moft heavy aggravation of every wrong ftep which he has thus got authorized or approved by Parliament. For this reafon, in confidering any particular ftep of his conduct, its being authorized or approved by Parliament can have no weight in his favour, whatever it may have againft him. If the ftep was in itfelf weak or wicked, or if it now appears from its confequences to have been fo, its having been approved of or authorized by Parliament, muft be fuppofed to have proceeded either from his having mifled the Parliament by falfe gloffes and afteverations, or from his having overawed a Majority by means of that crime which he has fince openly avowed.

Mr. Sands, April 16, 1740.

A s

As our duty to our Sovereign makes it neceſſary for us to return ſome ſort of Addreſs by way of anſwer to his Majeſty's Speech from the Throne, at the opening of a Seſſion, and as this practice has been eſtabliſhed by immemorial cuſtom, I ſhall be excuſed if I introduce my Motion with my ſentiments upon that ſurprizing turn which has been lately given to the affairs of Europe, by his Majeſty's wiſdom and conduct.

In order to do this, Sir, I muſt begin with obſerving, the diſmal proſpect we had of the affairs of Europe about eighteen or nineteen months ago. I think there is no maxim in politics more certain than this, that it is inconſiſtent with the liberties of Europe, to allow France to increaſe her own power, or to divide the power of Europe into ſo many branches, as to make it impoſſible for any one Prince or State, to think of oppoſing her in any of her ambitious ſchemes; for it is very certain, that, as ſoon as the thoughts of Oppoſition end, thoſe of Dependence begin; and conſequently, if France could once effect this purpoſe, all the Princes and States of Europe would become dependent upon her; and moſt of them would, at all times, think of preſerving their inſignificant ſhadow of ſovereignty only by being obedient to her commands, and aſſiſting her againſt thoſe who ſhould bravely dare to rebel. We ſhould then be in the ſame circumſtance as Europe, or, I may ſay, the world was, when the grandeur of the Romans was at its greateſt height. Some of the Princes and States of Europe, might be dignified with the deceitful title of *Socii Gallici Imperii*; but if ever any one of them ſhould ever dare to behave otherwiſe than as the moſt abject ſlaves, even that empty title they would be ſtript of, and their territory would be converted into a province of the French empire. Our Royal Family, like that of *Macedon*, might, for ſome time, be left in poſſeſſion of their throne; but if any one of our future princes ſhould endeavour to ſhake off his dependency, a powerful invaſion would be the certain conſequence; and if France were the ſole miſtreſs of the Continent of Europe, or

had

had it entirely at her command, our natural barrier would prove ineffectual: she would then come up against us with such a power as we could not oppose either by sea or land: our Royal Family would be cut off; our noble and great families would be all carried captives into France, and Britain would, from thenceforth, be divided and governed by French Intendants or Lieutenants, as *Macedonia* was by Roman Prætors or Proconfuls.

This confequence was forefeen, Sir: this confequence all Europe was fenfible of in the laft age: I wifh I could fay the fame of the prefent: but, by what fatality I know not, the prefent age feemed, a few months ago, to be ftruck with fuch a blindnefs as prevented their feeing this danger, though it was never more apparent. Several of the Princes of Europe, governed by a felfifh private intereft, had actually joined with France in pulling down the Houfe of Auftria, though that was the only power, on the Continent of Europe, that could, by itfelf, pretend to limit or fet bounds to the ambitious Court of France. By this means the Queen of Hungary was environed by fuch numerous hoftile armies, that it was impoffible for her to refift for any long time; and the confederacy againft her was fo powerful, that no counter-confederacy equal to it could be formed. This, I fhall grant, was, in fome meafure, owing to her own unfeafonable obftinacy, as well as to the felfifh views of fome of her enemies; for however unjuft fhe might think her pretenfions, in common prudence fhe fhould, upon the death of her father, have yielded to thofe that were the moft moderate, in order to enable her to refift thofe who were fo immoderate as to aim at the total overthrow of her Houfe.

This was, Sir, from the beginning of the prefent troubles, his Majefty's advice to her; but this prudent advice fhe would not, for a long time, give the leaft ear to; and this not only united her enemies amongft themfelves, but increafed the views and demands of each; which reduced his Majefty to the fatal
neceffity

neceffity of waiting till her obftinacy fhould be foftened, and the eyes of fome of her enemies be opened, by time and future accidents. This he was obliged to do before he could openly declare in her favour, or affift her in any other fhape than by granting her fums of money; but this he did with a fteady defign to take advantage of every accident that fhould happen : and the behaviour of the French in Germany, efpecially about the time of the battle of *Crotzka*, was fuch as furnifhed him with an opportunity which he wifely took care to lay hold of, and to make the beft ufe of it he could, whereby he prevailed upon both the kings of Pruffia and Poland to withdraw themfelves from the French alliance, and to make peace with the Queen of Hungary, upon terms which fhe readily agreed to.

By this prudent conduct of his Majefty, it became now poffible to form fuch a confederacy in Europe as might, with fome hopes of fuccefs, endeavour to oppofe the ambitious defigns of the Court of France; and to give courage to the other Powers of Europe to enter into fuch a confederacy, he refolved to fend a body of his Britifh troops to Flanders, in order to have a numerous army formed there; which, before the end of the campaign, raifed fuch terrors in France, as prevented their fending fufficient reinforcements to their troops already in Germany, and likewife prevented their joining the Spaniards with fuch armies as might have overwhelmed the king of Sardinia, or compelled him to defert the alliance he had before, by his Majefty's interpofition, entered into with the Queen of Hungary. At the fame time, proper orders were given to his Majefty's Admirals in the Mediterranean, to prevent the Spaniards from fending any reinforcements or provifions by fea to their army in Italy; and our fquadron there was reinforced and inftructed, fo as to enable it to execute thefe orders, againft whofoever fhould dare to abet the Spaniards in any fuch attempt.

By thefe means, Sir, the Queen of Hungary was, before the end of the campaign, reftored to the poffeffion of Bohemia, Weftphalia

Weftphalia was freed from the burden and terror of a French army, and the Spaniards were, during the whole campaign, defeated in every attempt they made againft Italy: but there were two things ftill remaining to be done; which were to drive the French entirely out of Germany; and to eftablifh, upon a more folid bafis, the alliance of the King of Sardinia, in order to drive the Spaniards entirely out of Italy, for which purpofe it was requifite to obtain the hearty concurrence of the Dutch. Thefe things were to be the work of the next campaign, and therefore as early as the feafon would permit, the army which had been formed in Flanders marched into Germany; and his Majefty not only joined it with a confiderable body of his electoral troops, but went in perfon to command the army, and by his valour and conduct, chiefly, the glorious battle of Dettingen was obtained, which compelled the French to evacuate Germany, and not only put the Queen of Hungary in poffeffion of all Bavaria, but opened a free paffage for her armies to the Rhine; fo that France, from being the invader of the dominions of others, had now enough to do to defend her own.

Whilft his Majefty was thus triumphing over the arms of France in the field, he equally triumphed over her councils in the Cabinet; for, notwithftanding the utmoft efforts of France to the contrary, he prevailed with the Dutch to fend a body of 20,000 men to the affiftance of the Queen of Hungary; and a definitive treaty of alliance was concluded at Worms, between his Majefty, the Queen of Hungary, and the King of Sardinia, by which, alliance, and affiftance of that Prince was eftablifhed upon a firm bafis: and experience has already fhewn the great ufe it may be of to us, in defeating the defigns of our enemies the Spaniards in Italy; which will convince that haughty nation of its being neceffary for them to cultivate a good correfpondence with Great-Britain, if they have a mind to be quiet in their own poffeffions, or to difturb the poffeffions of any of their neighbours.

Thefe

Thefe great and unexpected events, Sir, have been all brought about by the wifdom and vigour of his Majefty's Councils, and therefore we cannot in gratitude omit taking notice of them upon this occafion. I was very fenfible, that there were many Gentlemen in this Houfe, who could have fet them in a clearer light, and recommended them to your confideration with greater energy than I can; but I knew your affection and duty to your Sovereign, and the luftre of thofe events, was in itfelf fo refulgent, that I thought it required no high degree of eloquence to excite your grateful acknowledgments; therefore I ventured to undertake the tafk, and hope I fhall be forgiven my arrogating to myfelf the honour.

Honourable Edward Coke, Dec. 1, 1743.

ANECDOTE.

IN the Grecian and Roman Commonwealths, their tradesmen
and labourers gained laurels in the field of battle by their
courage, and returned to gain a subsistence for themselves and
families by their industry; but when they began to keep standing armies, their soldiers, it is true, for some time gained laurels in the field, but they returned to plunder, and at last to
subdue their country; which put an end to their freedom, and
of course to every thing that was praise-worthy amongst them.
God forbid our fate should be the same! It is a mistake to
imagine, that our tradesmen would be drawn away from their
labour by breeding them up to military discipline; on the contrary, they might be brought to use it as their diversion, and
then they would return with more alacrity to their usual labour.
In former times, our holidays, and even Sundays, were em_
ployed in the exercise of the *long bow*, and other warlike di-
versions; and I must think, that such days would be better
employed in that way, than in sitting at an alehouse, or loiter-
ing in a skittle, or nine-pin ground: but such a change of
manners is not to be introduced without the assistance of Government.

Mr. Sandys, Feb. 3, 1737.

OLIVER CROMWELL, when he turned every Member of
this House out of doors; when he bid one of his soldiers
take away our *mace*, that *fool's bauble*, as he called it, had
not a much more numerous regular army than we have at present on foot; and though the army under King James the Second behaved in a more honourable way, yet such a behaviour
is not much to be depended on; for I am convinced, even that
an army would not have behaved as they did, if the discontent-
ed had not had an army to repair to; or if proper measures
had been taken to garble them a little before hand.

Mr. Shippen, Feb. 3, 1737.

·Before I make my Motion for fettling on his Royal High-
nefes the Prince of Wales, one hundred thoufand pounds a
year, give me leave, Sir, to inquire into thefe feveral founda-
tions : and to begin with the laft, I fhall fhew, from many undoubted authorities, that the Prince of Wales has always had,
and ought to have, a fufficient provifion fettled upon him, in
fuch a manner, as to render him as independent of the Crown
as any other fubjeft can be. To recount all the precedents
that occur in our hiftories and records, would take up too
much of your time, and therefore I fhall take notice of only
the moft remarkable. King Henry the IIId granted to his
eldeft fon Edward, afterwards King Edward the Ift, the Duchy
of Guienne, before he was fourteen years of age; and the moment the Prince was married, he not only confirmed his former
Grant by a new Patent, but likewife granted him, and put
him in poffeffion of, the Earldom of Chefter, the cities and
towns of Briftol, Stamford, and Grantham, with feveral
other caftles and manors; created him Prince of Wales, to
which he annexed all the conquered lands in that Principality,
and appropriated him Lieutenant-Governor of Ireland, though
he was then but juft turned of *fourteen*; all which was done,
as the hiftorians exprefs it, *ut maturus ad res graviores gerendas
expertus redderetur.* By this generofity and benevolence of the
King towards his eldeft fon, that Prince was early in his youth
eftablifhed in a ftate of independence and grandeur; and thofe
paternal favours were afterwards fully repaid by that illuftrious
and heroic Prince, for he afterwards proved his father's chief
and only fupport. . Every one knows how by his conduft and
courage, at the battle of *Evefham*, he relieved his father out of
the hands of his enemies, and reftored his affairs after they
were brought into a moft dangerous and defperate ftate. Nay,
not only the King himfelf, but the nation reaped fignal fervices
from the free and independent circumftances in which the
King had fo early placed his fon. A ftate of independency
naturally ennobles and exalts the mind of man; and the effects
of

of it were moſt conſpicuous in this wiſe and brave *Prince*, for he afterwards became the glory of England, and the terror of Europe.

The next precedent I ſhall take notice of is, that of Edward the Black Prince, upon whom Edward the IIId his father, ſettled at different times the Earldom of Cheſter, the Duchy of Cornwall, the Principality of Wales, the Duchy of Guienne, and the Principality of Aquitain. That wiſe and grave Prince, Sir, was ſo ſenſible of the reaſonableneſs of the ancient maxim of England, with regard to the King's eldeſt ſon, that he took care every future Prince of Wales ſhould have ſomething to depend on, independent of his father, from the very moment of his birth : for which purpoſe he ſettled, by Act of Parliament, the Duchy of Cornwall in ſuch a manner, that the King's eldeſt ſon, and Heir Apparent to the Crown, has ever ſince been Duke of Cornwall as ſoon as born, and without any new Grant from the King ; from whence has ariſen the common proverb, *natus eſt, non datus, dux Cornubiæ.* Some of the latter Grants of that King might, indeed, proceed from the great perſonal merit of the ſon, but the firſt Grants could not proceed from any ſuch conſideration ; they could proceed only from his own wiſdom, and from the general maxim I have mentioned ; for the Prince was not then *three* years old, when his father ſettled upon him by Patent the Earldom of Cheſter ; he was but ſeven years old, when Cornwall was erected into a Duchy, and ſettled upon him by Act of Parliament as before-mentioned ; and he was but thirteen when the Principality of Wales was ſettled upon him. Soon after that time, indeed, his perſonal merit began to appear : But how came it to appear ? Its early appearance did appear, and could only proceed from his father's having em- ployed him in, and inured him to the ſtudy of weighty affairs, at an age when moſt Princes are induſtriouſly taught to think of nothing but baubles and toys.

The ſame conduct, Sir, that wiſe King obſerved during that brave *Prince's* life : he was continually heaping favours upon

D 2 the

the Prince his fon, and the Prince was continually repaying them
with glorious acts of gratitude and filial duty. When he was
feventeen, he fully repaid all former favours, by having the chief
fhare of the victory obtained over the French at the famous battle of Creffy. In the twenty-fourth, or twenty-fifth year of this
Prince's age, the King invefted him with the Duchy of Guienne, which new favour he foon afterwards repaid by fending
the *French* King home prifoner to his father, after having taken
him at the ever-memorable battle of *Poictiers*. And in the
two and thirtieth year of that Prince's age, a great part of
France having been conquered and fubdued by his valour, the
King his father erected *Guienne, Gafcony*, and feveral other
provinces of France, into a Principality, under the name of
the Principality of Aquitain, with which he invefted the Prince
his fon: this new favour the Prince likewife foon repaid, by
carrying the glory of the Britifh arms into Spain, and replacing
Peter upon the Throne of Caftile, after having defeated the
ufurper Henry at the battle of *Nejara* in that kingdom: for all
which glorious victories, and many other great fervices done
to his native country, the nation was fo grateful to his memory,
that immediately after his death, or at leaft as foon as their
grief for the lofs of fo brave a Prince would give them leave,
the Houfe of Commons addreffed the King to create his fon
Prince of Wales, and Duke of Cornwall, which that wife
King immediately agreed to; for his grandfon being then Heir
Apparent to the Crown, he became entitled, by the maxim I
have mentioned, to an independent fettlement: but as he was
not the King's eldeft fon, he had no pretence, from any former precedent, to the Principality of Wales; and his right by
the late Act to the Duchy of Cornwall, was thought to be doubt-
ful by the Lawyers of that age; the Lawyers being then, it
feems, as dexterous at ftarting doubts and fcruples, as the
Lawyers of the age we now live in.

Give me leave, Sir, to mention one other precedent; that
of Prince Henry, afterwards the glorious King Henry the Vth,
whom

whom his father Henry IV. in the very firſt year of his reign created Prince of Wales, Duke of Cornwall, and Earl of Cheſter, though the Prince was then but twelve years of age; all which grants were recorded upon the Parliament's requeſt, in order to prevent any poſſibility of a revocation : and though that King was naturally of a jealous and a fuſpicious temper, yet we find, during his whole reign, he was every now and then making new grants to the Prince his ſon, even tho' he was ſometimes maliciouſly made to believe the Prince was conſpiring againſt him. This Prince, it is true, fell into ſome exceſſes incident to youth and idleneſs ; but, from the firſt part of his life, and from his conduct after he became King, we may judge that thoſe exceſſes were rather owing to his father's jealouſy than to his own natural temper : for when he was but about ſixteen, he by his valour contributed greatly to his father's victory over the rebels at Shrewſbury ; and the very next year, having been entruſted with the command of his father's army againſt the rebels in Wales, by his conduct and courage, he gave them two ſignal defeats ; by which he gained ſo much eſteem, that the King, his father, from his own natural and unhappy temper, and not from any undutiful behaviour in his ſon, began to grow jealous of him, and therefore never afterwards employed him in any public affairs; ſo that the ex- ceſſes he fell into, probably proceeded from the idleneſs of his life, and the activity of his genius; or, perhaps, rather from a deſign of removing from his father all future occaſions of jealouſy. This, indeed, ſeems to be confirmed, or at leaſt rendered the moſt probable conjecture, by his conduct after he became King; for immediately upon his acceſſion, he baniſhed from his preſence all the companions and ſycophant upholders of his former debaucheries, and became one of the greateſt, and one of the moſt glorious Princes that ever ſat upon the Engliſh Throne.

The late King James the IId, when Duke of York, and the late Queen Anne, when Princeſs of Denmark, were both provided

D 3 for,

for. The Duke of York had a great fettlement made upon him by Parliament, foon after the Reftoration, though he was but Prefumptive Heir to the Crown, his brother King Charles being then in a capacity of having children, who would have given him a more effectual exclufion than could ever be attained by Parliament, till his own ridiculous meafures put it in their power : and the late Queen Anne, when Princefs of Denmark, had alfo a great fettlement made upon her by authority of Parliament, tho' King William and Queen Mary were both then alive, and in a capacity of having children; fo that the Princefs Anne, when that fettlement was made, was but the Prefumptive Heir to the Crown.

From thefe precedents it appears, that the maxim of having an independent provifion fettled upon the Prefumptive or Apparent Heir of the Crown, is a maxim that has ever been obferved in this nation.

Mr. Pulteney, Feb. 23, 1737.

Julius Cæfar had as great reafon as any man can ever have, to difcourage virtue, and reward the vicious : *Julius Cæfar* did fometimes threaten men for doing their duty ; but *Julius Cæfar* was always extremely fhy of putting fuch threats in execution. We are told, that when he went to feize upon the facred treafure of Rome, and was oppofed by *Metellus*, the Tribune, he threatened to kill Metellus ; and at the fame time told him, *Iftud nonne fcis adolefcentule, longe mihi difficilius dicere, quam facere.* This was threatening a man for doing his duty ; but *Julius Cæfar* took care not to put his threat in execution.

Mr. Lyttelton, Jan. 28, 1738.

I REMEMBER a ftory that was told of a great favourite of Charles the IId. This Gentleman, who was a true cavalier, fought for the father, and was banifhed with the fon, whom he attended all the time of his exile. Upon the reftoration of the Royal Family he continued ftill to follow his mafter's fortune,

but

but never minded his own; till his continual attendance at
Court, his giving into all the fashionable expences of the
times, and the figure which his intimacy with his Majesty
obliged him to support, at last exhausted every shilling of his
estate. But such was this Gentleman's modesty, (a virtue
you'll say very rarely to be met with in the favourite of a Monarch) that he never made one solicitation in his own behalf,
though he had many opportunities of doing it. At last the
King, being informed of his circumstances, took occasion one
day, as the Gentleman was soliciting a post for one of his
friends, to tell him, " Sir, you have been a very faithful and a very
" constant servant to me ; I have had very great satisfaction in
" your company, without your being a shilling the better for
" me, though I am persuaded your estate has suffered consider-
" ably in my service. As you are a man of sense, and fit for
" business, why do you not ask for something for yourself?"
The Gentleman made no other return to his Majesty at that
time, but a profound acknowledgment of the honour he had
received, by his Majesty's being so mindful of him ; but some
time after, being all alone with the King, " Pray, Sir," says
he to his Majesty, " be so good as to lend me half a crown."
" Half a crown !" answers the King, " what do you mean ?
" if you have occasion for a larger sum you may have it."
" No, no," replies the Gentleman, " this small piece does very
" well to begin with ; for I have often observed, that once put
" you in the way of giving, it is easy to keep you in it, and
" then you do not care how much you give."

There is something in this pretty applicable to our granting
money for the public service. The sum, Sir, originally asked
for, and granted, is but small, and makes no great figure, perhaps, in the public accounts ; but an accumulation of that
sum from time to time, obtained when we were in a giving
humour, makes at length, a most enormous article.

Sir Thomas Aston, Jan. 28, 1738.

IT was a maxim with *Julius Cæfar*, never to venture even a battle, if the difadvantages that might enfue from a defeat appeared to be greater than any advantages he could expect from a victory; and in Africa, we are told, that he bore with many infults and indignities, from the adverfe army, only becaufe by a little patience, he had reafon to expect being able to obtain a victory with lefs blood-fhed; and in refolving upon peace or war, the fame maxim ought to be obferved.

Horace Walpole, Efq; Jan. 28, 1738.

BOTH the circumftances of Europe, and the circumftances of Spain, are now, my Lords, very different from what they were in the reign of Queen Elizabeth, or in the time of Oliver Cromwell. In Queen Elizabeth's reign, Spain was the only formidable power in Europe, and we had as much reafon as any other of her neighbours to endeavour to reduce her power. For this prurpofe, Queen Elizabeth took the wifeft courfe that could be taken, by encouraging and fupporting the Civil War in the Netherlands; by which means, fhe at laft enabled the *Seven United Provinces* to throw off the yoke of Spain; and the whole power of Spain being applied towards fupporting their dominion over the Netherlands, they could neither fpare money for fortifying their fettlements in America, nor could they fend any regular troops thither for defending them; fo that even our private adventurers had great fuccefs, and often got rich-booties by privateering, and by incurfions upon thofe fettlements; for, as there was no good correfpondence between France and Spain, and an open war between Spain and Holland, the Spaniards could not make ufe of either French or Dutch veffels, for carrying on their trade with their fettlements in America; and befides, as the French were then involved in civil wars, they durft not venture to difoblige England, by affifting Spain, either openly or by underhand dealings.

In Oliver Cromwell's time, my Lords, we know that the Spaniards were engaged in a heavy war with France, which

rendered

rendered them unable to provide for the fecurity of their trade and poffeffions in America; and though, by our taking part with France in that war, we got the ifland of Jamaica, which was a valuable acquifition, yet I muft think, it would have been lucky for this nation, if Oliver had joined with France againft Spain; for it was his fatal union with France, that laid the foundation of the exceffive power of that kingdom, which has fince coft this nation fo much blood, and fo many millions of money. And now, my Lords, with regard to both thefe wars, I muft obferve, that notwithftanding our great fucceffes againft Spain, in Oliver's time, that nation was not eafily, or foon reduced to comply with fuch terms as we thought reafonable, for both Queen Elizabeth and Oliver Cromwell left the war to be put an end to by their fucceffors.

Lord Hervey, Feb. 22, 1738.

EVERY nation in Europe is proud of feeing the younger children of their Royal Family make a figure in the world. The provifion which his Majefty has been pleafed to make, is but very moderate. Twenty-four thoufand pounds a year, can never be thought too much to the four Princeffes; and 15,000 l. per annum is lefs, I believe, than any fecond fon of the Royal Family ever had before: the younger brother of Charles the IId had 10,000 l. fettled upon him; and the fmall allowance to the Duke, mentioned in this Bill, is a proof of his Majefty's moderation, and that he has the good of his kingdom, and the eafe of his fubjects, always firft in his thoughts.

Lord Delawar, Feb. 22, 1739.

AT the time of the Revolution, the Dutch provided a fquadron of fifty men of war, and tranfports for 14,000 men, of which a great number was cavalry, in three months time, for accompanying the Prince of Orange to England. I fay, my Lords, in three months time; for it was in July that the firft Refolution was taken to affift the Prince of Orange, and the

the States-General prepared fuch an expedition, that foon after the beginning of October, a fleet of 50 men of war, 25 frigates, 25 fire-fhips, and near 400 tranfports, with an army of 10,000 foot, and 4000 horfe, were ready to fail, and actually did fail upon the 19th of that month.

Lord Carteret, Nov. 18, 1740.

If then we fhould return to the country, my Lords, and tell the people, that our government durft not fend forces out to invade the enemy, for fear of their invading us, will not every man of common fenfe laugh us to fcorn ? Does not every one know, that the beft way to prevent an invafion is to invade ? Did not the Romans fend *Scipio* to invade the Carthaginians, at the very time that Hannibal was in Italy, and almoft at their gates? But the cafe with us is ftill ftronger; we could eafily have invaded the enemy when and where we pleafed ; whereas it was difficult and dangerous, if not impoffible for them to invade us at any time, or in any place. To pretend that we muft always keep a mercenary army of 30,000 men in Britain and Ireland, for fupporting our government againft an invafion with 4 or 5000, muft be ridiculous; or it muft be a very bad compliment upon the illuftrious family now upon the Throne ; becaufe, it is fuppofing that they have few or no friends in the nation, but thofe they keep in daily pay. And to fay that a common foldier, who has no property, who has neither *ara* nor *focus*, will fight againft a foreign invader with more courage and refolution than thofe that fight *pro aris & focis*, is, I am fure, a very unjuft reflection upon all the Gentlemen and all the men of fubftance in the kingdom.

Lord Carteret, Nov. 18, 1740.

I know, my Lords, I do not fpeak properly, when in talking of what happened in King Charles the Ift's time, I make ufe of the term *Cabinet Council*, becaufe it is a term of much later date ; for in thofe days, befides this Houfe, the King had no

other

other Council, but that which we ftill call the Privy Council, and of that Council there was always a Committee appointed to confider and take care of foreign affairs ; but the Refolutions of that Committee were not carried into execution, till they were approved of by the Privy Council : In that Council there then fat feveral great Officers, fuch as the Lord High Trea-furer, the Lord High Admiral, and others, who by their birth and quality, as well as by the importance of the pofts they en-joyed, added weight and dignity to the Council of which they were Members ; but thefe high offices are now fplit into Com-miffions, and fometimes granted to men who have neither birth, quality, nor character ; which is not done for the fake of difpatching bufinefs (for every one knows, the whole bufinefs of the nation, or office, is now chiefly directed by one, in the fame manner it was formerly) but for the fake of multiplying falaries and gaining votes. This has very much derogated from the honor of that Affembly, and is, I believe, the chief caufe of their power being now almoft entirely ufurped and exercifed by what is called the Cabinet Council ; but even what we now call the Cabinet Council, has not always the power and influence they feem to have ; for when any one Minifter happens to get the fole direction of all public affairs, the other Members of the Cabinet Council, or at leaft the majority of them, ferve only to give a fort of authority to what the Minifter has been pleafed to refolve on. *Duke of Argyle, Dec.* 8, 1740.

In Queen Elizabeth's time, though the war againft Spain began in 1585, and lafted till that Queen's death in 1603, which was feventeen years, yet in all that time there were but three or four expeditions of confequence undertaken againft the enemy, either in Spain, or in the Indies ; and though the pri-vate adventurers got fometimes a rich booty, yet the nation never reaped an advantage, nor kept poffeffion of any one place they had the good fortune to take. Again, in *Oliver Cromwell's* time,

time, though the war againſt Spain began in 1654, and continued till his death in 1658, yet no one expedition was undertaken, or, I believe, ſo much as thought of, againſt any one
of the dominions of Spain, except that one expedition by which
the war begun, and by which we got and kept the Iſland of
Jamaica,

The Lord Chancellor, Dec. 8, 1740.

My Lords, I muſt think it very unlucky in any one, that
argues in favor of our conduct in the preſent war, to mention
Queen *Elizabeth* or *Oliver Cromwell*; both of them began war
againſt *Spain* in a very different manner from what we have
now done.   Queen *Elizabeth* began the war, by ſending an
army into the *Low Countries*, to aſſiſt them in throwing off the
yoke of *Spain* ; at the ſame time ſhe ſent a ſquadron, with land
forces on board, to the Weſt-Indies, not with ſimple or am-
biguous orders for making repriſals, but expreſs orders to attack
the *Spaniſh* ſettlements; and accordingly they took and plundered *St. Jago*, one of the *Cape Verd* iſlands, as alſo moſt part
of the iſland of *St. Domingo*, the town of *Carthagena*, and the
towns of *St. Antonio* and *St. Helena* in *Florida*.   The very next
year after the return of this fleet, ſhe ſent another under the
ſame Admiral, *Drake*, to the coaſt of *Spain*, which did not lie
to be ſtared at off of any of their ports, but entered the harbour
of *Cadiz* and the river of *Liſbon*, and burnt a great number of
ſhips : and though the Admiral had no land forces on board,
yet he landed at ſeveral places upon the coaſt of *Spain*, and
ravaged the whole country round.   At the ſame time ſhe ſent
Cavendiſh to the *South-Seas*, where he ravaged the whole coaſt
of *Chili* and *Peru*, and returned to England with a booty vaſtly
rich.   The year following was the year of the *Spaniſh Armada*,
the fate of which I need not relate.   The next year, with the
aſſiſtance of ſome private adventurers, ſhe ſent a fleet and arm y
againſt *Spain* itſelf, where they landed at ſeveral places, beat an
army that was ſent againſt them, and might have got a great
booty,

booty, if they had not amufed themfelves with reftoring the dethroned King of Portugal. The four or five years next fol-lowing, that great Queen was chiefly employed in affifting Henry the IVth of France againft the Spaniards and his own rebellious fubjects; and in the year 1596, a new fleet and army was fent againft Spain under the Earl of Effex, who took the city of Cadiz, burnt or took all the fhips in the harbour, and after having done the Spaniards an infinite deal of fervice, re-turned to England with a moft inconfiderable booty.

Befides thefe, my Lord, there were feveral other expeditions of lefs note undertaken againft Spain in that reign; and if we did not, in that time, keep poffeffion of any of the places we took from the enemy in the Weft-Indies, it was becaufe we did not then fo much know the value of fettlements in that part of the world. But if Queen Elizabeth did not pufh the war againft Spain with fo much vigor as fhe might have done, there were two reafons for it, which do not now fubfift. In the firft place, our trade, which was then in its infancy, fuffered but very little by the war, and we were yearly getting great riches by plundering the enemy at fea or land; and in the next place, that gracious Queen was extremely fhy of loading her fubjects with any new taxes, or putting the public to any expence. When fhe found herfelf under no neceffity to fend out forces to attack the enemy, or affift her allies, fhe kept no army or fquadron at home, to be a burden and oppreffion upon her own fubjects. She raifed no armies, nor fitted out any fquadrons, but when fhe had immediate occafion for them, or was in imminent danger; and as foon as the fervice, or the danger was over, fhe difmiffed her armies, and paid off her fquadrons: I wifh I could fay, we had held the fame conduct ever fince, or that we now held fuch a conduct.

With regard to Oliver Cromwell, it is well known he began his war with Spain by the conqueft of Jamaica, which has fince brought in fo many millions fterling to England; and if it had not been for a miftake in his General, he would probably have

begun

begun it with the conqueſt of St. Domingo, which would have
been an acquiſition of much greater conſequence to this kingdom.
If he did not ſecond his blow in the Weſt-Indies, it was becauſe he engaged with the French in their war againſt the Spaniards in the Netherlands, by which he got poſſeſſion of the important city and port of Dunkirk ; and he died in little more than
two months after he had made this new and important acquiſition, which we might to this day have had in our poſſeſſion,
if the Parliament, upon the Reſtoration, had done their duty,
and annexed it to the Crown of England.

Earl of Cheſterfield, Dec. 8, 1740.

THE caſe of the Earl of Briſtol, in King Charles the Firſt's
time, may ſhow how dangerous it is to accuſe a favorite Miniſter, whilſt he is in the zenith of his power and intereſt at
Court.   Nothing could be more juſt than the accuſation brought
by that Earl againſt the Duke of Buckingham, yet it produced
an accuſation againſt that Earl, in which the King himſelf was
the accuſer, and his Attorney General the proſecutor.   This
was a moſt terrible ſituation which that noble Earl was brought
into by his fidelity to his country, and his own honor ; and if
the power of the Crown had been in the ſame condition it is
now, notwithſtanding the heinouſneſs of his charge againſt the
Miniſter, notwithſtanding his full and well-vouched defence as
to the charge exhibited againſt him, he might, probably, have
fallen a ſacrifice to the reſentment of that favorite Miniſter.

Earl of Carteret, Feb. 13, 1740.

IT is with regret I obſerve, that almoſt every Seſſion intro-
duces ſomething new, in diminution of the Liberties, or derogatory to the Conſtitution of this kingdom.   In former times,
the Grant of a Supply often ſtood a long Debate in this Houſe,
and was ſometimes abſolutely refuſed ; now it is always granted
nemine contradicente.   The Malt-Tax was never introduced till
towards the latter end of King William's reign, and was at
firſt

firft moft ftrenuoufly oppofed: Nay, even during the war in Queen Anne's time, it was often oppofed, and was looked on as a tax fo burdenfome upon the poor labourers and manufacturers of this kingdom, that no man imagined any Minifter would have the affurance to propofe renewing or continuing it, after the war was over. The Mutiny Bill was at firft thought to be a moft dangerous innovation, and was therefore moft violently oppofed, efpecially in time of peace; but it is now become fo familiar to us, that we pafs it regularly every year, without the leaft oppofition, as if a Standing Army and a Mutiny Act were two things abfolutely neceffary for the fubfiftence of our Conftitution. Not many years ago, the Members of this Houfe, when affembled, looked upon themfelves as the grand Inqueft of the Nation, and therefore thought themfelves in duty bound to inquire into every grievance and complaint, without any other foundation than a public rumour; but now every Motion, that tends to an inquiry into any complaint, is rejected; or if any fuch inquiry be fet on foot, it is committed to thofe who are themfelves fufpected of being the original and chief caufe of the complaint.

Thus, Sir, we have for feveral years gone on approaching, I am afraid, to the confines of flavery; and in this Seffion, we have made a new and a very extraordinary ftep. Till this Seffion we have always thought, that every Member of this Houfe had a right to vote for a Call of the Houfe. We are fellow-labourers for the public good: we are all joint-guardians of the Liberties of our Country, and every Member has a right to infift upon it, that his companion fhould attend and bear an equal fhare of the burden, or at leaft a fhare proportionable to his ftrength and capacity. But in this Seffion, Sir, we have feen a Motion for a Call rejected, though that Motion was the firft of the kind that had been made, though it was fupported by ftrong reafons, and though it was defired by near one half of thofe that were then prefent. This I muft look on as a moft dangerous innovation; for when we begin to encroach upon,

3   or

or derogate from our own Rights, no man can tell how far
it may go. I do not know, but I may live to fee the Queftion
put upon a Gentleman's rifing up to fpeak, *whether he fhall
have leave to fpeak?* And if ever fuch a Queftion fhould be
put, I fhall not in the leaft doubt of its being carried in the
negative, in cafe there fhould be a fufpicion of the Gentleman's intending to utter things difagreeable to thofe that may
then have the direction of the Majorities of this Houfe.

William Pulteney, Efq; Jan. 29, 1739.

I MUST be againft compelling the attendance of fuch Gentlemen in this Houfe; I am far from finding fault with any
of thofe Gentlemen that have returned; I think they have
done their duty in doing fo; but I cannot help comparing them
to the prefent King of Spain. He, fome years ago, refigned
his Crown, out of a pet, and, I think, it was a religious or
confcientious pet too. I wifh they had held him at his word,
and never allowed him to refume, as they might and ought to
have done; for his fecond fon, now Prince of Afturias, was
the natural fucceffor to his eldeft, who died King of Spain.
But they allowed him to refume his Crown, and we know
what difturbances he has fince bred in Europe. If the Gentlemen who left their Seats laft Seffion, had been taken at their
word; if we had ordered their Seats to be filled up by new
Elections, they could have complained of no injuftice: but
we have this Seffion allowed fuch of them as have returned, to
refume their Seats. In this, we have fhewn ourfelves to be as
indulgent as the fubjects of the King of Spain; and I hope
they will take care not to make fuch an ufe of the indulgence
they have met with, as his Catholic Majefty has done. They
have hitherto fhewn, that they do not incline to do; but, if
we fhould call in thofe that, for aught we know, are ftill in a
bad humour, I do not know what may happen. Evil company,
they fay, corrupts good manners. It is a dangerous experiment,

ment, to mingle the infected with thofe that are but juft recovered. For this reafon I was againft the Call.

Robert Tracey, Efq; Jan. 25, 1735.

No Legiflator ever founded a free Government, but avoided
a ftanding army, that *Charybdis,* as a rock againft which his
Commonwealth muft certainly be fhipwrecked, as the Ifraelites,
Athenians, Corinthians, Achaians, Lacedemonians, Thebans,
Samnites, and Romans; none of which nations, whilft they
kept their liberty, were ever known to maintain any foldier in
conftant pay within their cities, or ever fuffered any of their
fubjects to make war their profeffion ; well knowing, that the
fword and fovereignty always march hand in hand; and therefore
they trained their own citizens, and territories about them, perpetually in arms ; and their whole Commonwealths, by this
means, became fo many formed militias : a general exercife of
the beft of their people in the ufe of arms, was the only bulwark of their liberties, and was reckoned the fureft way to
preferve them both at home and abroad, the people being fecured thereby as well againft the domeftic affronts of any of
their own citizens, as againft the foreign invafions of ambitious
and unruly neighbours. Their arms were never lodged in
the hands of any who had not an intereft in preferving the
public peace, who fought *pro aris & focis,* and thought themfelves fufficiently paid by repelling invaders, that they might
with freedom return to their own affairs. In thofe days there
was no difference between the citizen, the foldier, and the
hufbandman; for all promifcuoufly took arms when the public
fafety required it, and afterwards laid them down with more
alacrity than they took them up: fo that we find among the
Romans, the braveft and greateft of their Generals came from
the plough, contentedly returning when the work was over,
and never demanding their triumphs, till they had laid down
their commands, and reduced themfelves to the ftate of private men. Nor do we find this famous Commonwealth ever

Vol. I.   E   permitted

permitted a difpofition of their arms in any other hands, till their Empire increafing, neceffity cenftrained them to erect a conftant ftipendiary foldiery abroad in foreign parts, either for , the holding or winning of provinces. Then luxury increafing with dominion, the ftrict rule and difcipline of freedom foon abated, and forces were kept up at home; which foon proved of fuch dangerous confequence, that the people were forced to make a law to employ them at a convenient diftance: which was, that if any General marched over the river *Rubicon*, he fhould be declared a public enemy. And in the paffage of that river, the following infcription was erected, *Imperator five miles, five tyrannus armatus quifquis fiftito; vexillum armaque deponito, nec citra hunc amnem trajicito*. And this made *Cæfar*, when he had prefumed to pafs this river, to think of nothing but the preffing on to the total oppreffion of that glorious Empire.

Mr. Hutchefon, Feb. 12, 1740.

SIR, it is a new doctrine in this nation, and abfolutely inconfiftent with our Conftitution, to tell us, that his Majefty may, and ought, in the difpofal of offices and favours, to confider Gentlemen's behaviour in this Houfe. Let his Majefty be never fo well convinced of the wifdom and uprightnefs of his meafures, he ought not to take the leaft notice of what is faid or done by any particular man in this Houfe. He is a traitor to our Conftitution that advifes his Majefty to do fo; and if reports are carried to his Majefty, with regard to the behaviour of any particular Member of Parliament in this Houfe, or at any Election, he ought to do with them, as it is faid King William did with the Papers of a Plot he had difcovered. By perufing one of them, he found reafon to fufpect fome of his Courtiers had been concerned; whereupon he threw them all into the flames, that they might not furnifh him with fufpicions againft thofe he took to be his friends.

The

The fame Monarch ſhewed another inſtance of his generoſity, and of his regard for our Conſtitution. A poſt in the army having fallen vacant, the Gentleman who had the next right to it, happened to be a Member of this Houſe, and one that had oppoſed the Court, which few Officers do now-a-days; the Miniſters, as uſual, were againſt his preferment, becauſe he had oppoſed the King's Meaſures in Parliament; but the King told them, he had always behaved well as an Officer, and he had nothing to do with his behaviour in Parliament.

Honourable Edward Digby, March 23, 1741.

WHATEVER notion ſome Gentlemen may have of abſolute power, Sir, it has been thought neceſſary in all countries for preſerving ſubordination and diſcipline in an army. In the Roman Commonwealth, from its very firſt original, the Generals of their armies had a moſt abſolute and unlimited power over every Officer and Soldier in the army. They could not only prefer and reduce, but puniſh even with death itſelf, by their ſole authority, and without the ſentence of any Court Martial. The ſtory of *Manlius*, who put his own ſon to death, for fighting the enemy againſt his orders, is ſo well known, that I need not put Gentlemen in mind of it. Not only particular men, but whole armies, were among the *Romans* ſubjeċt to be puniſhed by the ſole and abſolute power of their General; for we read that *Appius*, in the very infancy of that Commonwealth, cauſed every tenth man in the army to be whipped for flying from the enemy; beſides puniſhing ſome of the Officers with death. And, I believe, there is now no country in the world, where their armies enjoy ſo much freedom, or ſo much ſecurity againſt being oppreſſed by their Commanders, as both the Officers and Soldiers of our Britiſh armies enjoy.

Colonel Conway, Feb. 7, 1750.

THE

THE old Nabob *Meer Jaffier*, if ever Muſſulman had a friendſhip for a Chriſtian, had a friendſhip for me. When the news of my appointment reached Bengal, he immediately quitted *Muxadavad*; came down to Calcutta; impatiently waited my arrival ſix weeks; fell ill; returned to his Capital, and died! Two or three days before his death, in the preſence of his wife, and in the preſence of his Miniſter, he ſaid to his ſon and ſucceſſor, " Whatever you think proper to give to Lord Clive on your own account, the means are in your power : But as a teſtimony of my affection for him, I deſire you will pay to him, as a legacy from me, five lacks of rupees." I muſt obſerve, that the Nabob's death happened whilſt I was on my voyage, and ſome months before my arrival in Bengal. The principal and intereſt amounted to near ſeventy thouſand pounds. The whole of the money, added to about forty thouſand pounds more, which I prevailed on the Nabob to beſtow, is eſtabliſhed for a Military Fund, in ſupport of Officers, and Soldiers who may be invalided in any part of India, and alſo in ſupport of their widows.

Lord Clive, March 30, 1772.

IF Gentlemen will ſearch the Records in the Tower, they will find that the town of *Calais* in France, when it belonged to the Imperial Crown of theſe Realms, was not taxed till it ſent Repreſentatives to Parliament. Two Burgeſſes from Calais actually ſat and voted in this Houſe. Then, and not till then, was Calais taxed. The Writ out of Chancery, and the Return to it, in the reign of Edward the VIth, with the names of the Burgeſſes, are ſtill extant. I faithfully gave them to the Public from atteſted copies.

Mr. Wilkes, Feb. 1775.

THE adopting of the meaſures of ſupporting large ſtanding armies, to enforce the ſovereignty over their provinces, (an alluring motive) has ſubjugated them all in their turns, and ex-
                                        tinguiſhed

tinguifhed their conftitutional provifions and barriers againft tyranny.

To pafs over the leffer States, not only Marius, and Sylla, and *Cæfar*, but Auguftus and Tiberius, thofe able tyrants, who fyftematically ruined the Roman Empire and her liberties, atchieved it by troops raifed to maintain the Roman Sovereignty over their provinces. They did, indeed, fubdue thofe provinces; and their projeft reached ftill farther than they expefted; for it ftopped not till the Military Power, eftablifhed by them for that end, overturned the Imperial Power itfelf.— In lefs than fifty years from the death of *Auguftus*, thofe armies raifed to keep the provinces in awe, had no lefs than three Emperors on foot at the fame time; and thenceforward the Military Power difpofe of the Empire, and gave to whom it pleafed the throne of the *Cæfars*. Whoever will calmly examine thofe precedents, it is impoffible but they muft be convinced, that the like caufes muft have fimilar effefts. Oppreffed by an overgrown army, the Liberty of America, and *Ireland*, (for that ftands next in the minifterial plan) and afterwards that of Great-Britain, will follow of cdurfe;—the Monfter of Defpotifm will only grant even to the *latter* the favour intended for *Ulyffes*, that of being laft devoured.

Lord Irnham, Feb. 6, 1775.

THE cruel and perfecuting means devifed for enforcing our meafures againft America, exaftly refemble the mode adopted by *Marfhal Rozen*, King James the Second's French General in Ireland, in order to reduce the rebellious citizens, and other defenders of Londonderry. They, brave men, as the Americans are now, were ftyled traitors and rebels; and they, as well as our rebellious fubjefts in America, were to be ftarved into compliance; that is, the means employed were to be juftified by the goodnefs of the caufe. An order was fent by Rozen, obliging the garrifon of Derry to fubmit; which was to colleft the wives, children, and aged parents of the garrifon,

E 3

rifon, to drive them under the walls of the town, there to perifh in the prefence of their parents, hufbands, and other relations; and if they offered to return, to fire on them, and *maffacre them.* But weak, infatuated, and bigoted as that Prince was, his heart revolted at fuch a horrid expedient of fubduing his enemies; for as foon as it reached his knowledge, he immediately countermanded the barbarous order, and left the innocent and unoffending to their liberty,

Marquis of Rockingham, March 16, 1775.

OF thirty-three Sovereigns of England, fince William the Conqueror, thirteen only have afcended the Throne by *divine* hereditary Right; the reft owe their Royalty to the zeal and vigour of the People of England, in the maintenance of Conftitutional Freedom.

The Will of the People, fuperfeding an hereditary Claim to Succeffion, at the commencement of the twelfth century, placed Henry the Ift on the Throne of this Kingdom, with condition that he would abrogate the vigorous laws made fince the Norman Invafion, reftore the Government as in the days of Edward the Confeffor, and abolifh all unjuft and arbitrary Taxes.

King Stephen obtained the Crown, and Henry the IId kept it, on the fame exprefs terms: yet, Sir, in the days of King John, it was judged expedient, no longer to truft to mere oral declarations, which State chicane and fophiftry had of late years occafionally explained away, but to compel that Prince folemnly to regifter an affirmance of the antient Rights of the People in a formal manner; and this neceffary work was accomplifhed by the Congrefs at *Runnemede,* in the year 1115: an Affembly which ought never to be fpoken of by the Reprefentatives of the Commons of England, but with the profoundeft veneration.

An honourable and learned Member over the way mentioned, a few evenings ago, the introduction of foreign troops

into

into this Ifland in the Reign of Henry the IIId, as a precedent
to warrant the prefent ftretch of Regal Prerogative in the
cafe of the Hanoverian Mercenaries : as that Member is not
now in the Houfe, I fhall be more concife in treating of the
events he alluded to, than I otherwife intended. Sir, in the
Reign of Henry the IIId, (about the year 1233) the Barons,
Clergy, and Freeholders, refufed two diftinct Summonfes to
Parliament; and underftanding that the King, as Earl of
Poictou, had landed fome of his Continental Troops in the
weftern ports of England, with a defign to ftrengthen a moft
odious and arbitrary fet of Minifters, they affembled in a *Convention*, or *Congrefs*, from whence they difpatched Deputies to
King Henry; declaring, that if he did not immediately fend
back thofe *Poictouvians*, and remove from his Perfon and
Councils evil advifers, they would place on the Throne a
Prince who fhould better obferve the Laws of the Land.—Sir,
the King not only hearkened to that Congrefs, but fhortly after complied with every article of their demands, and pub-
lickly notified his reformation. Now, Sir, what are we to
call that Affembly which dethroned Edward the IId, when the
Archbifhop of Canterbury preached a fermon on this text,
The voice of the People is the voice of God. And when a learned
Judge, in the character of Procurator for the mafs of the
Freemen, furrendered the homage and fealty of the People of
England, alledging that the original compact, through which
they were bound to Allegiance, was diffolved, by the ufe and
aggrandizement of ill Counfellors; by the Adminiftration of
Government, which agreed not with the ancient Laws of the
Land, and by a total difregard to the advice and fupplications
of his Majefty's faithful but afflicted fubjects. Richard the
IId (like the unhappy Edward) fell a victim to defpotic obftinacy and favouritifm : and to this King, in the fame manner, was furrendered, by Commiffioners (or Proctors) the allegiance of his fubjects ; and a Prince of the Houfe of Lan-
cafter (founder of our prefent Moft Gracious Majefty's royal

line)

line) was invited over from banifhment, and elected by the People to the Throne. But, Sir, before I difmifs this Reign, it may be proper to obferve, that Richard entirely fubverted the Conftitution of the Upper Houfe of Parliament; for he made it an appendage to the Crown, introducing Peers by Creation in prejudice to the territorial Baronies: and with re-fpect to the other Houfe, he fent orders to the Sheriffs of the feveral Counties throughout England, to return only fuch Re-prefentatives to Parliament, as fhould, on every occafion, im-plicitly obey the royal mandate. Nay, Sir, both Houfes con-jointly went at laft fo far, as to commit their whole parlia-mentary power into the hands of a Cabinet Junto of Mi-nifters, having, however, firft obtained the Pope's leave for fo doing. I wifh Gentlemen, who contend for fupreme So-vereignty in the Crown and Parliament, denying any Rights of the People in pre-eminence to their joint authority, would apply fuch argument to the State of King, Lords, and Com-mons at that æra. I fhall next proceed to the general Con-vention and Congrefs, which, in 1461, enthroned the Earl of March in Weftminfter-Hall, by the name of Edward the IVth, the Primate of all England collecting the Suffrages of the People; and at that period, even the *Lancaftrian* Hiftorians date the commencement of his Reign.

But to come to modern occurrences: in 1659, a *Convention*, or *Congrefs*, reftored legal Monarchy in the perfon of King Charles the IId, who was then no farther diftant from this Ifland than the town of *Breda*; and being preffed by many of the Royal Partizans to iffue his Writs for a lawful Parliament, he made anfwer, that he would rather be indebted for his Re-ftoration to the uninfluenced fenfe of the People of England, taken in a free Affembly.

On the 26th of December, 1688, was held a *Convention*, or *Congrefs*, at St. James's, where the Prince of Orange pre-fided; and there were prefent moft of the furviving Members who had ferved in any one of the Parliaments of King Charles the

the Second, the Lord Mayor, the Aldermen, and about fifty of the Common-Council, &c. and on the 22d of January following, by virtue of notices iffued on the aforefaid 26th of December, at St. James's, the memorable Convention Parliament affembled in this Houfe, and perfected the glorious work of the Revolution.

I mean, Sir, from thefe examples and arguments, to deduce for an uncontrovertible truth, that all the fubjects of the Britifh empire have a right to be governed according to the fpirit of our ancient conftitution, by which no freeman could be taxed without his confent, either in perfon, or by his fubftitute : and notwithftanding the infringement of this right under fome of our Norman Kings and their fucceffors, yet we find William the Conqueror himfelf confirming it in his code of laws, the year before his deceafe. And the fame explicit declaration in its favour from our Englifh *Juftinian*, King Edward the Firft, in the charter of the 25th, and ftatutes of the 34th of his reign, admitted to be among the earlieft authentic records of Parliament extant, according to the prefent mode of fummons.

. I have, I think, fhewn, that our Kings, in former days, have not fcrupled to treat with a Congrefs ; that many of the beft of them owe their Crowns to fuch national meetings ; and that this nation has, on the one hand, been faved from defpotifm, and, on the other hand, from anarchy, by a *Convention* or *Congrefs* ; which furely poffeffes fome advantages over a Parliament : for being free from minifterial management, having neither placemen, penfioners, nor dependent retainers on their lift, are more likely to hear the fincere dictates of confcience, and the unpolluted fenfe of thofe they reprefent. But, Sir, however inadmiffible the voice of a Congrefs might be deemed as acts of legiflation, yet I conceive that their plea, in the character of *Advocates* for the conftituent body by whom they are commif- fioned, ought in juftice, as well as found policy, to be liftened to. A punctilious delicacy now in fafhion, which we ftyle the dignity of the Crown and Parliament, will, if madly perfifted in,

coft

coft at leaft half the blood and fubftance of Great-Britain. The moft haughty and powerful Monarch of his time, Lewis the XIVth, when there was a formidable commotion in the *Ce-vennes*, condefcended to depute two Marfhals of France to enter into a treaty with the male-contents. Peace was accordingly made, and the terms of it were afterwards faithfully fulfilled.

Look, Sir, into the hiftory of the proudeft, as well as moft renowned people that ever exifted, the Romans; obferve the conclufion of *their Social War*, and you will fee they were not above negociating a peace with thefe very infurgents, whom they had before, individually by name, profcribed as rebels. Rome found herfelf at that day reduced to the fame critical predicament which, I apprehend, we now ftand in; there was no other poffible means of reftoring concord, or faving the commonwealth from ruin. But, Sir, above all, I would wifh the Houfe to give due weight to a conclufive remark of the excellent author of the Commentaries on the Laws of England, where he is defcanting on the Revolution of 1688, which placed the fceptre in the hands of King William, and eventually brought in the illuftrious Houfe of Hanover to be guardians of the Proteftant religion, and affertors of the antient conftitutional rights of all the fubjects throughout the Britifh monarchy. " No practical fyftem of law (fays he) are fo perfect, as to point out before-hand thofe *eccentric* remedies, which national energency will dictate and will juftify."

Honourable Temple Luttrell, Nov. 7, 1775.

WHEN news was brought to Agelfilaus, King of Sparta, during a war in Greece, that a bloody fight had happened near the city of Corinth, but that the Spartans were victorious, and the number of their troops killed was but inconfiderable, compared with the lofs of the enemy; inftead of exultations of joy, that wife and humane Monarch, with a deep figh, cried out, " Oh, unhappy Greece! to have flain fo many warriors with thine

thine own hand, who, had they lived, might have proved a match for all the barbarians in the world ! ".

Honourable Temple Luttrell, Oct. 31, 1776.

BEFORE the Revolution there were but few difqualifications affecting the elected. I know but of two Acts of Parliament, one in the firft year of Henry the Vth, confining their refidence to the counties, cities, and boroughs, for which they ferved; the other, the twenty-third of Henry the VIth, refpecting Knights of fhires. There were, indeed, certain difqualifications, by the *lex et confuetudo Parliamenti*, as that neither aliens nor minors fhould be elected; that the Clergy fhould not be chofen, becaufe they fit in Convocation; perfons attainted of treafon or felony could not fit, becaufe they are unfit to fit any where : the Judges, my Lord Coke fays, cannot fit, becaufe of their attendance in the Houfe of Lords. In my poor opinion there may be another, and as good a reafon affigned; and that is, that it is highly improper to blend the legiflative and judicial capacities together.

Here let me remark, by the way, that at a time when the Judges of England are prevented, by the law and cuftom of Parliament, (which is the law of the land) from fitting in the Houfe of Commons, and the Judges of Scotland are declared incapable of being elected by the Act of 7 Geo. the IId, the very great impropriety of the Judges for the principality of Wales fitting in this Houfe.

I beg leave to recommend this matter to the confideration of the Honourable Gentleman who has this day moved to augment the Welch Judges falaries.

The Act, Sir, of the 5th and 6th of William and Mary, which laid a duty on falt, beer, ale, and other liquors, exprefsly declared, that no perfon concerned in farming, managing, or collecting the faid duties, fhall be capable of fitting in Parliament. It alfo difqualifies the managers of all other aids that fhall hereafter be granted. The 11th and 12th of King William excluded

cluded the Commiffioners of the Cuftoms. It went farther, and even forbids them from ufing any influence with voters under certain penalties. The Aft of the 4th of Queen Anne went ftill farther, and excluded various defcriptions of men, all of whom are declared incapable of being elected by the Act of the 6th of Queen Anne.

The 1ft of Geo. I. Section II. cap. 56. difables any perfon from fitting in the Houfe of Commons, who fhall have any penfion from the Crown, for any term or number of years, and fubjects fuch perfons as fhould fo fit to the penalty of 20l. per day.

The 17th of Geo. II. regulates the elections of Members to ferve for Scotland, and incapacitates the Judges of the Court of Seffions, Court of Jufticiary, and Barons of the Court of Exchequer in Scotland, from being elected Members of Parliament.

During the adminiftration of Sir Robert Walpole, various attempts were made to reftrain the influence of the Crown over this branch of the legiflature; Place and Penfion Bills were frequently brought in, and two or three times actually paffed the Houfe of Commons, but were as often loft in the other Houfe of Parliament. On the retreat or removal of Sir Robert Walpole, an Act of Parliament was however paffed in 1742, 15 Geo. II. which difabled the Commiffioners of Revenue in Ireland, the Commiffioners of the Navy and Victualling Offices, Clerks in various departments, and many other defcriptions of men, who, from their fituation, were fuppofed, natural enough, to be under influence, from fitting in Parliament; and fubjecting fuch as fhould, notwithftanding, prefume to fit and vote, to a penalty of 20l. a day.

In the 33d of George II. an Act paffed to oblige Members to deliver in a fchedule of their qualifications, and take and fubfcribe an oath of the fame. Thefe, Sir, are all the difqualifications on the perfons to be elected to Parliament, excepting that there are three Acts in the reign of Queen Anne, and one in in the reign of George the IId, difabling the Regifters, or their Deputies, for the three Ridings in Yorkfhire, and the county of Middlefex, from fitting in Parliament.

Sir Jofeph Mawbey, March 11, 1775.

THAT the office of Secretary of State is of very ancient eftablifhment in this kingdom, I am ready to allow, though they were not always confidered of equal importance as now. I have endeavoured to acqaire all the knowledge I could of that office; I think, therefore, I am warranted in faying, that there never was more than one Secretary of State · till towards the end of Henry the Eighth.

Two Secretaries of State only were appointed at the fame time in King Henry's reign. In the time of his fucceffor, Edward the Sixth, there were only two Secretaries of State, till towards the clofe of his reign; a third Secretary was then appointed in the perfon of Sir John Cheek. Of this appointment, as I expect to hear much from the oppofite fide of the Houfe, I · will prefently fpeak more fully.

In the reign of Queen Elizabeth there were but two Secretaries of State; there were no more in the reign of King James. In the reign of Charles the Firft there were but two, they were Secretary Windebank, at one time, and Coke, and afterwards the elder Sir Henry Vane fucceeded. At the Reftoration, Sir Edward Nicholas and Sir William Morris were the Secretaries. On or about the year 1670, Henry Lord Arlington fucceeded Sir Edward Nicholas, and Sir John Trevor Sir William Morrice. There continued to be only two Secretaries of State during the remainder of King Charles the Second's reign. There were but two in the reign of King James the Second. There were no more than two in that of King William, nor, I believe, in that of Queen Anne; at leaft, in that part of it which preceded the year 1705.

Having thus fhewn that originally, and till the end of the reign of Henry the Eighth, there was but one Secretary of

State,

State, and afterwards but two, (except in the fingle cafe of Sir John Cheek's, in Edward the Sixth's time) I now proceed to take more particular notice of that appointment.

I contend, Sir, that the precedent is not fuch as fhould have attention paid to it. It was eftablifhed in a time of faction, and exifted but a moment. Gentlemen know that the Duke of Northumberland plotted to bring the Crown into his own family, in confequence of the marriage of his fon, the Lord Guildford Dudley, with the Lady Jane Grey, who, after the King's fifters, Mary and Elizabeth, was prefumptive heir to the Crown. He prepared himfelf accordingly; fome of his creatures were put into old offices ; for others, new offices were created. Sir John Cheek had been the King's Preceptor ; he had, it may be reafonably prefumed, in confequence, an influence over the Royal Mind. Mr. Secretary Cecil had befides married Sir John Cheek's fifter, and Cecil had at firft objected to the fettlement of the Crown in favour of the Lady Jane, though he afterwards became a witnefs to it : it was of the utmoft importance to Northumberland's views to gain Sir John Cheek a new office ; a new appointment was therefore created for him, that of third Secretary of State ; he had befides *douceurs* given him. Sir William Petre was the other Secretary ; a man, I may fafely fay, without principle, who ferved four Crowned Heads in that capacity, as different in intellect and turn of mind as principle ; namely, Henry the Eighth, Edward the Sixth, Queen Mary, and Queen Elizabeth. Strype, in his Ecclefiaftic Memorials, in 1553, fays of Sir John Cheek :

" In the next month, viz. June, a third Secretary was appointed, (a thing not known before,) viz. Sir John Cheek, whofe love and zeal for religion made him fafe to the intereft of Lady Jane ; and a gift was added to him and his heirs, of Clare, in Suffolk, with other lands, to the yearly value of one hundred pounds."

That the appointment in his favour was merely the refult of political arrangement, to forward the Duke of Northumberland's

land's views, I think is beyond a doubt. He was appointed in
1553; King Edward died on the 6th of July following, and on
the 15th of the fame month the Lady Jane refigned her pretenfions to the Crown; fo that Sir John Cheek could only have
held that office for a month. That he was the Duke of Northumberland's agent, I have no doubt; he fled on Mary's acceffion; he was brought back, imprifoned in the Tower, and
ftripped of his fubftance: to fave his life he figned a declaration,
profeffing popery, and died in 1557, contemned, as he deferved
to be, by all good men, for wanting principle.—I truft the
Houfe will agree with me, that fuch a precedent, in fuch a time,
for fuch a purpofe, and for a month only, deferves not the leaft
attention.

I am, Sir, at a lofs to guefs upon what ground the Noble
Lord's (Lord George Germaine) right to a feat in this Houfe
will be defended. I contend that it is a new office, new in fact,
though not in name.

The 27th fection of the Act of the 6th of Queen Anne declares, in order to prevent too great a number of Commiffioners
from being appointed for the execution of any office, that no
greater number of Commiffioners fhall be appointed for the execution of any office, than have been employed in the execution
of fuch refpective office before the firft day of that Parliament.
It is incumbent, therefore, on the Noble Lord, or his friends,
to prove, that before that Parliament there exifted more than
two Secretaries of State, which I contend never was the cafe,
except during a fingle month of Edward the Sixth's time; a
precedent which, from what I have faid of it, I truft will not
have any weight.

The office of Secretary of State for the Colonies was firft
eftablifhed in 1768, in favour of the Earl of Hillfborough; he
was fucceeded, in 1772, by Lord Dartmouth; in 1775, the
Noble Lord (Lord Geo. Germaine) over the way took that
office.

Sir Jofeph Mawbey, March 11, 1779.

T H E R E

THERE are many precedents fince Queen Anne's time, to
fhew that there have been fix different appointments, of three,
and once *four* Secretaries of State. In the time of Edward
the VIth, there was a third Secretary of State ; and in 1708-9,
more bufinefs arifing, fhe thought it fit to appoint a third Secretary of State. There is an inftance when there were *four*
Secretaries, one of whom was a Commoner, that was in 1723;
thefe were the Duke of Roxburgh and two others ; one of
whom going with the King to Hanover, *Sir Robert Walpole*
was appointed *fourth* Secretary of State. A new writ iffued
on the 4th of May, 1723, he was re-elected, and his feat was
never queftioned ; and in 1730, it was not given in as a *new*
place, when the account of fuch was called for.

Mr. De Grey, March 11, 1775.

No Irifhman ever dreamt of the power of England to bind
Ireland ; fo far back as the year 1642, the Roman Catholicks
of Ireland, in their great Affembly of Trim, in the county of
Meath, folemenly refolved, that Ireland was an independent
kingdom, and its Crown imperial ; and in the year before, the
Parliament of Ireland had voted a fimilar Propofition. The
claims of the Irifh are not novel, they are as old as Henry the
IId, who gave them the laws and conftitution of England, and
granted them of courfe a Parliament. The Great Charter was
given them by his grandfon, Henry the IIId, and they had a
free and independent legiflature till the year 1719, when the
Lords of England thought proper to refolve, that a caufe which
had been tried in appeal by the Lords of Ireland, had been *coram*
non judice ; and then, and not before, did England think of
afferting by law the fupremacy of England over Ireland, though
the latter had, till that period, even after the Revolution, enjoyed the right of appeal to her own King, in his Parliament
of Ireland.

Mr. Courtenay, May 17, 1782.

WHEN

WHEN Auguſlus Cæſar modeſtly conſented to become the tribune of the people, Rome gave up into the hands of that Prince the only remaining ſhield ſhe had to protect her liberty. The tribunitian power in this country, as in ancient Rome, was wiſely kept diſtinct and ſeparate from the executive power : in this government it was conſtitutionally lodged where it ought naturally to be lodged, in the Houſe of Commons ; and to that Houſe the people ought firſt to carry their complaints, even when they were directed againſt the meaſures of the Houſe itſelf : but now the people are taught to paſs by the door of the Houſe of Commons, and ſupplicate the Throne for the protection of their liberties : hence the diſſolution of the late Parliament, pretendedly in obedience to the ſenſe of the people ; from addreſſes the ſenſe of the people have been collected, and not from the Houſe of Commons. But I warn the people to beware of this double Houſe of Commons, which Miniſters are erecting on the foundation of their deluſion ; the Commons of England in Parliament aſſembled ; and the Commons of England in corporation and county meetings diſperſed ; an artful Miniſter would craftily play off the one after the other ; he would make uſe of a pliant Houſe of Commons to oppreſs the people ; and he would make uſe of a deluded Houſe of Commons, diſperſed through the country, to awe a refractory or independent collected Houſe of Commons. If the proceedings of the late Parliament had been really diſagreeable to the people, why had they not petitioned that Houſe againſt thoſe proceedings? If they had petitioned, and their prayers had been diſregarded, or treated with contempt, then addreſſes to the Throne for a diſſolution of Parliament would have been extremely proper : when public œconomy became the general wiſh of the people, petitions were preſented not to the Crown, but to the Houſe of Commons; but means have been contrived of late ſo to delude the people, as to make them the very inſtruments of the degradation of that branch of the government, the deſtruction of which muſt neceſſarily be attended with the loſs of their liberty. ·

Mr. Burke, June 15, 1784.

I n 1751, there was in the Exchequer of Ireland, a furplus of 400,000 l. This, inftead of being a matter of joy, was the caufe of general confternation throughout the kingdom. It was feared that the Crown was become fo rich, that it could pay off the debt that was then upon the nation; and, having no farther occafion for the annual grants, would call no more Parliaments. The alarm was univerfal. " Good God! the " Crown out of debt !" was the general cry. " What's to " become of us ?" faid the Parliament. " And what further " employment is there for me ?" exclaimed the politician. In fhort the terror and difmay were indefcribable.

Lord North, May 30, 1785.

ATTACK.

ATTACK.

AS the Honourable Gentleman (Sir Robert Walpole) who
fpoke laft, has made grievous complaints of the treat-
ment he and his friends receive from other Gentlemen, I am a
good deal furprized, that he fhould at the fame time fall into that
very error, which he fo much complains of in others ; for to
fay that Gentlemen make Motions, only for the fake of having
an opportunity to declaim againft thofe in the Adminiftration,
or for the fake of making a figure in the Votes, is language, in
my opinion, as unparliamentary, and treating Gentlemen with
as little candour, as what he has blamed others for.

I muft fay it feems to be a very difficult matter to know how
to pleafe thefe great men the Adminiftration ; for I find that
when any encomiums are made upon them, when any thing is
faid in praife of their meafures, they immediately take it to be
meant by way of irony ; and if any Gentleman happens to
give them any names which may feem to be a little harfh, thofe
they underftand exactly as they are fpoke, and complain that
Gentlemen do not treat them in a parliamentary way : but,
whatever other people may do, I am none of thofe who have
beftowed panegyrics either upon the prefent or upon any Adminiftration ; and I hope I never was or ever fhall be guilty of
calling names.

Mr. Shippen, Jan. 23, 1734.

UPON fuch a flight view, Sir, as I have taken of the accounts now upon the table, it is not poffible for me to enter
into the particular articles : but I cannot help taking notice of
one, which to me feems very extraordinary. There is near
250,000 l. charged, not for the building of fhips, but for the
building of houfes ; whether fuch houfes were neceffary, I fhall
not now proceed to determine : but if they were, I think it

is too large a fum for any Adminiftration to have expended, without a previous authority from Parliament; and that, I am fure, was never afked for : what the prefent age may think of fuch a fum, I do not know, but I am fure our ancefters, even of the very laft age, would have been extremely fhy of loading the people with at leaft fix-pence in the pound upon all the lands in Great-Britain, for building houfes for the Officers belonging to the Admiralty: and I muft think it a little extra-ordinary to fee Minifters, of their own heads, undertake to do that, which even Parliaments of old would fcarcely have thought of doing. It is true, that Parliaments have of late become very good-natured ; they have put great confidence in Minifters, and have generally, I fhall not fay blindly, approved of all minifterial meafures : this may, perhaps, have made Minifters prefume a little farther than they would otherwife have done ; but I am very fure, that till very lately, no Minifter would have dared to have drawn the nation into fuch an ex-pence, without an authority from Parliament for fo doing.

Sir William Wyndham, Feb. 24, 1735.

THAT there are difcontents among the people, Sir, and that thofe difcontents are too general, I fhall readily agree; but whether they are owing to difaffection, I fhall not pretend to determine ; I am fu e they are not owing to reafon: for there is no country in the world where the liberties and properties of the fubjects are facredly preferved, nor are more there any fubjects who pay lefs for the eafe and fecurity they enjoy, than the fub-jects of this kingdom: but there are fome men who feem to think they ought to pay nothing, nor be at any trouble, for preferving to themfelves the bleffings of peace and fecurity. To pleafe fuch men, or to prevent their being diffatisfied, is impoffible ; for government muft always be expenfive: fome men muft be employed for managing and tranfacting the affairs of the fociety ; and fome muft now and then expofe themfelves to danger for the defence of the fociety : and it is both reafon-

able

able and neceſſary, that thoſe who ſpend their whole time, or a
great part of their time in government affairs, as well as thoſe
who venture their lives for the preſervation of others, ſhould
be rewarded by thoſe, who by their means are enabled to pro-
ſecute their own private affairs with ſafety, and without inter-
ruption. There are other men, and thoſe not a few, who are
ſo fond of novelty and change, that they are continually wiſhing
for public convulſions and revolutions : ſuch men are of ſo odd
a temper, that they become diſſatisfied with the ſecurity they
enjoy; and a long uninterrupted courſe of public happineſs,
renders them completely miſerable ; and there are others who
never can be pleaſed, unleſs they have the entire direction of
all public affairs ; therefore when they are not employed, and
chiefly employed, they are continually ſpreading virulent libels
and ſeditious pamphlets againſt thoſe that are ; by which means
many unwary perſons are caught, and are made to believe that
the nation is ruined and undone ; though every man in the nation, who is tolerably frugal and induſtrious, finds himſelf in
an eaſy and thriving condition.

Col. Mordaunt, Feb. 3, 1738.

I HATE, Sir, all expedients, and I diſdain all Miniſters
(looking at Sir Robert Walpole) who uſe them. Some Miniſters, Sir, there are, who live upon expedients, and who cannot
do their dirty work without them. Expedients, Sir, in the
hands of weak Miniſters, are the inſtruments of defeating the
moſt beneficial, and promoting the moſt deſtructive meaſures.

Mr. Pulteney, May 12, 1738.

THOUGH the manner in which the Honourable Gentleman
who ſpoke laſt delivered himſelf may well excuſe me from ſay-
ing any thing in anſwer to a ſpeech ſo very unparliamentary, and
ſo very inconſiſtent with all the rules of common decency ; yet
I think I ought to ſhew ſo much regard to the Houſe as to declare, that I abhor dirty expedients as much the Honourable

F 3 Gentleman

Gentleman would be thought to do : as for his common-place railing againft Minifters, it gives me very little trouble, fo long as I am confcious I do not deferve to have it applied to me. Were I ambitious of fhewing my wit, I might have a fair opportunity of doing it, by railing againft mock-patriots as much as the Honourable Gentleman has been pleafed to do againft corrupt Minifters, and both perhaps might be equally inftructive to the Houfe. But, railing of all kinds, Sir, has always been looked upon as the laft expedient of difappointed ambition, and a poor expedient it is. Were I one who for many years had unfuccefsfully endeavoured, by all the arts that malice and falfhood could fuggeft, to work myfelf into thofe pofts and dignities that I outwardly affected to defpife, I know not how far, Sir, my temper might be foured, as to make ufe of fuch an expedient ; but really, Sir, if I did, I fhould make but a very poor figure in the world.

Sir Robert Walpole, May 12, 1738.

THE meafures which the Gentleman who fpoke laft (Sir William Wyndham) and his friends may purfue, afford me no uneafinefs. The minds of the nation and his Majefty, are obliged to them for pulling off the mafk. We can be upon our guard, Sir, againft open rebellion, but it is hard to guard againft fecret treafon. The faction I fpeak of, Sir, never fat in this Houfe; they never joined in any public meafure of the government, but with a view to diftrefs it, and to ferve a popifh intereft. The Gentleman who is now the mouth of this faction was looked upon as the head of thefe traitors, who 25 years ago, confpired the deftruction of their country, and of the Royal Family, to fet up a Popifh Pretender upon the Throne. He was feized by the vigilance of the then government, and pardoned by its clemency : but all the ufe he has ungratefully made of that clemency, has been to qualify himfelf according to law, that he and his party may, fometime or other, have an opportunity to overthrow all law.

I am

I am afraid, Sir, that the Honourable Gentleman (Sir William Wyndham) and his friends, will not be fo good as their word, to withdraw themfelves from Parliament, for I remember that, in the cafe of a favourite Prelate who was impeached of Treafon, the fame Gentleman, and his faction, made the fame refolution. They then went off like Traitors as they were, Sir, but their retreat had not the deteftable effect they expected and wifhed, and therefore they returned. Ever fince, Sir, they have perfevered in the fame treafonable intention of ferving that intereft by diftreffing Government. But I hope their behaviour will unite all the true friends of the prefent happy Eftablifhment of the Crown in his Majefty's Perfon and Family, more firmly than ever; and that the Gentlemen who, with good intentions, have been deluded into the like meafures, will awake from their delufion, fince the Trumpet of Rebellion is now founded.

Sir Robert Walpole, March 13, 1739.

AFTER what had paffed laft Seffions, and after the repeated declarations of the Honourable Gentleman who fpoke laft, (Mr. Pulteney) and his friends, I little thought that we fhould have this Seffion been again favoured with their company. I am always pleafed, Sir, when I fee Gentlemen in the way of their duty, and glad that thefe Gentlemen have returned to theirs; though, to fay the truth, I was in no great concern left the fervice either of his Majefty, or the Nation, fhould fuffer by their abfence. I believe the Nation is generally fenfible, that the many ufeful and popular Acts which paffed towards the end of laft Seffion, were greatly forwarded and facilitated by the feceffion of thofe Gentlemen; and if they are returned only to oppofe and perplex, I fhall not at all be forry if they fecede again.

Sir Robert Walpole, June 14, 1739.

F 4

I must own, Sir, I can fee but one reafon for raifing, at
this prefent juncture, this additional number of troops; and that
is, to ftrengthen the hands of the Minifter againft the next
Election, by giving him the power of difpofing of Commiffions
to the fons, brothers, nephews, coufins, and friends of fuch as
have interefts in Boroughs, into fome of which, perhaps,
troops may be fent to procure the free election of their Members, in imitation of the late Czarina fending her troops into
Poland to fecure the free election of a King.

But ftill there is one thing more fatal than all I have yet
named, that muft be the confequence of fo great a body of
troops being kept on foot in England, and will be the finifhing ftroke to all our Liberties. For as the towns in England
will not be able much longer to contain quarters for them,
moft of thofe who keep public houfes, being nearly ruined by
foldiers billetted on them ; fo on pretence of the neceffity of it,
barracks will be built for quartering them, which will be as fo
many fortreffes, with ftrong garrifons in them, erected in all
parts of England, which can tend to nothing but by degrees
to fubdue and enflave the kingdom.

But if ever this fcheme fhould be attempted, it will be incumbent on every Englifhman to endeavour to prevent it by
all methods ; and as it would be the laft ftand that could ever
be made for our Liberties, rather than fuffer it to be put in
execution, it would be our duty to draw our fwords, and never
put them up till our Liberties are fecured, and the authors of
our intended flavery brought to condign punifhment.

Lord Gage, Nov. 29, 1739.

Notwithstanding the bad fuccefs of my laft Motion,
for inquiring into the late conduct of our public affairs, it fhall
not difcourage me from offering another of the fame nature;
becaufe, I think, our making fome fort of inquiry, during
this Seffion of Parliament, abfolutely neceffary for quieting the
minds of the People, and for reftoring, in fome degree, the

character

character and credit of our Government. What fort of company fome Gentlemen may keep, I do not know ; but to me, that keep all forts of company, the difappointment upon the former Motion's being rejected, appeared evident in the face of every man, who had not reafon, upon his own account, or the account of fome of his friends, to dread the confequences of that inquiry ; and whatever we may think within doors, it will be thought without, nay, it is now generally faid, that if fome people were not confcious of their own guilt, they would not fo vigoroufly oppofe an inquiry: for an innocent man, when he finds himfelf accufed or fufpected, will always defire to be brought to a fair and legal trial, that he may have an opportunity to vindicate his character againft thofe whifpers that are fpread about againft him. This, Sir, is the language now held without doors ; and the certain confequence will be, that if we let this Seffion pafs over without any inquiry, it will be faid, that a Majority of us have been partakers in the guilt, and partners in the plunder of our Country.

From hence, Sir, I muft hope, that every innocent man in this Houfe, (and now that one man is gone from amongft us, I hope, all of us are fo) will be for the Queftion I am now to propofe, becaufe I have taken care to prevent its being liable to the two chief objections that feemed to prevail againft my laft Motion. Thefe were, its being too extenfive as to time, and too extenfive as to matter. An inquiry for twenty years back was thought to be without precedent, and that it would be fuch a precedent as might be of dangerous confequence in future times. This was one of the chief objections againft it, and an objection which, I believe, had weight with fome whofe concurrence I hope to be favoured with in this Motion. And the other objection was, its comprehending all our foreign as well as domeftic affairs, which muft of courfe have brought all the papers relating to our foreign negotiations before our Committee. To this it was objected, that it would endanger the difcovery of fome of the moft important fecrets of our Government

ment to our enemies, which might be of the moft fatal confequence now that we are engaged in one war, and in great
likelihood of being foon obliged to engage in another. This
likewife feemed to have weight, and, I believe, prevailed with
fome Gentlemen to be againft my former Motion; for which
reafon I fhall now only move, That a Committee be appointed
to inquire into the conduct of *Robert* Earl of *Orford*, during
the laft ten years of his being Firft Commiffioner of the
Treafury, and Chancellor and Under Treafurer of his Majefty's
Exchequer.

Sir, I hope the time of inquiry propofed by this Motion will
not be thought too extenfive; for confidering the chief crime
of a domeftic nature he has been accufed of, our inquiry cannot, I think, be confined within narrower bounds. The crime
I mean, is that of applying not only all the favours of the
Crown, but even the Public Money, towards gaining a corrupt influence at Elections and in Parliament. This he is generally accufed of by the voice of the People without doors,
and, I believe, there is not a Gentleman in this Houfe that has
been chofen in oppofition to what was called the Court Intereft,
who was not fenfible of fome fuch practices being carried on
againft him, before and at the time of his Election. Every
Gentleman muft be fenfible, that it is very difficult to fix fuch
practices upon a Minifter, becaufe they are not only carried on
in an hidden manner, but by Tools and Under-Agents, who
do not appear at the Election as Agents for the Minifter, but
as Agents for the Court Candidate; and generally fpend their
money very freely; though it is often known, that neither they
nor their Candidate had ever any money of their own to fpare:
nay, thofe Agents are often known to be Treafury-Agents,
though in the common courfe of juftice it is impoffible to prove
that they are: it will even be difficult for a Committee of this
Houfe, with all the powers we can give them, to trace this
practice up to its original fource: but, confidering the general
fufpicion without doors, and the many ftrong reafons there are
for

for believing that fufpicion to be well grounded, we ought certainly to aim at it; and if we do, we cannot begin later than
the time when canvaffing may be fuppofed to have begun for
the chufing of the laft Parliament, which, I reckon, was about
ten years ago; for as that Parliament was chofen in the fummer 1734, we muft fuppofe that the Candidates, efpecially
where there was like to be an oppofition, begán to take mea-
fúres for fecuring their intereft in the fummer 1732, which will
juft come within the term of ten years, computing back from
this time.

For this reafon, I hope, this will appear to be the fhorteft
time I could move for: and as it is much fhorter than the
time propofed by my laft Motion, I hope I fhall have the concurrence of mány Gentlemen who then appeared againft me;
efpecially as I have likewife in this taken care to obviate the
other objection, of its being too extenfive as to the matters
propofed to be inquired into; for as this Noble Lord had by
none of his Offices any thing to do with foreign affairs, this
Motion cannot be faid to relate to, or comprehend any affairs
of that nature, unlefs it be fuppofed, that this Minifter directed
every other branch of public bufinefs, as well as that of the
Treafury; which, I am fure, none of his friends will pretend
to fay, becaufe this would be as great a crime as any he is
accufed of. This Motion cannot therefore be fuppofed to relate to any Foreign Affairs, and, confequently, an inquiry into
this Nobleman's conduct, cannot be fuppofed to endanger the
difcovery of any of the fecrets of our Government. Nay, if
he, whilft he was in office, confined himfelf to the duty of
his office, our inquiry, in purfuance of this Motion, can comprehend but one branch even of our Domeftic Affairs, and that
branch too, which, of all others, has the leaft to do with our
Foreign Affairs. An inquiry into the conduct of a Secretary
of State, a Secretary at War, a Commiffioner of the Admiralty, or even the Lord High Chancellor, might be faid to have
fome relation to Foreign Affairs; but I cannot fuggeft to myfelf

felf what a Commiffioner of the Treafury can have to do with
·Foreign Affairs, or how an inquiry into his conduct can have
the leaft relation to any Foreign Affairs whatever: confequently,
I hope, this Motion will appear to be quite free from this objection, which feemed to be urged with fo much weight againft
my former: and as much has in this Seffion been faid, upon
former occafions, about the neceffity of an immediate inquiry,
I fhall add no more, but move to refolve, That a Committee
be appointed, as I have before-mentioned.

Lord Limerick, March 23, 1741.

THE Laws and Liberties we now enjoy, were procured for
us by fuch of our anceftors, as were utter ftrangers to every
fyftem but what conduced to honour and virtue. A Government fupported upon any other bafis ought not to fubfift a moment longer, nor is fuch a one worth contending for; no, not
even by thofe whofe depraved minds are not to be gratified by
the corrupteft Government, becaufe thofe who act or fight for
hire only, are always looking out for the beft market. So that
I hope we fhall not let this Seffion pafs without a good Militia
Bill; for a ftanding army, even in time of war, was never
yet an object that fuited the genius of this Nation, fuppofing it
kept up with the ftricteft œconomy, becaufe it is not our natural defence; and I can aver, there hath nothing happened
within thefe twelve months and upwards to render it more acceptable: for be it ever fo formidable, it cannot be every
where, much lefs can it prevent invafions or infurrections,
when, to our late memorable fhame, we were twice baffled by
a *banditti* rabble; and, in all probability, we had been ferved
fo a third time, but for the prefence of his Royal Highnefs the
Duke: whereas a well-armed and well-difciplined Militia,
difperfed over the face of this Kingdom, muft fupprefs all rifings
in the firft inftance, befides the great benefits we fhould have
of them in every maritime county, to put a ftop to that
abominable trade of fmuggling, without having recourfe to a
much

much more abominable practice, of putting your laws in execution by a military force : a precedent, give me leave to tell
you, Sir, that muft be fatal to the Liberties of this Kingdom,
if not timely prevented.

Sir, the conduct of our late and prefent Patriots, as they
prefume to call themfelves, proves the neceffity there is for
fome alteration in your Conftitution ; becaufe, how inhumane
is it for that eloquence, which was given by Providence for its
defence and prefervation, to be employed in its ruin and deftruction ! Punifhments there are for the thief, the murderer,
and the bare-faced traitor ; but alas.! to the grief of all well-
difpofed minds, there is none for the *fordid orator :* I fay, Sir,
there is none for the *fordid orator,* who fhall one day difplay
his eloquence in the caufe of his country, to fhew his parts and
gain attention ; and the next fhall convince his injured countrymen, that he is a proftitute to venality, and the purchafed flave
of a corrupt Miniftry. What pity it is that fuch wretches
cannot be brought to condign punifhment, without doing
violence to the laws of their country, who one day fling out
farcafms againft the Meafures of an Adminiftration, as ruinous
and deftructive, for no other caufe but to be admitted prin-
cipals in it : and the next day purfue the very fame meafures
which they had fo emphatically exploded, without the leaft jot
or tittle of alteration in the whole minifterial Syftem. Surely,
Sir, if there is one of that abject ftyle in being, how can he
ftand clear of that *occultum quatiente animo tortere flagellum ?*
—Or why fhould he not expect every moment to be hurled
down into that execrable, that moft deteftable pit, where the
worm never dies, and the fire is never quenched !

Sir, I fhould have no objection to addreffing his Majefty,
could I perceive the leaft tendency to reftore the Conftitution
to its ancient purity. The Royal Family upon the Throne,
under whom we enjoy fo many bleffings, found us in poffeffion of the Triennial Act ; and although it might be proper
to repeal it upon an extraordinary occafion, yet to continue
Parliaments

Parliaments to their prefent length, hath, I fear, been productive of many political misfortunes, fubfequent to that alteration. Yet, if ever the good people of South-Britain deferved a triennial holiday, it is for that fteady loyalty they have
fo lately fhewn, in oppofition to thofe of the Northern Parts
of this Kingdom; who have alfo diftinguifhed themfelves, but
not at all to their honour or credit. The Repealing of the
Septennial Act would bring us a little nearer to that happy
fituation of Independency, which Annual Parliaments would
undoubtedly compleat.

Thus, fuch as now think it ill policy to be unattached, or
unfafhionable to be difengaged, may then come to have nobler
views, than to proftitute their legiflative truft, conferred upon
them by their Conftituents; who, in all probability, could be
no otherwife influenced in their choice, (for fo fhort a period)
but merely from a perfonal regard. As I am one of thofe that
fhall be ever proud of being fo unfafhionably *degagée*, as to deteft nothing fo much as an attachment to any fide, or fet of
men whatfoever; fo, according to that laudable practice, of
our anceftors, I fhall wait to fee fome of the many grievances
we labour under firft redreffed, before I can give my affent to
the Addrefs moved for.

Major Selwyn, Nov. 18, 1746.

ABOUT the latter end of May, or the beginning of June,
the Miniftry were acquainted with the fate of Falkland Ifland.
At that time they learned, that the Governor of *Buenos Ayres*
had fent a frigate or two, to warn our troops to quit the
Ifland; that our Commanding Officer had threatened to fire
upon them if they would not depart; that the Spaniards, in
confequence, declared their refolution of employing force;
and that there was no doubt they would put their threat in
execution. Where their pride is concerned, the Spaniards are
tenacious of their words: and it could not be fuppofed,
that the Governor of *Buenos Ayres* would, in this cafe, belie

2   the

the character of his nation. But who is this Governor, this mighty Potentate, againſt whom the King of Great-Britain is going to draw his ſword? I will tell the Houſe. When at Gibraltar, in an inferior ſtation I confeſs, I happened in an excurſion to meet this Governor, this *Don Franciſco de Buccarelli*, whom our Miniſters conſider as great and formidable. For a Spaniard, he was not a bad companion; but I do not believe he had, at that time, the moſt diſtant hope of ever entering into a competition with the King of Great-Britain. But our Miniſters were made for rendering abſurdity faſhionable. As they have, for theſe two years, degraded their Royal Maſter by a quarrel with a wretched Libeller, ſo now they commit his dignity in a conteſt with a little *Spaniſh* Officer. The terrible foes that rouſe his vengeance, are *John Wilkes*, and my old friend *Buccarelli*. How much more honourable would it have been, to have at once conſidered the King of Spain as the aggreſſor, as the delinquent? It is evident, from the coolneſs and deliberation with which *Buccarelli* acted, that he acted under the authority, and by the expreſs command of the King of Spain. If he had not, he would have, ere now, forfeited his head. Why then did not our Miniſters, upon the firſt intelligence, deem this act of hoſtility the moſt explicit and effectual Declaration of War? Why did they not immediately arm the nation, and prepare for ſtriking as deciſive a blow, as that which ſecured us the ſuperiority of the late war? This ſtep would have brought into our ports their ſhips and ſailors, and effectually ruined their Marine. Of this truth no perſon of common ſenſe can entertain the leaſt doubt. Inſtead of adopting this vigorous meaſure, they let the affair ſleep for three or four months, as if time had no wings. And, when at laſt waked out of their lethargy, what have they done? What harbours have they improved? What forts have they repaired? What cities have they fortified? Have they ſtrengthened the lines at Quebec? Have they ſecured that ſpot, which, if taken by the enemy, will ruin our fiſhery, if it is not already

ruined

ruined by their indolence, timidity, or ignorance? Have you taken any Meafures for defending thofe Sugar Iflands, which, from their fituation, are expofed to the infults of the enemy? What precautions have you taken for the fafety of *Minorca?* I know, that when the troops from *Ireland* arrive, the garrifon will confift of nine battalions. But whofoever told you this number would be fufficient, knows nothing of the fervice. I am confident, that every Officer of judgment and experience, will coincide with me in opinion. You fee then where you are vulnerable. More inftances might be pointed out; but that were impiety! I fhould hold myfelf inexcufable for what I have already faid, were I not fenfible that our enemies know them as well as we do. Such then is the fituation of this country, to which our Minifter, in the courfe of laft Seffion, promifed a ten years peace. I ftood up in my place, and ventured to call his prophecy in queftion; I gave my reafons, but they were called the fuggeftions of faction. The Minifter, trufting to his own fagacity and forefight, paid no regard to the forebodings of the gallant Admiral, who now fits at the head of the Marine Department. The illuftrious feaman, than whom I know not a better Officer, nor a more excellent citizen, declared, that whoever occupied next year the place then held by him, would be forced to call for an augmentation of fix thoufand failors. Thefe words fhew that I was not fingular in my opinion, and that other refpectable perfons felt the approach of war. I know not what the opinion of the Minifter may be, but I ftill continue of the fame. I fmell war; a calamity which might have been eafily prevented, had our negociators acted with fpirit and refolution in the affair of Corfica.. I happened then to be at Paris; and can with the greateft truth affirm, that the French would have deemed your interpofition the part of a friend. Tired and exhaufted with fuch an effufion of blood and treafure, they would have thanked you for any honourable pretence to withdraw from that fcene of fo many difafters. But you acted then like poltroons, and pol-

troons

troops always bring upon themfelves a fucceffion of infults. And now, that like bullies, you hector and blufter, and run fwaggering about, what will you do? Where is there a man among you who can make the proper arrangements for war? Whom will you appoint Commander in Chief? He, alas! who could fill that office with dignity and ability, is no more; and no friend of Britain will refufe his memory a tear. For when fhall we fee his like again? Regardlefs of money, and ftudious only of true glory, he fought the applaufe and affection of his country, and he acquired them. His honour (the late Marquis of Granby) and integrity were unqueftioned: his courage, which was of the moft ardent and decifive kind, and covered him with laurel, fo much the more honourable, that he did not employ the weight and authority thence derived to his own private emolument, but for the public good. Such virtue, rare at any time, was to be doubly prized in fuch an age as this. Such talents might have given life and vigour to our military counfels. But, fnatched away when we moft needed his heart and his hand, he is, alas! no more.

It is, however, fome confolation under this diftrefs, that we have fuch an able Secretary at War. His fuperior talents will make us amends for the lofs of fo great a character. That clearnefs for which his difpatches are fo remarkable, is a fufficient earneft for his future atchievements. In the laft war, fome of his letters to the Governor of *Gibraltar* were, if I remember right, unintelligible, fome were contradictory, and all confufed and perplexed. Hence the lofs of *Minorca*. If his head produced fuch effects, when he acted only an under part, what may we expect from it, where he is the fupreme director? It is not that the Noble Lord cannot write with fufficient perfpicuity, where the queftion is to deftroy his Majefty's fubjects. There I confefs the power of his eloquence. There he is quite intelligible. There he can infpire the foldiers with alacrity. I wifh the Miniftry joy of fuch a fuperintendant of the military

VOL. I.   G   department;

department; but I am forry I cannot pay my country the fame
compliment.

Colonel Barré, Nov. 13, 1770.

THE Noble Lord at the head of the Treafury (Lord North)
is the greateft of all Contractors ;—he is a Contractor for men ;
—a Contractor for your flock, Mr. Speaker, (addreffing himfelf to the Chair); a Contractor for the Reprefentatives of the
people. The Noble Lord propofed to give a place of a thoufand a year, provided a Noble Duke would prevail on the moft
infignificant Member in that Houfe to vacate his feat in Parliament.

The Noble Duke behaved like a man upon the occafion;
like a friend, like a brother: he rejected the villainous propofition that Noble Lord had the affurance to make.

I am not acquainted with the Noble Lord. I have never fpoken
to him ; I have never had the honour of being introduced to him ;
but I fincerely wifh him to fave his country and his own life. I
exhort him to call off his butchers and ravagers from the Colonies ; to retire with the reft of his Majefty's evil advifers from
the public government, and make way for honeft and wifer
Counfellors ; to turn from his wickednefs and live ; it is not yet
too late to repent.

Lord George Gordon, April 13, 1778.

THERE is but one anfwer I have to give, as applicable to
Adminiftration in a body. Oppofition are well warranted to
reply to them in the words of a celebrated author, (Swift's Gul-
liver) a little altered and enlarged ; where, at the conclufion of
his well-known Travels, he fays, he could bear them well
enough in fome refpects; he could make allowances for their
incapacity, ignorance, folly, corruption, love of place, and emolument; he could pity them for their blunders, their wants,
weakneffes, and grofs ftupidity; he felt for their miferable fituation, knowing not whether to rufh headlong on certain ruin,

or

or retreat with fafety: but defpicable, unprincipled, and detefted as they are, I had neverthelefs learned to treat their perfons with refpeft: yet, when fuch men grow abufive and infolent, urge their claims of merit for what they deferve an axe; when I behold fuch men, in the very midft of thefe dire difafters and national misfortunes, endeavouring to contend that thofe misfortunes do not exift, or if they do, that they ought juftly and folely to be imputed to Oppofition; to fee a lump of deformity and difeafe, of folly and wickednefs, of ignorance and temerity, fmitten with pride, immediately breaks all meafures of patience; it being hardly conceivable, that fo much pride, vice, and folly, can exift in the fame animal.

Mr. Fox, May 13, 1775.

I DO not rife, my Lords, with any intention to oppofe the Motion for the Addrefs to his Majefty. The Speech from the Throne, muft, in my mind, give very general fatisfaftion; and I fhall never defcend to the meannefs of a faftious Oppofition. If I were called upon to deliver my fentiments on the Speech, I fhould rather find fault with it for its omiffions than for what it contains. It fpeaks a language of zeal and earneftnefs, and, as far as it goes, is congenial with my feelings and ideas. But, my Lords, having faid this, I may be permitted to ftate my reafons for with-holding confidence from the prefent Adminiftration. I have no wifh to inflame—I am not inftigated by envy; I do not fpeak haftily, but on the moft mature deliberation—I muft declare, that I have no confidence in the prefent Minifters.

. My Lords, when I look back but a very few months to the events in our hiftory, I do not hefitate to pronounce it as my opinion, that the prefent Minifters have in one great meafure attacked, if they have not deftroyed, the conftitution of the country. This is a bold affertion; but I do not throw it out lightly and at hazard; it is the refult of inquiry and difcuffion. I fay, my Lords, that the conftitution of the country muft be deftroyed, when a fet of men can feize on the reins of govern-

G 2   ment,

ment, and take the clofet of the King by affault. I am not weak enough to hazard this charge, eight months after the event, without having ferioufly weighed it in my mind ; and I fhould have delivered it at an earlier period, but that I was absent in another place (Ireland). My fituation at that time I accepted in duty to my Sovereign and country—I was introduced into it by no party—I was neither the adherent nor the dupe of any faction. I received it in the moft honourable manner from the Crown ; and I maintained myfelf in the fituation by the pureft and moft upright means, by acting under the principles of the conftitution, and ftudying the happinefs and welfare of the country. When I faw the bold and unconftitutional attack that was made on the dignity of the Crown, and on the fyftem of the country, I thought it high time to lay at his Majefty's feet the commiffion (Lord Lieutenant of Ireland) which I had received. There was a time, my Lords, when this Houfe was voted to be ufelefs. On this occafion the bold faction did not proceed to this indecent length : but where, my Lords, was the virtue, where the energy, where the influence and ufe of this Houfe, when they could fee and fuffer fuch an infringement to be made on the conftitution ? This Houfe, in that moment, was evidently a cypher, and in fo far I aver the equilibrium of the legiflature was overturned. I fpeak from no envy nor difappointment. The manner in which I accepted and refigned my office, will acquit me from the imputation of interefted motives ; and I do not fpeak from any factious defire of fetting up an indifcriminate oppofition to his Majefty's government.

I have reafons, from the conduct of Minifters fince they came into office, for diftrufting them. The treaty with the Americans is concluded ; both of that and of the definitive treaties with France and Spain, they are certainly the legitimate children of the preliminary articles ; but having adopted the iffue which they fo violently condemned, it furely became them to have nurtured the offspring with the greateft care and tendernefs,

nefs, to have made them at leaft as vigorous and promifing as poffible; inftead of which, have they taken the meafures which prudence and policy pointed out? What is become of the commercial treaty with America, from which fo much good fortune was promifed: has it not terminated in air? The Gentleman who was employed to negociate that treaty is returned from Paris; the whole is broken off, and broken off for reafons, which, if his information was right, were cenfurable. Thefe reafons were not communicated to the public, but they were perfectly well known to individuals. I am not willing to take up rumours, and argue from the hearfay evidence of the day; but reports are circulated with great opennefs, that this treaty has not only been broken off, but is not likely to be renewed; for reafons by no means favourable to the King's Minifters.

Preliminary articles are figned with Holland; but give me leave to fay, my Lords, that they alfo are but the legitimate offfpring of the meafures of the former Miniftry; the advantages procured in that treaty were fecured, and it will be required— it muft be known why thefe preliminary articles have not yet been wrought up into a definitive treaty. Why have we not yet begun even to reap the advantages of this peace? Why have not our Minifters been more vigorous and decifive in giving the finifhing hand to a treaty, which they boaft to be fo profitable?

The critical and very ferious affairs of the Eaft-Indies, properly make a paragraph in the Speech from the Throne: it certainly was time that the nation fhould begin to reap the advantages of the elaborate inquiries which had taken place. I muft confefs, I have not undergone the fatigue of reading thofe voluminous reports and papers which are on the table of the Houfe of Commons; but the fubject muft be inftantly difcuffed, and I much doubt, whether, by being delayed fo long, we fhall not want other information, and more recent materials than any of which we are now poffeffed.

G 3 The

The ftate of the funds, my Lords, call for the moft ferious confideration: at this inftant, they are more depreffed than almoft at any period during the late diftrefs and exertions of the nation, nay, even in the moment of threatened invafion: and, indeed, it was likely to be fo, when, along with the other caufes, there was fo immenfe a fum as three or four and twenty millions of unfounded debt, part of which bore an intereft of eight per cent. Was it not fingular, that his Majefty's Minifters fhould not have thought fit to recommend from the Throne, the immediate and earneft confideration of the funds, and to take notice of their late extraordinary fall—a fall which could not be the effeft of chance, but of a fixed and alarming caufe? It would not have been improper to have ftated what they mean to do in this bufinefs, that the minds of the ftockholders might be quieted.

I now come, my Lords, to mention a matter of the moft delicate kind; and, when I prefume to touch it all, I do it with pain to myfelf and anxiety. But your Lordfhips may conceive that I feel myfelf particularly interefted in whatever belongs to Ireland. Surely Minifters, on this delicate ground, fhould have given us fome general confolatory expreffion, merely to quiet the fufpicions that muft be excited by their total filence—if they had done no more than juft echoed the Addreffes of the Houfe of Lords and Commons, and framed any general words which might have fhewn their difpofition to harmony and union.

I faid, my Lords, that I did not mean to give any oppofition to the Motion for the Addrefs, nor to fuggeft any Amendment. I have delivered to you my reafon for diftrufting the King's Minifters—I fhall certainly watch their conduft, and in doing fo, without being inftigated by factious motives, I fhall, in my place, ftate whatever appears to me to be cenfurable or injurious.

Earl Temple, Nov. 12, 1783.

I HAVE

I HAVE watched the debate with great attention, and have endeavoured to find out if any thing fell in the courfe of it, that would afford the leaft hopes of an union of parties, but in vain. Nothing of that kind has been hinted at; and I am forry to have obferved, that thofe who have taken part in the debate, and are known to be the moft intimate with the Right Hon. Gentleman, (Mr. Fox) and the neareft about him, have all, more or lefs, indulged themfelves in perfonal afperities : which pretty plainly fhews, that the Right Hon. Gentleman (Mr. Pitt) has not been fincerely inclined to union all along. The fort of attack that has this day been made on my Right Hon. Friend is what he by no means deferves; and I am the more forry, becaufe, undoubtedly, fuch is the ftate of the country, that all the abilities of this Houfe are wanted to reftore it to its proper ftate of vigour and profperity. The great and extraordinary talents of the two Right Hon. Gentlemen are univerfally acknowledged; but as far as regards that circumftance, I am not forry for the contefts that have occurred, fince this Houfe has affembled after the recefs of the laft fummer, as they have given occafion for a farther difplay of the abilities of each of the Right Hon. Gentlemen, that has called forth greater admiration and greater wonder. I cannot but exprefs my aftonifhment to hear Gentlemen complaining that there is no charge made againft the Right Hon. Gentleman, (Mr. Pitt) nor any fault imputed to him. In the prefent cafe it would have been a little extraordinary if there had been any charge or imputation, becaufe there is not the fmalleft occafion for either. The Queftion has nothing perfonal in it; it throws no difgrace on the Right Hon. Gentleman oppofite to him, nor on his colleagues. When Sir Robert Walpole had a Motion for his removal made againft him, there was not any charge thought neceffary; it was held to be enough that he had loft the confidence of this Houfe; and when, upon the divifion, it appeared that Sir Robert had but a majority of one in his favour, he thought that a fufficient hint, and he no longer appeared as a Minifter. But no charge had been called

G 4   for—

for—[A cry from the Treasury Bench of, *yes there was !*]—But I muſt deny that there was any. After Sir Robert had been made a Peer, I am perfectly aware that a Secret Committee was inſtituted for the purpoſe of inveſtigating all the tranſactions of the paſt ten years of his life, and every body knows in what manner the Secret Committee was put an end to. In the preſent caſe it has been aſked, " what, no *fault* imputed ?" So far from any faults being capable of being imputed to the Right Hon. Gentleman, I proteſt I do not know any perſon leſs culpable. The fact is, the Houſe has thought proper to deny its confidence to the Right Hon. Gentleman, not with any view to proſcription in future, but merely on account of the grounds upon which he came into office; and no Miniſter can think of ſtanding after this Houſe has withdrawn its confidence. It never has been done, nor indeed ever attempted. Let the Right Hon. Gentleman reflect a little how extraordinary it is, therefore, for him to perſiſt in keeping his place. Not that I mean to blame him for it. I like his ſpirit. He has ſhewn it, and proved, what I always thought he would prove, fit to be a Miniſter. But let the Right Hon. Gentleman look to the manner in which a period has been put to former Adminiſtrations. The Earl of Shelburne loſt his ſituation by the peace he made ; a peace which I always conſidered as a good thing for the country, but of which I now entertain ten times a better opinion than before ; becauſe if the war had continued, and the diviſions and conteſts we had been lately engaged in taken place, the country muſt have been utterly ruined. The Earl of Shelburne, upon a majority of ſixteen only againſt him in this Houſe, though with a conſiderable majority in the other Houſe, thought fit to retire. My Noble Friend in the blue ribbon alſo, had not had a majority againſt him two years ago, but he neverthelefs thought it right to retire, when he ſaw his majority rapidly decreaſing. My Noble Friend has done wiſely in ſo retiring. I thought and ſaid ſo at the time, having, as I recollect, ſtood up pretty nearly in the ſame place in which I now ſtand, and adviſed my

Noble

Noble Friend to take the hint and retire. Ministers may imagine whatever they please, but it is impossible for them to remain after this House has denied them their confidence. I am well known to be a friend to the prerogative of the Crown, but that prerogative has been lately exercised in so lavish a way, that though I would not point it out as a *fault* imputable to the Right Hon. Gentleman, (Mr. Pitt) yet certainly it has been used in such a manner, as to excite and deserve the notice of this House. The Crown has an undoubted right to distribute honours, but it never has been held to be a right or a constitutional exercise of the prerogative to lavish honours and titles in such a manner as has of late been the case. This House has seen four peerages within the last month, and I understand there is a promise of thirteen or fourteen more. It is not a little extraordinary that three out of four are bestowed on Gentlemen from Cornwall, a county that was ever remarkable for more of what is called rotten boroughs than any other county in the kingdom. I do not mean to abuse the Gentlemen who have received these honours, but it cannot escape the notice of the House, that it is extraordinary they should happen to be created just now, and three of them out of such a county. The Duke of Northumberland has but lately come into that county, and, tottering as he is under the load of ribbons and honours, and other favours of the Crown, he has been decked with one more honour. How the Noble Duke came by his former honours, you all know; perhaps it might be guessed at, why he has an additional honour granted him at this time. When I say this, I declare I mean nothing derogatory to the Noble Duke; I have a very high respect for him; but I thought it right to observe a little upon this matter, since my Right Hon. Friend has been ridiculed, because he could not, when Minister, make a single Peer. The fact certainly was so. My Right Hon. Friend has also lately been sneered at, and it has been said, that his majorities did not increase. I will venture to say, that the House, under such temptations, has evinced unexampled integrity,

grity, and daring difintereftednefs. Had my Right Hon. Friend had it in his power to make one-half, and promife feven out of the fourteen Peers he had mentioned, I would have undertaken to have anfwered for his majorities having increafed, rather than decreafed.—With regard to the reafon of making thefe Peers juft now, I conceive it not to have been fo much, becaufe the perfons fo to be honoured were wanted to do the bufinefs in the Houfe of Lords, but becaufe there were others wanted to do bufinefs in the Houfe of Commons. The advifing his Majefty to difmifs his Minifters about Chriftmas was a rafh and foolifh thing; but having done fo, the prefent Minifters fhould complete the bufinefs. They fhould have inftantly diffolved the prefent Parliament. That would have been acting rightly and wifely; not that I mean to fpeak inconfiftently with my former opinion againft a diffolution. All I mean now is, that a meafure which I by no means approve, could only have been rendered of any effect by being immediately followed up by another meafure, which I likewife, abftractedly confidered, deemed equally rafh and improper. I voted for Mr. Fox's India Bill, becaufe I thought upon the whole the Bill a good one. There were parts of it, undoubtedly, which wanted, and which I was pretty certain would now receive the neceffary improvement. Mr. Pitt's Bill I will call by no nick-name; I will apply no watch-word of a party to it; I will barely fay it does not appear to me to have been any thing like effectual, or equal to the real neceffity of the cafe. With regard to the patronage the Bill gave, I had, at any time, rather truft a large influence, broad and oftenfible, in the hands of a Minifter, properly refponfible, than the fmalleft portion of an influence, fecret in its nature, in any hands whatever. Before I fit down, however warmly I may have delivered myfelf, I hope I have not fpoken offenfively; I am fure I had no intention to do fo.

Mr. Rigby, Feb. 8, 1784.

AMERICAN

A M E R I C A N   A F F A I R S.

THERE are two things which Miniftry have laboured to deceive the People in, and have perfuaded them to; firft, that it was an affair of Bofton only, and that the very appearance of one fingle regiment there, would quiet every thing.

I have foretold the falfehood of both; I was converfant with that country more, more years, perhaps, than any man; I knew the caufe of Bofton would be made the caufe of America; I knew the mode of the Military would not be effectual.

The manner of proceeding againft Bofton, was a profcription of a People unheard;—unheard in any Court, either in the common Courts of Juftice, or the higher, of Parliament, in both of which, evidence of facts are ftated in proof of criminality; but the Americans were denied to be heard. The People of America condemned, and not heard, have a right to refift.

By whofe advice vindictive counfels were purfued—by whofe advice falfe reprefentations were made—by whofe advice malice and ill-will were made principles of governing a free People;—all thefe are queftions that will be afked. I mean no perfonal charge on any man farther than his mifdoings call for.

There ought to be fome inftant proceeding towards a fettlement before meeting of the Delegates. My object is to put the foot on the threfhold of Peace, and to fhew an intention of reconciling; I will, unlefs I am fixed to a fick bed—I will attend this bufinefs throughout, till I fee America obtain what I think fatisfaction for her injuries—ftill attentive that fhe fhall own the fupremacy of this country.

It would be my advice to his Majefty to end this quarrel the fooneft poffible; his repofe is our duty. Who by mif-advice had planted a thorn in his fide, by a conteft with a People determined on their purpofe?—

I wifh

I wiſh to offer myſelf, mean as I am—I have a Plan, a Plan of a Settlement; ſolid, honourable, and laſting.

America means only to have ſafety in Property, and perſonal Liberty. Theſe, and theſe only were her object. Independency was falſely charged on her.

I diſclaim all metaphyſical diſtinctions.

The Declaratory Act leaves you a right to take their money when you pleaſe.

I mean to meddle with no man's opinion; and leaving all men to follow the Plan of their own opinions of former profeſſions, my Plan is to eſtabliſh for the American an unequivocal, expreſs right of not having his Property taken from him but by his own Conſent, in his own Aſſembly.

Eight weeks delay admits no farther heſitation, no, not of a moment; the thing may be over; a drop of blood renders it *immedicabile vulnus.*

Whether it can ever now be a true Reconciliation, muſt be owing to the full compenſation that America ſhall receive. Repeal the mutual ill-will that ſubſiſts, for it is not the repeal of a little Act of Parliament that will work Peace. Will the repeal of a bit of parchment avail? Will, think you, three millions of People in Arms be ſatisfied by ſuch a repeal? It muſt be a repeal on the principle of Juſtice? There muſt be no procraſtination; you are to a moment—now—inſtantaneouſly. Every hour, that a beginning is not made towards ſoftening, towards healing! the very news of which might work wonders—endangers the fixed Liberty of America, and the honour of the Mother Country.

The ſucceſs and permanent effect of the beſt meaſures may ariſe from mutual good-will.

My Motion is part of a Plan; and I begin with a proof of good-will. My Motion is, " to addreſs the King to remove " the Forces from the town of Boſton."

The Congreſs, they are more wiſe, and more prudent than the meeting of ancient Greece. Your Lordſhips have read

Thucy-

Thucydides. He mentions nothing of ancient ſtory more honourable, more reſpectable, than this deſpiſed meeting.

The Congreſs is treated harſhly—I wiſh we would imitate
their temper; firm, indeed, if you pleaſe—but Congreſs is conducted with firmneſs and moderation. I wiſh our Houſe of
Commons as freely and uncorruptly choſen.

The proceedings from hence ariſe from ignorance of the
circumſtances of America.—The idea of *coercion* by Troops,
where they were not the natural reſource, was wanton and
idle.

Anger was your motive in all you did. " What! ſhall
" America preſume to be free? Don't hear them—chaſtiſe
" them!" This was your language *caſtigat auditque*—the ſevereſt Judge, though he chaſtiſes, alſo hears the party.

All the miſchief has ariſen from your anger; for your not
adapting your means to your ends; troops and violence were
ill means to anſwer the ends of Peace.

I underſtand Government is not altogether ſatisfied with the
Commander of your troops; he has not been quick enough to
ſhed blood; his moderation is ridiculed: but I know that Gentleman, an Officer of long ſervice, has acted prudently; it was
want of wiſdom to place an army there—I have heard of armies
of obſervation, but this is an army of irritation.

In the civil war of Paris, where thoſe great men, the Prince
of Condé and Marſhal Turenne commanded the two parties—
Marſhal Turenne was ſaid often to have been near the Prince.—
The Queen was angry; ſhe did not ſee why, when he was ſo
near the Prince, he ſhould not take him; ſhe was offended,
and with ſome anger aſked, " *Quand vous etiez ſi pris, pourquoi*
" *n'avez-vous pas pris le Prince?*" That great Officer who
knew his buſineſs, anſwered coolly, " *J'avois peur, Madame,*
" *qu'il ne m'eut prit.*"

The Miniſtry tell you, that the Americans will not abide by
the Congreſs;—they are tired of the Aſſociation;—true, many
of the Merchants may be—but it does not now depend on the
Merchants,

Merchants, nor do the accounts come even from the principal
Merchants, but from the runners of Miniftry. But were the
diffatisfaction among the Merchants ever fo great, the account
is no way conformable to the nature of America.

The nation of America, who have the virtues of the People
they fprung from, will not be flaves. Their language is, if
Trade and Slavery are companions, we quit the Trade; let
Trade and Slavery go where they will, they are not for us.

Your anger reprefents them as refractory and ungrateful, in
not fubmitting to the parent they fprung from; but they are in
truth grown an acceffion of ftrength to this country; they know
their importance; they wifh to continue their utility to you;
but though they may be fick of the Affociation, thofe fons of
the earth will never be diffuaded from their Affociation.

After the repeal of the Stamp Act, two years after, I was in
the country an hundred miles off; a Gentleman who knew the
country, told me, that if regiments had landed at that time,
and fhips had been fent to deftroy the towns, they had come to
a refolution to retire back into the country.—It is a fact—a
Noble Lord fmiles; if I were to mention the Gentleman's name,
it would not increafe his fmile.

I wifh the young Gentlemen of our time, would imitate
thofe Americans that are mifreprefented to them; I wifh they
would imitate their frugality; I wifh they would imitate that
Liberty which the Americans love better than life; imitate that
courage which a love of Liberty produces.

One word more. I will fend my Plan, if the ftate of a
miferable conftitution ftretches me on a fick-bed. It is to put
an end to the quarrel. " What before you know whether they
" will come to terms?" Yes, let my expectations be what they
will, I fhould recall the troops; it partakes of a nullity to accept fubmiffion under the influence of arms.

I foretel, thefe Bills muft be repealed.—I fubmit to be called
an idiot if they are not; three millions of men ready to be
armed, and talk of forcing them?

4   There

There may be dangerous men, and dangerous men and dangerous councils, who would inftil bad doctrines, advife the enflaving of America; they might not endanger the Crown, perhaps, but they would render it not worth the wearing.

The caufe of America is allied to every true Whig. They will not bear the enflaving of America. Some Whigs may love their fortunes better than their principles; but the body of Whigs will join; they will not enflave America. The whole Irifh nation, all the true Englifh Whigs, the whole nation of America, thefe combined make many millions of Whigs, averfe to the fyftem. France has her full attention upon you; war, is at your door; carrying a queftion here, will not fave your country in fuch extremities.

This being the ftate of things, my advice is, to proceed to allay heats; I would at the inftant begin, and do fomething towards allaying and foftening refentment.

My Motion, you fee, refpects the army, and their dangerous fituation. Not to undervalue General Gage, who has ferved with credit,—he acts upon his inftructions; if he has not been alert enough to fhed blood;

Non dimicare quam vincere maluit.

And he judged well. The Americans too have acted with a prudence and moderation, that had been worthy of our example, were we wife;—to their moderation it is owing, that our troops have fo long remained in fafety.

Mal-Adminiftration has run its line—it has not a move left—it is a check-mate.

Forty thoufand men are not adequate to the idea of fubduing them to your Taxation. Taxation exifts only in Reprefentation; take them to your heart, who knows what their generofity may effect?

I am not to be underftood as meaning a naked, unconditional repeal; no, I would maintain the fuperiority of this country at all events.

But

But you are anxious who shall disarm first. That great Poet, and, perhaps, a wiser and greater Politician than ever he was a Poet, has given you wisest counsel, follow it:

Tuque prior, tu parce; genus qui ducis Olympo.
Projice tela manu. ⸻

Who is this man that will own this system of force as practicable? And is it not the height of folly to pursue a system that is owned to be impracticable.

I therefore move, that an humble Addrefs be presented to his Majesty, most humbly to advise and beseech his Majesty, that, in order to open the ways towards an happy settlement of the dangerous troubles in America, by beginning to allay ferments and soften animosities there; and above all, for preventing in the mean time, any sudden and fatal catastrophe at Boston, now suffering under the daily irritation of an army before their eyes, posted in their town, it may graciously please his Majesty, that immediate orders may be dispatched to General Gage, for removing his Majesty's forces from the town of Boston, as soon as the rigour of the season, and other circumstances indispensable to the safety and accommodation of the said troops may render the same practicable.

The Earl of Chatham, Jan. 20, 1775.

I ENTIRELY agree with the Honourable Gentleman who seconded the Motion for an Addrefs to his Majesty, that every man ought now to speak out; and in a moment so important as the present to the whole empire, I think it ill becomes the dignity and duty of Parliament to lose itself in such a fulsome, adulatory Addrefs to the Throne as that now proposed. We ought rather, Sir, to approach our Sovereign with sound and wholesome advice, and even with Remonstrances against the conduct of his Ministers, who have precipitated the nation into an unjust, ruinous, felonious and murderous war. I call the war with our brethren in America an unjust, felonious war,

becaufe

becaufe the primary caufe and confeffed origin of it is, to attempt to take their money from them without their confent, contrary to the common rights of all mankind, and thofe great fundamental principles of the Englifh conftitution, for which Hampden bled. I affert, Sir, that it is in confequence a murderous war; becaufe it is an attempt to deprive men of their lives, for ftanding up in the juft caufe of the defence of their property and their clear rights. It becomes no lefs a murderous war, with refpect to many of our fellow-fubjects of this ifland: for every man, either of the navy or army, who has been fent by government to America, and has fallen a victim in this unnatural and unjuft conteft, has been murdered by Adminiftration, and his blood lies at their door. Such a war, I fear, Sir, will draw down the vengeance of heaven upon this devoted kingdom.

I think this war, Sir, fatal and ruinous to our country. It abfolutely annihilates the only great fource of our wealth, which we enjoyed unrivaled by other nations; and deprives us of the fruits of the laborious induftry of near three millions of fubjects, which centered here. That commerce has already taken its flight, and our American Merchants are now deploring the confequences of a wretched policy, which has been purfued to their deftruction. It is, Sir, no lefs ruinous with regard to the enormous expences of the fleets and armies neceffary for this nefarious undertaking; fo that we are wafting our prefent wealth, while we are deftroying the fources of all we might have in future.

I fpeak, Sir, as a friend to England and America, but ftill more to univerfal liberty, and the rights of all mankind. I truft no part of the fubjects of this vaft empire will ever fubmit to be flaves. I am fure the Americans are too high fpirited to brook the idea. Your whole power, and that of your allies, if you had any, and of all the German troops you can hire, cannot effect fo wicked a purpofe. The conduct of the prefent Adminiftration has already wrefted the fceptre of America out of the

VOL. I. H hands

hands of our Sovereign, and you have now scarcely a Post-master left in the whole northern continent; more than half the empire is already lost, and almost all the rest is in confusion and anarchy. The Ministry have brought our Sovereign into a more disgraceful situation than any crowned head now living. He alone has already lost, by their fatal counsels, more territory than the three great united powers of Russia, Austria, and Prussia have together robbed Poland of; and by equal acts of violence and injustice from Administration.

England was never engaged in a contest of such importance to our most valuable concerns and possessions. We are fighting for the subjection of a country infinitely more extended than our own; of which every day increases the wealth, the natural strength, and population. Should we not succeed, it would be a bosom friendship soured to hate and resentment. We shall be considered as their most implacable enemies; an eternal separation will succeed, and the grandeur of the British empire pass away. Success seems to me not equivocal, but impossible. However we may differ among ourselves, they are perfectly united. On this side the Atlantic, party-rage unhappily divides us; but one soul animates the vast northern continent of America, the General Congress, and each Provincial Assembly. An appeal has been made to the sword, and at the close of the last campaign, what have we conquered? Bunker's-hill, with the loss of 1200 men. Are we to pay as dearly for the rest of America? The idea of conquest is as romantic as unjust.

The Honourable Gentleman who moved the Address, says, " The Americans have been treated with lenity." Was your Boston Port Bill a measure of lenity? Was your Fishery Bill a measure of lenity? Was your Bill for taking away the Charter of the Massachusett's Bay a measure of lenity, or even justice? I omit your many other gross provocations and insults, by which the brave Americans have been driven into their present state. He asserts, that they avow a disposition to be independent. On the

the contrary, Sir, a'l the declarations both of the late and the prefent Congrefs, uniformly tend to this one object, of being put on the fame footing they were in the year 1763. This has been their only demand, from which they have never varied. Their daily prayers are for liberty, peace, and fafety. I ufe the words of the Congrefs laft year. They juftly expect to be put on an equal footing with the other fubjects of the empire. If you confine all our trade to yourfelves, fay they; if you make a monopoly of our commerce; if you fhut all other ports of the world againft us, tax us not too. If you do, then give us a free trade, fuch as you enjoy yourfelves; let us have equal advantages of commerce, all other ports open to us; then we can, and cheerfully will pay taxes.

It muft give, Sir, every man who loves his country, the deepeft concern, at the naming in the Addrefs foreign troops, Hanoverians and Heffians, who are now called to interfere in our domeftic quarrels, not to dwell this day on the illegality of the meafure. The militia, indeed, are now employed, and that noble inftitution is at prefent complimented by Minifters, who hate the very name of a militia, becaufe the embodying of thefe forces enables Adminiftration to butcher more of our fellow-fubjects in America.

Mr. Wilkes, Oct. 26, 1775.

I AM ftill clear, my Lords, as to the right this country has to exercife its fovereignty over America by taxation. I had no hand in paffing the Stamp Act, in the Declaratory Bill, in the Bill laying·Duties upon Teas, and other commodities, in the partial repeal of that Act, nor yet in the infanity of fending the tea to America without repealing the duty. From thefe and other caufes, together with the imbecillity of Adminiftration, this country is reduced to a fituation fo deplorable, that the wifeft and honefteft man in the kingdom can propofe nothing that promifes an happy and honourable iffue. I feel that I fpeak in fetters; I therefore will not prefs arguments on

either

either fide to their full extent. The next eafterly wind will carry to America what fhall fall from any, and from every Lord in the Houfe. I do not wifh that the nakednefs of my country and its weaknefs, fhould ftand confirmed by the authority and fanction of teftimonies given here. It is a time to act, and not to talk. Much is to be done, and little faid. The die of war is caft, the fword is drawn, and the fcabbard thrown away. With great refpect to your Lordfhips, wife as you are, and no doubt the great hereditary council of the King and kingdom, yet allow me to fay, you are not enabled to decide upon matters of fuch tranfcendent importance and difficulty, without having the fulleft materials before you, which you moft certainly have not. This is a queftion for the Minifters to decide, who muft be fuppofed to have the fulleft information: the execution will likewife lie with them. They have decided; and it is to be wifhed they have at laft fome well-confidered plan: not only taking into pay all the troops that can be got, at any rate, but alfo how they can be fupported, fupplied, and enabled to act with effect; in fhort, a plan confifting of a great variety of efficient parts. If I had the honour of being in the King's Council (which thank God I have not) I fhould expect the ampleft information before I fhould decide; but decide I would, and abide by the decifion. Retired, however, as I now am, and uninformed, I have not prefumption enough to give an opinion, nor do I hold myfelf fpecially called upon to do it. My country is, indeed, reduced to a deplorable condition. We are driven between Scylla and Charybdis, and it will be tranfcendently difficult to fteer the veffel of the ftate into a fafe port. I muft be allowed freely to confefs, that I have not a good opinion of the King's fervants. Paft experience will not juftify confidence. I cannot, therefore, anfwer to myfelf or to my country, the trufting fuch men with the expenditure of ten millions; and laying the foundation of lavifhing many more, our laft ftake; thereby accelerating that bankruptcy, which, fooner or later, I fear, by adopting either meafure, is become

inevitable.

inevitable. Nor am I, on the other hand, fo friendly to them, as by declaring our utter inability to reduce America, to furnifh them with a golden bridge for concluding an inglorious peace, on any the moft ruinous and difgraceful terms. I cannot confent to throw this once great and glorious country at the feet of America ; and there humbly implore fuch peace, as fhe, in her generofity and magnanimity fhall condefcend to grant us. I am not yet made to the idea of hanging out a white flag of furrender. To thofe who lament the prefent moft melancholy ftate of the Colonies, once fo profperous and flourifhing, beyond the example of any others known in the annals of time, I cannot help obferving, that I rejoice in the teftimony, becaufe it does honour to the government of England, under whofe care and influence they had profpered fo wonderfully. I do verily believe, that till the late troubles, they had infinitely lefs to complain of than the Mother Country herfelf; and that, feparated as they are by the vaft Atlantic, it was not in the nature of things, that there muft not be much to complain of, tho' not fufficient to juftify their ingratitude to the Parent State. I cannot blame a determination to make peace, fword in hand ; the fooner it can be had upon reafonable, fafe, and honourable terms, the better for both countries. I never did declare, whether I thought it was confiftent with found policy to impofe any new tax upon America, and it will hardly be expected that I fhould decide it now, I have heard it called an unjuft war ; I know not who in this Houfe have a right to call it fo. Infinite fagacity and difcretion are neceffary to the attainment of what all alike, I am perfuaded, muft eagerly wifh. When the happy and favourable moment for conciliation fhall arrive, I hope the Minifters will feize it, and I fincerely wifh them fuccefs. At leaft at fuch a crifis, I will not hang upon the wheels of Government, and thereby render what is already but too difficult, the more impracticable.

Earl Temple, March 5, 1776.

H 3   My

My Lords, I have not the arrogance to think, that what I
shall submit to your Lordships has escaped the vigilance of all
your Lordship's judgments: I have not the vanity to imagine,
that the arguments my circumscribed talents may suggest to me
to use, can have the good fortune to persuade the majority
of this House, unless they should meet with the support of men
of greater weight. Some there are who chance to be absent,
whose great authorities I must lament the loss of. But, my
Lords, if what I may offer should throw any light upon a subject as interesting as ever arose since Britain has extended her
power beyond the confines of the isle, I shall at least have the
satisfaction to think, I have not buried my ideas; I have not
been wanting in that duty, which, from the rank we hold in
life, is mine, is that of every Lord in this House. My Lords,
for a paltry set of words, for an unreasonable claim of power,
for a fascinating assertion of impracticable authority, for an
airy nothing, a visionary shadow of ideal revenue, impossible to
be raised but by the consent of that people whose contributions
we so much thirst after, and whose consent we do despise, has
Britain been duped into an unnatural war, where victory or
defeat must each enfeeble this lately great empire: a war carried on against a part of our fellow-subjects, whose numbers,
at least, equal a fifth of the whole; and who in extent of
country so far exceeds the size of Britain, that the comparison
of her is but as a speck in the disk of the sun. I will not dwell
on the disadvantages our army must labour under from the far-
extended distance of the war; a common map, to the com-
monest understanding, must demonstrate more than rhetoric can
paint. But, my Lords, it has been your pleasure to enter into
this war; the matter has been laid before you, and often has
been debated, and your Lordships, in your judgments, have
deemed it necessary to correct the saucy freedom of high-
minded sons, grown up to manly age; to check in your American children that independent spirit, that strange love of
liberty, which, where permitted to take root, does so infatuate

mankind, and which has long been the honour and safety of this Ifle. You have thought it right to curb their ideas of property, which lead them to imagine, we have no right to take any part of that property away from them without their free confent. My Lords, I refpect the Decifions of the Majorities of this Houfe; but if thefe Decifions may have arifen from any peculiar circumftances now no more exifting; if they may have fprung from falfe or miftaken intelligence; if the whole difpofition of things, from various accidents and events, may have become totally different; perhaps it may not be unworthy your Lordfhips wifdom to reconfider what you have decided, to revife your judgments, to retrace the fteps we may have too haftily trod. My Lords, in the beginning of our unhappy contefts with America, thofe who debated the matter on the fide of the ruling Power of Government, ftated not only the neceffity, but the great facility of forcing to a compliance with all the demands of Government, fuch Colonies as fhould dare to offer their vain refiftance: we are told they had not ftrength for war, they had not means of war, they had not union among themfelves, that they wanted money, that they wanted difcipline, that they wanted Officers: and, to fum up the whole, to make them contemptible even as fubmiffive fubjects, that they poffeffed not courage to face an Englifh Soldier, whofe birth on this fide the Atlantic endowed him with that intrepid fpirit, an American, whom even neceffity had inured to toils, could never afpire to reach. The Decifions, my Lords, of Adminiftration, gave them union; the refufal to hear their Petitions, confined the whole in a firm knot of calm, deliberate, defperate determination to refift. Money, which is but the type of property, was foon fupplied by a type of equal fenfe and ufe; even perfonal freedom gave way to public fecurity, and perfonal property was facrificed to the neceffities of the rifing State. The difaffection was general, and Britifh Governors now no longer adminifter Law in Britifh America. How true the charge of wanting martial fpirit proved, let thofe

relate

relate who firſt ſaw the blood of civil war ſpilt at Lexington, .To 'thoſe who ſaved the honour of the day, at the bloody forcing of the lines on Bunker's-Hill, to thoſe who ſaw the Britiſh valour checked, may I ſafely refer for a full confutation of the abſurd ſuppoſition, that men deſcended from the ſame line as ourſelves, whoſe all is at ſtake, who think their cauſe juſt, would, like the moſt enervated Aſiatic tribe, yield a bloodleſs victory. My Lords, the hiſtory of human nature teaches us, that the greateſt talents often lie hid in the moſt diſguiſed obſcurity, till accident, till the buſtle of the times, calls forth the genius, and lights the ethereal ſpark ; then do theſe meteors caſt an unexpected blaze : an Apothecary's late 'prentice leads forth armies, diſplays the warrior's ſkill, the warrior's intrepidity, and meets a death a Roman might have envied : another, who, in peaceable times, might have never roſe to greater praiſe than a jockey's ſkill, amidſt every rigour of an inclement ſeaſon, in an inclement country, aſtoniſhes us with a march a Hannibal would have admired, and carries the alarm of war to the walls of a great city, which muſt pro- bably have yielded to the boldneſs of the undertaking, had not a *Carleton* ſaved it. I am not making a panegyric on American prowefs, though great atchievements, even by an enemy, will ever meet my praiſe. But, my Lords, theſe are facts in- capable of diſpute. To come now, my Lords, to that which has caſt the deepeſt ſtain on the glory of the Britiſh arms, to that which muſt rouſe the indignation of all who feel for her diſgrace : the army of Britain, equipped with every poſſible eſſential of war, a choſen army, with choſen Officers, backed with the power of a mighty fleet, ſent to correct revolted ſub- jects, ſent to chaſtiſe a reſiſting city, ſent to aſſert Britain's au- thority, has for many tedious months been impriſoned within that town by the Provincial Army, who, their watchful guards, permitted them no inlet to the country, who braved all their efforts, and defied all their ſkill and abilities in war could ever attempt. One way, indeed, of eſcape was left; the fleet is

yet

yet refpected; to the fleet the army has recourfe, and Britifh
Generals, whofe names never met with a blot of difhonour,
are forced to quit that town which was the firft object of the
war, the immediate caufe of hoftilities, the place of arms,
which has coft this nation more than a million to defend.

The Duke of Manchefter, May 10, 1776.

I HAVE been reading a work given us by a country, that is
perpetually employed in productions of merit—I believe it is
not yet publifhed—the Hiftory of Philip the IId; and there
find, that that tyrannical monarch never dreamt of the tyranny
exercifed by this Adminiftration. Gods! Sir, fhall we be told,
that you cannot annalyze grievances! that you can have no
communication with Rebels, becaufe they have declared for
Independency! Shall you be told this, when the tyrant Philip
did it after the fame circumftance in the Netherlands. By
Edict he allowed their fhips to enter their ports, and fuffered
them to depart in peace; he treated with them; made them
Propofitions; and pofitively declared that he would redrefs all
their grievances. And James the IId, when he was failing
from France, at the head of a formidable force, affifted like
you by foreign troops, and having a great party in the kingdom, ftill offered fpecific terms; while his exceptions of pardon were few, amongft the reft my honourable friend's anceftor, *Sir Stephen Fox.* But you will offer none;—you fimply
tell them to lay down their arms, and then you will do juft as
you pleafe. Could the moft cruel conqueror fay lefs? Had
you conquered the devil himfelf in hell, could you be lefs liberal? No! Sir, you would offer no terms;—you meant to drive
them to the declaration of Independency: and even after it
was iffued, ought, by your offers, to have reverfed the effect.
You would not receive the Remonftrance that I brought you
from New-York, becaufe it denied your Rights to certain
Powers;—yet the late King of France received the Remonftrances from his Parliaments, that exprefly denied his Rights

to

to the Powers he was in the conftant exercife of—anfwered
them, and even redreffed fome of the Grievances which thofe
very Remonftrances complained of; though he refufed to
grant what he thought more peculiarly entrenched upon his
own Authority.

In this fituation, Sir, fhocking to fay, are we called upon
by another Proclamation to go to the Altar of the Almighty,
with war and vengeance in our hearts, inftead of the peace
of our Bleffed Saviour; he faid, " *My peace I give you*," but
we are on this Faft to have war only in our hearts and mouths;
war againft our brethren.—'Till our churches are purified from
this abominable fervice, I fhall confider them, not as the
temples of the Almighty, but the fynagogues of fatan. An
act not more *infamous*, refpecting its political, than *blafphemous*
and *profane* as a pretended act of national devotion, when the
People are called upon, in the moft folemn and awful manner,
to repair to Church, to partake of a Sacrament, and at the
foot of the Altar to commit facrilege; to perjure themfelves
publicly by charging their American brethren with the horrid
crime of Rebellion, with propagating " *fpecious falfhood*," when
either the charge muft be *netorioufly falfe*, or thofe who make
it, not knowing it to be true, call Almighty God to witnefs
to not a *fpecious*, but a moft *audacious* and *blafphemous* falfhood.
Mr. Burke, Nov. 2, 1776.

I HAVE read, Sir, a late Proclamation of that great General
and Preacher, Mr. Burgoyne, which is fhocking to a civilized
and generous nation. As a State Paper it difgraces our
country. The Imperial Court have often employed many
kind of irregular troops, Croats, Pandours, and Huffars, but
their names difgrace no public act. If they plunder, they do
not torture. The pious Preacher, Mr. Burgoyne, complains
of this froward and ftubborn generation; and at the very moment of mentioning his confcioufnefs of Chriftianity, difplays
a fpirit of cruelty repugnant to every principle of humanity.
He

He boafts that he will give ftretch to the Indian forces under his direction, and they amount to thoufands. Merciful Heaven! Thoufands of Indian favages let loofe by the command of a Britifh General againft our brethren in America! Human nature fhrinks back from fuch a fcene. At his heels, leafht in like hounds, fhould famine, fword, and fire, crouch for employment. Mr. Burgoyne's feelings as a man, I fear, will not hereafter be as univerfally acknowledged, as the military talents of the great General. In the prefent cafe I have that pity for him and his employers, which they have not fhewn to others, What, Sir, has been, and continues, the conduct of the Indian favages in war? Is it not to exercife the moft wanton cruelties on their enemies, without diftinction of age and fex? The conduct of this war goes on a par with its principles. Has the feeble old man, the helplefs infant, the defencelefs female, ever experienced the tender mercies of an Indian favage? He drinks the blood of his enemy, and his favourite repaft is on human flefh. Is a ftretch given to thoufands of thefe cannibals by command, in a public Manifefto of one of the King's Generals? I am bold, Sir, to declare, that fuch orders are unworthy the General of any Chriftian King. They are only becoming a Jewifh Prieft to a Jewifh King, a Samuel to a Saul, in the moft bloody and barbarous of all hiftories, the Hiftory of the Jewifh Nation. The orders of the Jewifh Priefts were, now go and fmite the *Amalekites*, and deftroy all that they have, and fpare them not; but flay both man and woman, ox and fheep, camel and afs. General Burgoyne threatens the Americans with all the vengeance of the State, not its juftice, that the meffenger of wrath will meet them in the field, devaftation, and famine, and every concomitant horror. Not the fword of even-handed juftice falling on the head of the bold rebel, but the favage horrors of the tomahawk, from the thoufands of Indians under his direction, on the innocent women and children. I remember, Sir, an honourable Gentleman, (Lord Advocate of Scotland) whom I fee in his place, a Gentleman

very

very high in the Law, not only humanely propofing, according to
the ideas, and in the language of his own country, but dwelling
with rapture on what he claffically called a Starvation Bill for
the poor Americans. I rely, however, Sir, on the fpirit of
the Americans, that they will neither fuffer the fate of the
Amalekites, nor retaliate the attempt on the favages of Europe.
Governor Johnflone, Nov. 18, 1777.

No man can have a more determined abhorrence of the employing the Indian favages in our wars than I have; becaufe
no man, in this Houfe at leaft, has had occafion to know fo
much of this matter, as it fell to my lot to have during the laft
war. My horror of their cruel fervices does not arife from
the paintings of imagination, but from what I have known of
the fact; there is not fo hellifh, fo unfair an engine of war,
as the fervice of the Indian favage, when mixed in with the
wars of civilized nations. What then muft *we* think of it,
what muft be *our* feelings, when they are employed in a war,
between parts of the fame nation, branches of the fame family,
in the war between us and our brethren?

The mutual feelings of humanity, and a fpirit of honour,
have, amidft civilized nations, defined even rights, and given
laws ʌto a ftate of war; have laid a reftraint on havock, and
given limits to deftruction and bloodfhed. There are even in
rigours of war, the *jura belli*, which civilized nations have
adopted, and do almoft univerfally obferve. The war of the
favage, inftead of being a conteft of right by power, regulated
and reftrained by any feelings of honour or humanity, is an
unreftrained effufion of the paffions of revenge and blood-
thirftinefs, *eft certare odiis*, is a war of univerfal ravage and
devaftation to utter deftruction; inftead of giving laws to war,
it gives the name and effect of right to every cruel exertion of
paffion, revenge, and barbarity, *jufque datum fceleri.*
Governor Pownall, Feb. 6, 1778.

WHEN

WHEN America was firft fettled, the whole right to conqueft, difcovery, and divifion of lands was in the King;—it was in his power to grant them to any body, and on any condition. This power he ufed in America, in all cafes without, and in fome againft the confent of Parliament, who never, indeed, fuppofed, that fuch feudal Rights were vefted in them.

At what time the King gave up, or Parliament ufurped thefe Rights, is not now my bufinefs to inquire; but I muft maintain, that unlefs America had confented to fuch a ceffion, America is not bound by it, but her Rights remain the fame as when firft eftablifhed by her Charters.

A late decifion in the King's Bench has fully eftablifhed this doctrine. The King may lay any impofitions on a conquered country by his own authority, till he has by Proclamation, or otherwife, given up that power by eftablifhing another.

Sir Cecil Wray, April 6, 1778.

ARMY.

A   R   M   Y.

" I HAVE fpoken fo often againft maintaining an extra-
" ordinary number of land forces in time of peace, that I
" fhould now chufe to be filent, if I had not the firft day of
" the Seffion entered my claim to difpute the continuance of
" the four thoufand Augmentation Troops ; and if I did not
" think it my duty to oppofe every propofition, which feems
" to carry the leaft appearance of danger to our Conftitution.

" I afk pardon, if I take the prefent Queftion to be of this
" nature. Nor can I be perfuaded, that the frequent impo-
" fitions of unneceffary Taxes, or the repetition of any
" grievance, ought to beget an infenfibility, or a flavifh ac-
" quiefcence in it. On the contrary, I think it ought to
" awaken and double our attention, left it fhould in time
" plead a prefcriptive right, and gradually grow into an
" eftablifhment.

" If I may be permitted to confider the King's Speech as
" the compofition of his Minifters, which, though I know by
" experience to be a more dangerous, is yet a more parlia-
" mentary way, than to confider it as an Edict from the
" Throne, I will obferve, that it does not afk the advice and
" opinion of the Commons, how far they will ufe their great;
" effential, and undifputed Right of raifing money; but it
" pofitively prefcribes the exact provifion we are to make, both
" by fea and land, for the fervice of the enfuing year : and
" whether that be not a new method of fpeaking to Parlia-
" ments, is with all deference fubmitted to the wifdom of this
" Houfe, which is the beft-judge of its own Privileges and
" Power.

" Surely, Sir, it is very melancholy to hear, one Seffion af-
" ter another, that, though we are in a ftate of tranquillity,
" as the language is, yet we can neither be fecure at home,

" nor

" nor refpected abroad, without continuing above eighteen
" thoufand land forces in pay.

" This way of reafoning entirely mifreprefents our circum-
" ftances and condition. For it would fuggeft, that we can-
" not enjoy the bleffings of a good Reign, without enduring
" at the fame time the hardfhips of a bad one ; which is a
" contradiction in itfelf, and inconfiftent with the notions we,
" as Englifhmen, muft ever entertain of our legal liberties ;
" in maintenance of which, our predeceffors in Parliament
" thought fit to alter the lineal fucceffion of our Royal Fa-
" mily. This way of reafoning farther fuppofes, that the
" mutual confidence betwixt his Majefty and his People is
" deftroyed; that there is a diftruft on one hand, and a
" difaffection on the other, for which there is not the leaft
" ground or pretence. For his Majefty, by his refidence
" amongft us this laft fummer, has not only given us the
" cleareft proof of his preferring the welfare and happinefs
" of thefe Kingdoms to. that of his own foreign Dominions,
" but has for ever fecured the love of his fubjects here, by his
" moft gracious affability and perfonal condefcenfion to them.
" He has for ever fecured that tranquillity at home, on which
" he is pleafed with fo much fatisfaction to congratulate his
" Parliament. Nor can this tranquillity be affected by the
" clamours in Ireland, againft a late Patent for coining ; for
" there is a large army in that Kingdom fufficient to curb tu-
" multuous fpirits, and to awe patronizing malcontents,
" fhould any fuch be found. Nay, if more forces are judged
" neceffary, either for the honour or fafety of the Government
" here, that Kingdom is able and willing to maintain more on its
" own Eftablifhment ; and therefore all arguments drawn from
" thence relating to the prefent Queftion muft be inconclufive.
" The Houfe may perhaps think fit, at a proper feafon, to
" liften fo far to the complaints of our fellow-fubjects in ano-
" ther Kingdom, as to call for this obnoxious Patent, and to
" examine into the grounds of it. For the mif-government

4   " of

" of Ireland has been frequently under the examination of the
" Houfe of Commons here, and fuch examinations have fre-
" quently proved fatal to as great Minifters as England ever
" bred : which may be matter of reflection to their fucceffors,
" and to thofe it may concern ; but never can be any induce-
" ment to any Englifh Parliament, to pay one Soldier more
" than is abfolutely neceffary for our own ufe.

" Now all Rebellions, all Confpiracies, feems to be totally
" extinguifhed, not more by the late feafonable exertion of par-
" liamentary juftice, than by the wife and prudent conduct of
" thofe in the Adminiftration. They have fo carefully re-
" viewed, and modelled the forces of this fummer in every
" part of the nation, that, we are to hope, there are not left
" even fo many as three or four Serjeants and Corporals, who
" fhall have fool-hardinefs enough to undertake again to draw
" the whole Army into wild and chimerical attempts. They
" have freed the Church from all apprehenfions of danger, by
" promoting only the moft orthodox and learned part of the
" Clergy to the epifcopal Dignity, and other ecclefiaftical
" Preferments. They have preferved the State, by advancing
" only men of diftinguifhed ability and experience to all great
" Offices and Civil Employments. They have, which is
" above all, reconciled their own animofities, and have no
" other contentions now, but who fhall beft ferve his Majefty
" and the Public, without any views of accumulating im-
" menfe wealth to themfelves, or of aggrandizing their own
" private families. Such an Adminiftration can never need
" the affiftance and protection of above eighteen thoufand dif-
" ciplined troops. Such an Adminiftration fhould not fuffer
" the Army to run away with the reputation of their good and
" great works, or to affume the glory of raifing our Credit,
" enlarging our Trade, and eftablifhing our prefent Profperity.
" Nor are our Foreign Affairs in a lefs flourifhing con-
" dition than thofe at home, fo far as I am capable of judging
" from

" from the common appearance of things, without being in
" the fecrets of the Cabinet.

" We can have no apprehenfions from our neareft neigh-
" bour France. For that Kingdom is engaged to us by many
" ftrict Treaties; and I have heatd the French *bona fides*, of
" late years, as much afferted and extolled in this Houfe, as
" I have formerly heard it ridiculed and exploded. Befides,
" we have a vigilant Minifter at Paris, who, by his own fkill
" and penetration in Politics, as well as by good advite and
" affiftance from hence, is not only promoting the Britifh in-
" terefts there, but influencing and directing the French
" Councils.

" Nor can we have any pretence to keep up thofe forces on
" account of danger from Spain. For if that Monarchy fhould
" be indifcreet enough to entertain the leaft harfh remem-
" brance of any pretended ill ufuage from Great-Britain; if
" it fhould refent our glorious and feafonable conqueft over
" their fleet in the Mediterranean, for which we ftruck a Me-
" dal with pompous infcriptions; if it fhould infift on a refti-
" tution of Gibraltar and Port Mahon, which, in my humble
" opinion, can never be furrendered without the higheft in-
" famy, as well as injury to England. I fay, if any thing of
" this kind fhould remain in the breaft of the Court of Spain,
" notwithftanding our Treaties, and daily Negociations there,
" it is our comfort, that we need fear no invafion from their
" Armada: that the mutability of their Councils, their pre-
" tenfions in Italy, their diftance from Great-Britain, render
" it impracticable for them to annoy or diftrefs us. And if
" King Philip's Refignation of the Crown was a good argu-
" ment the laft year for continuing the four thoufand Augmen-
" tation Troops, then his Refumption of it now muft be a
" good one for difbanding them this year.

" The Emperor's perfonal obligations to Great-Britain are
" fuch, that it is impoffible for him to entertain any ill in-
" tentions againft us, either on account of the Oftend Eaft-

" India Company, or of his Majesty's glorious endeavours to
" remove the religious grievances in Germany, and to pro-
" mote the Proteſtant intereſt there, of which he is the great
" Guardian.

" The Dutch are our natural allies, and always ready to
" aſſiſt us. Nor is it their fault, that we have ſometimes
" diſputed amongſt ourſelves, concerning the expence of tranſ-
" porting their auxiliar forces. They are bound to us by
" antient ties of gratitude, for their original preſervation, and
" by, what is yet a ſtronger cement, their own intereſt and
" ſafety.

" As to the two northern Crowns, Sweden and Denmark,
" they have in their turns received our protection, and taſted
" of our bounty. We all remember the famous æra, when
" two hundred and fifty thouſand pounds, as well as many
" ſmaller ſupplies ſince, were raiſed on that account. Beſides,
" we are to hope our expeditions into the Baltic, under the
" conduct of a brave Officer here preſent, have been as effec-
" tual as they have been expenſive; and that our fleet has not
" only awed them into a reconciliation betwixt themſelves, but
" into an abſolute ſubmiſſion to Great-Britain.

" The Czar is ſtretching his conqueſts into remote parts of
" the world; and if what we hear of a late Treaty be true, that
" it is made entirely in favour of Great-Britain, without any
" regard to foreign principalities, we can apprehend nothing
" from our new ally, who is otherwiſe ſo fully employed.
" For however extenſive our mediating care may be, I preſume
" we are not engaged with him to oppoſe the intended ſucceſſion
" of the Crown of Poland, or to ſettle the balance of Empire
" in Perſia.

" If ſuch then is our proſperous ſituation at home and abroad,
" why ſhould we be denied the promiſed happy conſequences of
" it? Why ſhould we be afraid of reducing our land forces?
" Why ſhould we not at leaſt ſtrike off the four thouſand aug-
" mentation troops, in compaſſion to a nation loaded, and al-
" moſt

" moſt ſunk with debt ? For ſhould a ſtorm ariſe after this
" calm, ſhould any new event produce a rupture in Europe,
" it will be time enough, if we are either prompted by our own
" heroic diſpoſition, or bound by any inviolable Treaties, to
" enter into the quarrels of the Continent. I ſay, it will be
" time enough, when the war ſhall be actually declared, to
" lend our aſſiſtance to thoſe, who we voluntarily eſpouſe, or
" to perform our engagements to our reſpective allies, if they
" ſhould not be found romantic or impracticable. We have
" the opinion of a moſt eminent author in civil learning, That
" it is more grievous to any nation, to bear the leaſt extra-
" ordinary taxes in times of peace, than to endure the greateſt
" impoſitions in times of war. Becauſe a war may prove ad-
" vantageous, may terminate in conqueſt and glorious acqui-
" ſitions. But a continuance of extraordinary taxes without
" it, muſt inevitably end in poverty and ruin.

" Now I can never be ſo unjuſt to his Majeſty's mild and
" gracious Government, as to aſcribe our preſent tranquillity
" to the continuance of an extraordinary number of troops,
" any more than I can believe, it would ceaſe at the reduction
" of part of them. This would be a dangerous, as well as an
" abſurd doctrine, with relation to us at home. For ſhould it
" be admitted, that above eighteen thouſand land forces, have
" not only procured our preſent tranquillity, but that they are
" abſolutely neceſſary for the ſecurity of the kingdom; then it
" will follow, that the ſame number will be always abſolutely
" neceſſary ; that a military power is the moſt pacific form of
" Government ; and that an army will be a better preſerver
" of peace and plenty, a better guardian of our civil and re-
" ligious Rights, than the Law of the Land. This doctine
" too, conſidered with regard to the reſpect and influence we
" may have abroad, is as abſurd as ill grounded : for that re-
" ſpect and influence can never proceed from the number of
" land forces we may think fit to burthen ourſelves with in
" time of peace, but it muſt proceed from the advantages of

" our

" our natural fituation, from our naval ftrength, from our ex-
" tended commerce, from our vaft riches, which have enabled
" us to carry on long and expenfive wars; to maintain, when
" our allies failed in their quotas, three great armies at once
" in their different nations; and thefe advantages will ever
" enable us to hold the balance of power in Europe, unlefs
" worn out with unneceffary and infupportable taxes.

" But if not fo much as the four thoufand augmentation
" troops are to be parted with, if they are to be continued till
" the pretences of all the Princes of Europe fhall be adjufted,
" till the different interefts of different nations fhall be recon-
" ciled, till the claim of Bremen and Verden fhall be fully fet-
" tled and acquiefced in, till the long expected form of a Con-
" grefs fhall be compleated, I freely own, I am not without
" my apprehenfions, that our immenfe national debt, inftead
" of being annually reduced, will be daily increafed: that our
" prefent grievances, for grievances we have in the midft of
" all our tranquillity, inftead of being fpeedily removed, will
" become perpetual, and we may dream of bleffings we fhall
" never enjoy."

Mr. Shippen, Nov. 22, 1724.

' My fentiménts concerning a ftanding army, in time of
peace, are well known here; and it may feem unneceffary, perhaps be thought impertinent in me, to debate anew on a worn-
out and exhaufted topic, when other Gentlemen, who entertain
the fame fentiments, are pleafed to be filent. But furely the
queftion before you is not become a Motion of courfe; furely
as long as the grievance is continued on one hand, fo long
there is a right of complaint on the other; and that complaint,
I fhould think, may without offence be continued, till it can be
proved that the Britifh Government is in its nature military, or
ought to be made fo.

' I do not intend to trouble you with what I have formerly
urged, or to ufe any argument drawn from the expence and

burthen,

burthen, or from the terror and oppreffion which have been brought upon this and other nations, by raifing and keeping up a greater number of forces, than were abfolutely neceffary in time of peace : not but that the gradations, by which armies, with all their inconveniencies, have been firft introduced into free ftates, and afterwards impofed upon them, ought to be had in perpetual remembrance. We ought never to forget, that fuch fteps have been ufually taken, to gratify the views of am-'bitious Princes; to carry on the fchemes of evil Minifters, to terrify Parliaments into obedience, and to make the Members of them dumb fpectators of the miferies of their country.

' I will not infift on thefe arguments, however juft in themfelves, however proper on other occafions, becaufe they would be unapplicable to the prefent fituation of our affairs. For we have a Prince whofe aim is to continue us the bleffings of peace and plenty; we have a Miniftry who have merits above my commendation ; we have a Parliament, which acts with a fpirit fuperior to all influences, and to all temptations. Befides, every year has its particular circumftances, and thofe particular circumftances ought to guide our refolutions, when we are marking our annual parliamentary provifions for the public fervice. I thought our circumftances both at home and abroad, were fo profperous the laft Seffion, that we might without hazard have difbanded at leaft the four thoufand augmentation troops. But the Majority of the Houfe was of another opinion. There was then indeed a Rendezvous, though not a formed Congrefs, of Plenipotentiaries, vyirg with each other in the fplendor of their equipages and the magnificence of their entertainments at Cambray, which had for fome time employed our fpeculations, and promifed great events to the world. And it was thought good policy to fhow the negociating Powers, by continuing our army, that, if they would not accept of his Majefty's plan for fettling the balance of power, and for eftablifhing the tranquillity of Europe, Great-Britain was ready to do her part toward compelling them to a com-

I 3   pliance,

pliance. But that policy proved ineffectual, and that negotiation appears at laft to have wanted fubftance as well as form,
and to have produced nothing to Great-Britain, but an increafe
of the civil lift debt, as we were given to underftand the laft
Seffions, in a Debate on that fubject, by one that knew the
fecret.

' But we are now told, that prudent and powerful alliances
are actually made, and that what was only attempted at Cambray, has been fully accomplifhed at Herenhaufen: nor can
there be any doubt, of his Majefty's extenfive care over
all his concerns both foreign and domeftic; but that his alter-
nate refidence here and abroad, as it hath procured, fo it
would, with the advice of a good Miniftry, and without the
aid of a great army, preferve to us, through the whole courfe
of his reign, that fecurity, and thofe bleffings we now enjoy.
For, whether at home or abroad, his influence is irrefiftible,
becaufe his councils are wife and his defigns are juft. Nor
am I altered in this opinion by what has happened at Glafgow
and other places in Scotland, or at Thorn in Poland.

' For, if I am rightly informed, the tumult at Glafgow was
no more than a mob, compofed chiefly of women, a mere
mock-refemblance of an Amazonian army, that might have been
quelled by the interpofition of the civil power, without recourfe to that military vengeance which was executed there.
Such commotions we fee arife almoft in every nation, when
the occafions of the public call for new and extraordinary taxes;
and yet they are generally defpifed, as impotent efforts againft
eftablifhed Governments, and left to be punifhed by the laws
of the country. But, now all is quiet, now all is fafe in Scotland, not the leaft murmur is heard againft Adminiftration.
The Highland Clans have been difarmed without any difturbance; they rejoice, we are told, in their fubmiffion, and are
brought to a perfect fenfe of their duty to his Majefty, by the
obliging behaviour and prudent conduct of the General, whofe
province it was to enforce the act of Parliament againft them.

' As

' As to the important affair of Thorn, which by the way
was no act of retaliation, as some, who neither confider the
circumftance of time nor things would infinuate, but the
effect of a fpirit of perfecution ; we are affured, that his Majefty has done more towards obtaining the defired fatisfaction
for the barbarous and unchriftian cruelties committed there,
and gained greater conceffions from the Catholic Princes, by
his pacific mediation and by his perfonal intereft, than he
could probably have done by rougher expedients, by threatening,
or even entering into a religious war. Nor can malice itfelf
fuppofe, that, whilft he is refenting the violation of Treaties,
he would do any thing that would but look like an infraction of
the limitation in the Act of Succeffion, which reftrains the
Crown from involving Great-Britain in any foreign difputes,
except where her own immediate interefts and alliances are
concerned.

' I hope we conceive no ill omens from the French King's
marriage to the daughter of the Pretender to the Crown of
Poland ; no diftruft, that fuch an alliance can fhake our late
Proteftant Treaty with that young Prince ; no jealoufy that he
will follow the example of the Emperor and the King of Spain,
by engaging in a clandeftine League without our knowledge,
and to our prejudice. I muft own, that would be a melancholy
confideration. For then an army of twice eighteen thoufand
men would not be fufficient to defend that caufe, which his
Majefty has hitherto afferted, with fo much glory to himfelf, and fo much advantage to the Proteftant part of Europe.

' It was a notorious faying, and the avowed policy of our
late famous Statefman, who lived till after the Revolution, and
was thought a fecret inftrument in it, that notwithftanding the
noife and clamour of the people againft foldiers in time of peace,
the cafieft and beft way of governing England was by an army ;
and that a Minifter fo guarded, might profecute his meafures
with fafety and fuccefs, and foon make the boafting affertors of
Liberty and Property, as tame as a flock of turkies, and drive

. I 4   them

them which way he pleafed. This gives us a true idea of fome forts of modern policy, and of the infolence of that man in authority, who ruined the Prince by the very methods he would have enflaved his own fellow-fubjects, but not of the genius of the people of England. For he found another fpirit in them; he found they perpetually ftruggled with him in defence of the Church and State, when he was endeavouring to facrifice both, as well as he did his own honour and confcience, in order to erect an arbitrary and unlimited dominion in thefe kingdoms. Nor could they endure his return into power after the Revolution, though he was countenanced by King William himfelf, and though his meritorious perfidy was ftrongly pleaded in his favour. But they continued their oppofition to him, till they had accomplifhed his difgrace; and ftill his memory is as deteftable, as his Adminiftration was wicked, though he neither aggrandized his family, nor augmented his eftate by the fpoils of the Public.

' Now we are to hope the military principles of this Statefman are dead with him, and we are fure good Minifters will never purfue the maxims of bad ones, becaufe the means of their actions muft neceffarily be as different as the ends are. It is therefore unintelligible to me, how the keeping up an army in time of peace, which has formerly been thought criminal advice in a Minifter, as being incompatible with our Conftitution, fhould now be annually recommended to Parliament by our modern patriots, as the only method of fecuring us in the poffeffion of our Laws and Liberties. I fay, this is unintelligible to me; and till the feeming paradox can be reconciled to reafon, I muft beg leave conftantly to oppofe the Queftion.'   *Mr. Shippen, Jan.* 28, 1726.

I am forry to hear a parrallel drawn by any Member of this Houfe, between the army kept up by the late King James, and the army intended to be kept up at prefent. King James's army was raifed againft law, was maintained againft the con-

4   fent

fent of the people, and was employed in overturning the liberties of the people : the prefent queftion is about an army which
is to be kept up according to law, and by and with the confent of the people. If we look into the *Petition of Right* itfelf,
what does it fay ? Why that an army raifed, or kept up, without
confent of Parliament, is contrary to the conftitution; but it
never was faid, that an army kept up by confent of Parliament, is illegal, or any way contrary to the conftitution ;
in this refpect, no parallel can therefore be drawn between
the prefent army, which is to be kept up only by confent
of the people, and maintained by them, and that army
which was raifed and maintained by King James himfelf ;
and was fo far from being by the concurrence or confent of
the people, that it was to be employed *againft* them ; and I am
perfuaded, that no man here expects that the prefent army is
to be employed in fuch manner.

I really believe, and I hope I am right, that there is but very
little diffatisfaction in the nation, and that the Jacobite party is
now become very inconfiderable ; but ftill that party is not to
be ridiculed and made a joke of : we are not fo much to defpife
all attempts that may be made by them, as not to take any
meafures to provide ourfelves againft them ; fuch a fecurity is
the beft thing they can wifh for ; they would be glad to be
defpifed in fuch a manner. Gentlemen may fay what they will
of the little confequence of any endeavours that have been, or
may be ufed by them ; but the late rebellion is a certain teftimony that they are not to be too much defpifed. The fate of
the kingdom was at that time brought even to the decifion of a
day ; and if the Rebels had been fuccefsful at Prefton, I do not
know what might have been the confequences ; I dread to think
of them : but let them have been never fo fatal, if the liberties
of this nation had been overthrown by the fuccefs of thofe
Rebels, it would have been entirely owing to our having fo few
regular forces on foot at that time. We have efcaped that
danger, but do not let us expofe ourfelves every day to fuch
dangers for the future ; which muft be the neceffary confequence
of

of reducing any part of the fmall army now on foot, and de-fired to be continued.

A parliamentary army never yet did any harm in this nation; but reductions of that army have often been fatal. I have been affured by a Minifter of very great confequence of the Court of France, that the reducing our army after the Peace of Ryfwick, very much encouraged the Court of France to take fuch meafures, and to make fuch bold fteps as they afterwards did. They would have been more cautious, if we had kept ourfelves in a capacity of pouring in a numerous army upon them; but they faw that we had put it out of our power, and therefore they defpifed us. The reduction of the army after the Peace of Utrecht, had not, by good luck, all the ill con-fequences that were defigned, but the reduction was certainly made with no good intent. I have a good opinion enough of the late Queen; fhe had not, perhaps, any ill intentions; but I am convinced, that her Minifter had laid a fcheme for overturn-ing the Proteftant fucceffion: and they had no other way of executing this fcheme, but by getting free of all thofe brave officers and foldiers who had ferved their country fo faithfully in the late wars; this was what made the army be reduced at that time fo low as it was: the Minifters knew, that thefe honeft officers would not ferve them in the execution of their de-ftructive fchemes; but they took care to fupply their place with a body of above 6200 men, who were privately kept in pay, and maintained under colour of Chelfea-hofpital; and the con-fequence fhewed what fort of men thefe new troops were, for almoft every man of them appeared in arms in the late Re-bellion againft the government. We have heard the Treaty of Utrecht, upon which this reduction was made, applauded by fome; whether it deferves any fuch applaufe I do not know; but I am certain that fince that time we have been obliged to enter into feparate treaties and negotiations almoft with every power in Europe, for amending and explaining the blunders of that Treaty: and if we are now right, whoever afcribes our

being

being fo to that Treaty, may be faid to be like a man, who, after breaking another's bones, and feeing them fet again very right, and well cured by an able Surgeon, cries, you are obliged to me, Sir, for this great cure that has been performed upon you. *Mr. Horatio Walpole, Jan.* 26, 1732.

I CANNOT but be againſt even giving this Bill a fecond reading, becaufe at firſt view it apppears to be for fupporting a numerous ſtanding army in time of peace : this I need not any time to confider of ; this appears evidently to be the purport and intention of the Bill now read to us ; and this, my Lords, is againſt the very words of the *Petition of Right,* and alters the very nature of our conſtitution. All the confufions and diforders that have been brought upon this kingdom for many years, have all been brought upon it by the means of ſtanding armies : it was, my Lords, a ſtanding army that took off King *Charles* the Firſt's head, and turned that very Parliament out of doors which had eſtabliſhed them ; and the very fame army that had murdered the father reſtored the fon : it was by King *James* the Second's keeping up a ſtanding army, that the affections of the people were alienated from him ; and by that very army, in whom he had put his only truſt, he was turned out ; for by their joining the other fide, the fcales were turned againſt him, and he found himfelf at laſt obliged to fuccumb under the juſt refentments of an injured people. In this country, in every country, my Lords, where numerous ſtanding armies have been kept up, we may find that innumerable evils and ſtrange confufions have been brought on by the means of fuch armies : and therefore I ſhall always be againſt giving the leaſt countenance to any Bill, that feems to tend towards keeping up a ſtanding army in time of peace in this country.
Earl of Aylesford, Feb. 24, 1732.

I SHALL readily grant that there is a continual rivalſhip between the two' great contending powers of Europe ; there
always

always will, I hope, be such a rivalship; for if ever that rival‑
ship should ceafe, which it never can, but by one of them being
fwallowed up by the other, it would be an unlucky thing for
this nation, as well as for all the reft of *Europe:* but, my
Lords, are we to keep up a numerous ftanding army as long
as that rivalship shall continue? If so, we muft never think of
any reduction: no, my Lords, that rivalship has already con‑
tinued for many ages, and yet we have always fupported our‑
felves againft both, without having ever kept up a ftanding
army: this new fort of defence has been but lately thought on,
and never can be a proper defence for this nation: the only way
we have to fecure ourfelves at home, to make ourfelves con‑
fiderable abroad, and to force a refpect from both thefe con‑
tending powers, is to do as we have always formerly done, to
put our whole truft in our natural ftrength, which confifts in
our fleet, and in the natural bravery of our men in general:
as long as we truft to this, and obferve a neutrality as to both
thefe contending powers, we shall be courted by both: wo
may fall in fometimes with the one and fometimes with the
other, according as may beft fuit with our own intereft, and
with the circumftances of affairs at the time: by fuch a ma‑
nagement we shall always be able to hold the balance of *Europe*
in our own hands, and never will have any occafion either to
court the friendship, or to fear the refentment of any power on
earth.

But, my Lords, if we begin to purfue contrary meafures, if
we be always the firft to enter into alliances with the powers of
Europe, and the original contracting parties in moft treaties,
we thereby give the power of holding the balance of '*Europe*
out of our hands; and the neglecting our fleet and militia, for
the fake of keeping up a ftanding army, will foon render us
contemptible to every one of our neighbours, unlefs we refolve
to keep up a much more numerous army than what is propofed
by this Bill; and fuch a propofition will, I hope, never be ap‑
proved of by a majority of either Houfe of Parliament.

A ftand‑

A ftanding army and military law, has, my Lords, been always inconfiftent with the liberties of the people; the officers and foldiers under fuch a regulation, are always obliged to give the moft implicit obedience to the commands of their fuperior officers; they muft obferve and execute the orders they receive without any referve or hefitation; they muft not inquire whether their orders be according to law, if they do, they are guilty of mutiny, and may be immediately fhot for any fuch difobedience: the chief Commander of an army muft always be vefted with an arbitrary and abfolute power over the army; and if his army be numerous, he may eafily, by their means, extend his power over the whole people of the country where fuch army is kept up: and therefore, my Lords, in all countries where the people have any regard to their liberties, they ought never to keep up a greater number of regular forces than are abfolutely neceffary for the fecurity of the government, and for the prefervation of the country againft any fudden in-vafion or inroad that may be made by a foreign enemy. In this country we have the happinefs to be furrounded by the fea; we know how difficult and expenfive it is to make any invafion upon us with any great body of men; any fuch invafion we muft have a timely warning of, and by having our militia in good order, and our men, as they were formerly, all trained up to arms and military difcipline, we fhould always be able to draw, upon any occafion, and in any place within the ifland, a great army together, to oppofe our enemies, if they fhould happen to have the good fortune to efcape our fleet at fea,

In our prefent circumftances, my Lords, and confidering the happy fituation of our country, I muft be of opinion, that 12,000 men are abundantly fufficient for all the good ufes we can have for them, and therefore I fhall give my affent to the reduction propofed.

Earl Strafford, March 6, 1733.

I CAN-

. I CANNOT imagine how fome people have got into that way
of thinking, that the liberties of all 'the countries in *Europe*
have been overturned by ftanding armies : I do not know one
country in *Europe* whofe liberties have been overturned by their
ftanding army. It is a miftake to fay fo of the Romans ; the
liberties of *Rome*, were in a great meafure overturned, by the
luxury and corruption that had crept in among the people long
before the time of *Julius Cæfar :* and in his time, their ftanding army were fo far from being the only means of overturning
the liberties of Rome, that the greateft part of the ftanding
army joined againft *Julius Cæfar :* but he had a devilifh head of
his own, fo that by his own good conduct, and bravery of his
troops, he got the better of his enemies, though they had the
greateft number of regular troops of their fide. If the *Romans*
at that time had had no ftanding army, would not the people,
would not the very mob have done the fame ? Every man who
had courage, or who could be perfuaded to go to fight, would
have joined that party he liked beft : the Commander who
could make the beft ufe of thofe that joined him, would have
got the advantage, and the victorious army would have had it
in their power to have fettled the future form of government
upon what footing they had a mind.

It is the fame with refpect to all the other countries of
Europe, where arbitrary power is or ever was eftablifhed : in
France, it is certain that their liberties were overturned long
before they had fuch a thing as a ftanding army : the oldeft
regiment or corps of regular troops in *France*, is what they call
the regiment of *Picardy*; that regiment was raifed only in the
firft or fecond year of the reign of our Queen *Elizabeth*; and
it is well known, that long before that time the liberties of the
French people were entirely deftroyed. In *Spain* we know that
it was their priefts that deftroyed the liberties of the people ; and
it is by means of their Inquifition, that their arbitrary government is to this day fupported : by means of that terrible fpiritual
court, their priefts fupport their own defpotic rule not only
over

over the people, but likewife over the court, and even over their army too. In *Sweden*, my Lords, it was likewife their priefts that formerly eftablifhed an arbitrary rule in that country; and it was by their army that their liberties were reftored. In *Denmark* it was a Houfe of Commons that furrendered up their liberties to the Crown; they firft gave up their own liberties, and thereby enabled their King to get himfelf declared the abfolute and the arbitrary Sovereign over the whole country.

Thus, my Lords, we may find that a ftanding army never had in any country the chief hand in deftroying the liberties of their country: nor indeed can it be fuppofed that they ever will. Can it be fuppofed that any man of common fenfe, who has a good poft in the army, and has the laws of his country for his protection as long as he behaves well, can it, I fay, my Lords, be fuppofed, that any fuch man will ever join in meafures for fubjecting himfelf to the uncontroulable will and giddy pleafure of any one man? He muft know that true honour and virtue, or a faithful performance of his duty, could then be no protection to him; his life, his eftate, and every thing that is dear to him, muft then depend on the mere pleafure of a court: and every man knows, that about courts, true honour and virtue often fails a facrifice to whifpers, to deceitful infinuations, and to falfe and private accufations: is it then reafonable to prefume, that the Gentlemen of the army, who are by their education bred ftrangers to the low arts and vile practices ufual about courts, will ever give up that honourable dependence they have upon their own behaviour, and the laws of their country, for the fake of a flavifh dependance upon any court whatever? For my part, it is not poffible for me to fufpect any fuch thing, and therefore I cannot from thence draw any argument againft keeping up a ftanding army in this country.

Duke of Argyle, March 6, 1733.

I AM

I AM one of thofe, and I believe there are a great many more, who are againft the fecond reading of this Bill, prefented by a Noble Duke (the Duke of Marlborough) for the better fecuring the conftitution, by preventing the Officers of the land forces from being deprived of their commiffions, otherwife than by judgment of a Court-martial.   I did not, it is true, rife up im-mediately after the Motion was made, to give my reafons for being againft a fecond reading, becaufe I thought the Bill was of a nature fo very extraordinary, and the objections to it fo ftrong and evident, that I thought it unneceffary for me, or any other Lord in this Houfe, to give himfelf or the Houfe the trouble of explaining them : but fince the Noble Lord who fpoke laft, infifts fo much upon it, in order to fatisfy him, I fhall give him fome of thofe reafons which prevail with me to be againft a fecond reading of the Bill now before us : and if either that Noble Lord, or any other, can give fufficient an-fwers to thofe reafons, I fhall moft readily join with thofe Noble Lords who are for reading this Bill a fecond time.

With me, my Lords, one of the principal objections againft the Bill is, that I look upon it as an open and a direct attack upon the Prerogative of the Crown.   It is an attack upon a Prerogative, which his Majefty and his anceftors have enjoyed ever fince our monarchy had a being ; and we all know how nearly connected the Privileges of this Houfe are with the Pre-rogative of the Crown : we know, my Lords, that the laft open and direct attack that was made upon the Prerogative of the Crown, ended in the total fubverfion of our monarchy, and an entire diffolution of this Houfe ; and therefore I cannot but be furprized, to fee a Bill of this nature brought firft into this Houfe : if fuch a Bill had paffed the other Houfe, and had been fent up to us from thence, I do not doubt but that every one of your Lordfhips would have eafily feen through the defign ; you would have feen the fnare that was laid againft the mo-narchical eftablifhment of our government, upon which the Pri-vileges of every Lord in the nation abfolutely depend.   This
                                                                     would

would have given your Lordſhips a juſt claim; and this, I doubt not, would have made you receive ſuch a Bill in the manner it deſerved.

I have often heard, my Lords, of a compaĉt between the King and the people; and a compaĉt, upon which, it is ſaid, our conſtitution and government depend; if there be any ſuch, the nature of it muſt certainly be mutual. On the one part, our Kings are obliged not to uſurp, or encroach upon the liberties of the people: but ſurely there muſt be a counterpart, and by that there muſt be an obligation on the part of the people not to uſurp or encroach upon the Powers and Prerogatives of the Crown: for it would be a very unjuſt compaĉt, if, on the one hand, the King was moſt ſtriĉtly tied down, and, on the other hand, the people left at full liberty to encroach as often, and as far as they pleaſed, upon the Prerogatives of the Crown. This cannot be the caſe; the compaĉt muſt be mutual; and as his preſent Majeſty has never once attempted, nor deſires, in the leaſt to encroach upon the Liberties or the Privileges of the people, it would be very unjuſt and unfair in us, to make any encroachment upon him. Nay, it would be moſt unwiſe, and might be attended with the moſt fatal conſequences; for a breach of covenant on one ſide, would diſſolve all the covenants on the other, which would at once unhinge the whole of our conſtitution.

It has always been thought neceſſary, my Lords, to give our Kings the ſole power of naming, preferring, and reforming at pleaſure the Officers of our armies, in order to give our Kings that power and influence over our armies; which is abſolutely neceſſary for ſupporting and promoting a proper military diſcipline among them, without which they would be of no uſe againſt a foreign enemy, and might ſoon become moſt oppreſſive to the people, for whoſe ſafety they were raiſed and maintained. This power was thought ſo neceſſary at the time of the Revolution, and it was then thought to be of ſo little danger to the freedom of the conſtitution, that at that time, when the liberties of the People were fully confidered, when every thing was removed that could be of dangerous confequence to them, there was not the leaft mention made of taking this Power from the Crown, or even of laying it under any reftraints: and I do not know any thing that has happened, which can give us the leaft ground for being of an opinion different from that, which was the opinion of our anceftors at that time.

The happinefs of our Conftitution, my Lords, depends upon that equal Divifion of Power, which is eftablifhed amongft the three Branches of our Legiflature: the executive Power, and the defending of the People againft their enemies, is now, and always has been, entrufted folely with our King; it muft always be abfolutely neceffary to give our Kings proper Powers for thefe purpofes: the fupreme and ultimate determination of all difputes about property is lodged folely in this Houfe; and the raifing of money for the public ufe, or laying Taxes upon the People, is what now feems to be principally the province of the other Houfe. Thus the three Branches of the Legiflature are a check upon one another, which prevents its being in the power of any one of them to opprefs the People, or to deftroy the other two. Under this Eftablifhment we have been happy for many ages, under this the nation has grown up to a very high pitch of riches and power; and while this Eftablifhment continues, it is more than probable, we fhall always be happy.

But, my Lords, by the Bill now before us, we are to eftablifh a fourth Power, a new fort of Power, which, I am perfuaded, will foon become independent of the other three. This is making a moft confiderable alteration in the Conftitution; an alteration that may be attended with fuch fatal confequences, that it makes me tremble to think of it: to eftablifh a General for life at the head of a well-difciplined army, commanded by Officers who could not be removed but by the confent of one another, would foon put it in the power of

that

that General to make himfelf mafter of both King and Parliament : the tranfition from *Dux* to *Rex* would foon become
eafy to him ; by this the Conftitution might be entirely overthrown, and the nation might be involved in a multitude of
calamities.

It is true, my Lords, that by what is propofed in the Bill now
before us, an Officer may ftill be removed from his Command in
the Army, upon an Addrefs of either Houfe of Parliament; but
as the Parliament cannot always be kept fitting, this Addrefs
could not be fpeedily obtained : and if an Officer fhould be difcovered to be confpiring the overthrow of the Government, and
fhould, notwithftanding, be continued in his Commiffion, and in
the poffeffion of that power in the army which he had, by virtue
of his Commiffion, till the next Seffion of Parliament, both Houfes
might, perhaps, addrefs for turning him out : but his power in
the Army might, perhaps, by that time be fo well eftablifhed,
that it would be out of the power of both King and Parliament
to diveft him of his Command : and as for a trial by Court-
Martial, I believe it would not be fo much as pretended, that
a fentence could be got againft fuch an Officer, or indeed,
againft any Officer who had a great influence in the army: it
is not to be prefumed that Officers would be ready to condemn
one another, unlefs it was for a crime which they themfelves
could no way approve of, efpecially when they knew that they
could not be removed by any other authority.

Since then, my Lords, I can fee no manner of occafion for
the Regulation now propofed; fince I am of opinion, that it
would be great injury done to his Majefty, that it would tend
to deftroy all military difcipline in the Army, and would greatly
endanger, if not totally fubvert our happy Conftitution, I cannot therefore agree to the giving it a fecond reading.

Lord Hervey, Jan. 17, 1734.

THE Honourable Gentleman who fpoke firft for the Motion,
has indeed made the beft excufe for the Miniftry that can be
K 2   made

made, Minifters are but men, fometimes weak men; and though it would be unjuft to fuppofe them endued with a fpirit of prophecy, yet, I think, they fhould at leaft be poffeffed of a tolerable fhare of prudence. I fhould not, indeed, wonder, if one or two Meafures went wrong upon a Minifter's hand, through unavoidable accidents; yet I think it ftrange, that every Meafure fhould go wrong; that not one of the numerous expedients that have been fet on foot for fecuring the tranquillity of Europe, or providing for the fecurity of Great-Britain, fhould prove effectual. Sir, I own this gives me ftrong apprehenfions of what I am not inclined to exprefs on the occafion. I own that I was apt to think, that the round of Negociations and Treaties we have been carrying on for thefe ten or twelve years paft, with all the Powers of Europe, might have procured us, at leaft, fome refpite from a burden which our forefathers never knew; I mean, Sir, that of a ftanding Army. I call it a ftanding Army, becaufe it has continued for thefe many years; and we have always been told the fame things over and over again, as reafons why it is continued. I have, during many years, told the Houfe every Seffion, that we fhould have a return of the very fame reafons next Seffion; but Gentlemen never feemed to believe me, though they have hitherto found my words but too true. Now, Sir, as the fame caufes have fubfifted for above thefe forty years, without being any worfe for the wearing, I am apt to think that they may fubfift forty years longer; and while the fame caufes fubfift, the fame effects muft follow: fo that in reality a ftanding Army may be thought as much a part of our Conftitution, as the more lawful Prerogative, or Privilege, which either Prince or People may claim. But, Sir, though even the Gentlemen who are moft converfant in Public Affairs, will, I believe, be puzzled to find out one new argument in favour of a ftanding Army, yet there is nothing eafier than to bring twenty againft it. The reafon of this, Sir, is becaufe it produces but one fingle good, which is the fecurity of the Adminiftration; but

it

it begets many inconveniencies, two of which are the impoverishing the People, and the increase of Taxes.

And here give me leave to say, Sir, that no country can give more melancholy instances of the effects of a military force than England can. The very army which was raised by the Parliament in defence of the subjects, against some encroachments made by Charles the Ist upon their liberties, afterwards gave law to the Parliament itself, turned Its Members out of doors, razed our Constitution to the foundation, and brought that unhappy Prince to the block. This catastrophe, Sir, was not owing to the People; for of them, nine parts in ten were well affected to the person and cause of the King; but to their Army, which, like other wild beasts, turned upon and destroyed their keepers. After the Restoration of the Royal Family, the Prince then upon the Throne raised a few guards, which never swelled to above 5890; and yet so jealous was the nation even of that small number, that he never could get his Parliament, prostitute as it was, to pass over one Session without taking notice of them. This, Sir, was the more extraordinary, as the Parliament was never asked for any money for their support; and the money which was then raised for the support of the Government, was nothing when compared with the sums that have been granted since. The next Parliament proved as uneasy to him on this head as the former had been; and were so distrustful of his intentions, that they appointed Commissioners of their own, for applying the money granted for disbanding them, and it was paid into the Chamber of London. Nay, Sir, as a farther proof of the apprehensions the Nation was under from a standing Army, they came to a Resolution, ' That the continuance of standing Forces in this ' Kingdom, other than the Militia, is illegal, and a great ' grievance and vexation to the People.' I have mentioned this period of our history, Sir, to shew, that notwithstanding the venality of that very Reign, the Parliament never could be brought to concur with what might one day overthrow both

K 3   their

their own and the People's Liberties. If the nation was then fo jealous of an inconfiderable number, which did not coft it a fhilling, ought we confent to keep on foot fo formidable a number as eighteen thoufand? Sir, it is in vain for any Gentleman to fay, that the Army is under the direction of a wife and a juft Sovereign, who will never harbour a thought inconfiftent with the good of his fubjects. I am as thoroughly perfuaded of his Majefty's perfonal virtues as any Gentleman; but an Army, when it once finds its own power, may very probably refufe to take laws, even from that very Sovereign under whofe immediate direction they are. The Parliament's Army, Sir, was as abfolutely under the direction of the Parliament in the time of Charles the Ift, as any Army is now under the direction of his Majefty; and yet it is well known, they obeyed orders no longer than they found it convenient for themfelves.

The period, Sir, from which we are to date the rife of our ftanding Army in Britain, is the ninth year of the late King William, when the Parliament granted an Army of ten thoufand men for the fervice of the current year. This was done, in confideration of the powerful faction at that time fubfifting in the kingdom in favour of King James. And if ever a ftanding Army can be of ufe at any time, it is at fuch a juncture. But nothing, Sir, can make fo palpable an infraction of the fubjects rights, as eftablifhed at the Revolution, go down. Though this nation was then bleffed with a Prince that had hazarded every thing to free us from oppreffion and tyranny, and therefore could never be fuppofed to have any defigns upon our Conftitution; yet many Gentlemen, who were friends of the Revolution upon principles of liberty, with one confent remonftrated againft a ftanding Army, though but kept up from year to year, as fubverfive of the People's Rights, and of the Revolution principles.

Some I know, Sir, who appeared early for the Revolution, were fo much delighted with the funfhine of a Court, that

they

they joined in all its meafures, though fome of them were found
to be directly oppofite to the principles upon which the Revolution was founded : but we find that they, who ever were
acknowledged to be the fincere well-wifhers of that caufe,
forfook them, and could never be brought to concur with them
in any one meafure. On this account, Sir, thefe Gentlemen
were branded by fome, who then fat in the Houfe; with the
name of Jacobites and Republicans, two denominations of
men equally enemies to the prefent eftablifhment. But, Sir,
there was this difference betwixt their antagonifts and them,
that the former never refufed to concur with any meafure propofed by the Court, and the latter never voted for any ftep that
was difliked by their country.

Their late deliverance from a Prince, who, by means of his
Army, aimed at arbitrary Power, made them look back with
fo much horror upon the precipice they had juft efcaped, that
there was an exprefs Provifo againft ftanding Armies in times
of peace, inferted in the Claim of Right, which we may in
fome meafure call the laft great Charter of our Liberty. I
own that it gives me great concern to fee Gentlemen, who
have always valued themfelves upon treading in the footfteps of
thofe who brought about the Revolution, act a part fo inconfiftent with the principles of their anceftors, by voting for this
Queftion. I know a fet of men under a different denomina-
tion, who have always been more moderate in their pretences,
but more fteady in their adherence to thofe principles. I am
not at all inclined to revive any party diftinction; but I will
venture to fay, Sir, that let any man compare the conduct of fome
Gentlemen who have affected to pafs for Whigs, with that
of Gentlemen who have always been looked on as Tories,
he fhall find the latter acting a part moft confiftent with the
Revolution Principles. He will find them oppofing the Crown
in every encroachment upon the People, and in every infringement of the Claim of Right. He never will find them complimenting the Crown at the expence of the People when in

K 4 Poft,

Poft, nor diftreffing it by oppofing any reafonable Meafure when out. Can fome Gentlemen, Sir, who now affect to call themfelves Whigs, boaft of fuch an uniformity of conduct? Can they fay that times and circumftances never influenced the Meafures they purfued? Or that when they were in Office, they always acted in confequence of the Principles they pro- feffed when they were out? Sir, I believe I have fat long enough in this Houfe to convince Gentlemen, if there were occafion, of very great inconfiftencies in certain characters. But, Sir, I forbear it, becaufe the eyes of fome of thefe Gen- tlemen feem to be now open, and I hope thefe diftinctions are in a great meafure either entirely abolifhed or better un- derftood.

As no Queftion, Sir, is of greater importance, fo none has been fo frequently debated in this Houfe as the prefent. Yet I never heard any Gentleman make a doubt, that a ftanding Army in time of peace was a grievance to the People of Great- Britain. But, Sir, the Tories always oppofed this Grievance. When his late Majefty, upon the Rebellion againft him being fuppreffed, for the eafe of his fubjects, ordered ten thoufand of his troops to be difbanded, I remember a particular friend of mine, who always paffed for a Tory, propofed that it fhould be inferted in our Addrefs to his Majefty on that occafion, *That nothing could more endear his Majefty to all his fubjects, than his reducing the Land Forces to the old eftablifhment of guards and garrifons, as his Majefty found it at his Acceffion to the Throne.* This, Sir, happened in the fourth year of his late Majefty's Reign; and had his Majefty thought fit to have made the propofed reduction, or, rather, had he been advifed by his Minifters to have done it, and had the Military Eftablifhment continued on that footing till now, we fhould have difcharged upwards of twelve millions of our national debt, and yet have enabled his Majefty to have made good fuch engagements with his allies, as tended to fecure the public tranquillity.

As

As to what the Honourable Gentleman, who spoke laft, mentioned with regard to reftraining the Liberty of the Prefs, and concerning the general depravity that obtains among the People, I fhall leave him to be anfwered by other Gentlemen, who can do it much better than I can. But I agree with the Honourable Gentleman fo far as to own, that the People are at prefent very much diffatisfied; and, as I think that ferment ought to fubfide gradually, I am willing to give my vote for a larger number of forces this Seffion, than perhaps I may think neceffary to be kept up the next. I therefore move, That the number of Land Forces for the fervice of the current year may be twelve thoufand men.

Mr. Shippen, Jan. 28, 1738.

THE keeping up of a numerous ftanding Army in time of peace, is abfolutely inconfiftent with the liberties of this country. Gentlemen talk of an army of eighteen thoufand men, as always neceffary to be kept up in this Ifland. This, Sir, is the true fecret of this day's Motion: thefe Gentlemen know, that when peace is reftored, the nation will infift upon a reduction being made; therefore, think they, let us now increafe the army, that when peace is reftored we may ftop the mouths of the difaffected, (as they call them) by making a reduction of the troops we are now to add; and thus, Sir, we fhall have a ftanding Army of eighteen thoufand men faddled upon us for ever. As I am of opinion, that an army of eighteen thoufand men is at leaft ten thoufand more than we ought to have in time of peace; as I am of opinion, that fuch a numerous army can be neceffary for no end, but that of enabling a Minifter to trample upon the liberties of his country, I think the Motion ought to be rejected with difdain.

As for Minifters, they muft not expect regard and efteem from their equipage, but from the wifdom and addrefs of their negociations: for a Minifter with a blundering head, or one that is fent upon ridiculous errands, will make as forry a figure

with

with an equipage of regular troops, as an equipage of foot-men; and I am afraid the afs's ears will appear much more conspicuous under a well-burnished head-piece, than ever they did under a well-powdered peruke.

Mr. Pulteney, Feb. 14, 1735.

As the keeping up of a great number of land forces in this Island is quite unneceſſary, and even inconſiſtent with the na-ture of oer happy Conſtitution, and the freedom of our Go-vernment; therefore, when any war is like to break out in which we may probably have a concern, we are always obliged to take foreign troops into our pay : whether we have always been in the ,right ,when we have done ſo, is what I ſhall not now controvert; but I have always obſerved, that no foreign Prince would lend us any of his troops, without our engaging not only to pay them, but to grant him a ſubſidy, perhaps greater than the pay of thoſe troops, upon their own footing, would have amounted to; and that, even in caſes where the Prince ſtood obliged, perhaps by former Treaties, to aſſiſt us with troops at his own expence; and often in caſes, when his own preſervation was more immediately concerned in the event of the war than ours.

Mr. Walter Plumer, Jan. 26, 1736.

In a free country, I am afraid that a ſtanding Army rather occaſions than prevents mobs : where a Magiſtrate has a guard of regular troops to truſt to, he is apt to neglect humouring the People he deſpiſes and ſometimes oppreſſes; in which caſe the People as long as there is any ſpirit among them, will certainly grow tumultuous. If a tumult happens with any juſt cauſe of complaint, a little gentle uſage and calm reaſoning, generally prevents any miſchief, and prevails with the People to return to their duty : but a Magiſtrate with an army at his back will ſeldom take this method, for few men will be at the pains of perſuading, when they know they can compel. But

2   in

in a free country, if a tumult happens from a juft caufe of complaint, the people ought to be fatisfied, their grievances ought
to be redreffed; they ought not furely to be immediately knock-
ed on the head, becaufe that they happen to complain in an irregular way. To make ufe of regular troops upon every fuch
occafion, is like a tyrannical fchool-mafter, who never makes
ufe of the foft arts of perfuafion and allurement, but always
makes ufe of the rod : fuch a man may break the *fpirit*, but never can improve the *minds* of his fcholars.

Sir John Barnard, Feb. 3, 1737.

OUR armies have known no other power than that of the
Secretary at War, who directs all their motions, and fills up
every vacancy without oppofition, and without appeal.

But never, my-Lord, was his power more confpicuous than
in raifing the levies of this year; never was ever any authority
more defpotically exerted, or more tamely fubmitted to; never
did any man more wantonly fport with his command, or more
capriciouſly fport with pofts of preferment; never did any tyrant appear to fet cenfure more openly at defiance, treat mur-
murs or remonftrances with greater contempt, or with more
confidence or fecurity diftribute pofts amongft his flaves,
without any other reafon of preferment, than his own uncontroulable pleafure.

And furely no man, my Lords, could have made choice of
fuch wretches for military commands, but to ſhew, that nothing
but his own private inclinations ſhould influence his conduct,
and that he confidered himfelf as fupreme and unaccountable :
for we have feen, my Lords, the fame animals to-day cringing
behind a counter, and to-morrow fwelling in a military drefs ;
we have feen boys fent from fchool in defpair of improvement,
and entrufted with the military command : fools that cannot
learn their duty, and children that cannot perform it, have been
indifcriminately promoted : the drofs of the nation has been
collected together to compofe our new forces, and every man
who

who was too ftupid or infamous to learn, or carry on any trade, has been placed, by this great difpofer of honours, above the neceffity of application, or the reach of cenfure.

Did not fometimes indignation, and fometimes pity, check the fallies of mirth, it would not be a difagreeable entertainment, my Lords, to obferve in the Park, the various appearances of thefe raw Commanders, when they are expofing their new fcarlet to view, and ftrutting with the firft raptures of fudden elevation : to fee the mechanic new-modelling his mien, and the ftrippling tottering beneath the weight of his cockade ; or to hear the converfation of thefe new adventurers, and the inftructive dialogues of fchool-boys and fhopkeepers.

I take this opportunity, my Lords, of clearing myfelf from any fufpicion of having contributed, by my advice, to this ftupendous collection.

Duke of Argyle, *Dec.* 9, 1740.

SIR, let us at leaft, not adopt that damn'd *Machiavilian* doctrine, *that a free People cannot be governed but by force*, who may fo eafily be won by love and affection. An army, Sir, was never kept up in any country in time of peace, but, fooner or later, it was ufed againft the Liberties of the People, and at laft enflaved them.

Sir, I lament that the People of this country have now too unequal terms to contend upon, for fecuring their Properties and their Independency. *Machiavel* fays, iron will prevail over gold ; but, by this army added to the other power, our managers poffefs both—fo are regardlefs of complaints, and of gratifying the expectations of the People. To whom can they fly for refuge, or from whom can they expect redrefs, if not from perfons now at the helm of affairs, famed through the land for being the fupporters of Liberty, and for their deteftation of Tyranny and Oppreffion ?

If the People do complain, perhaps they have juft caufe for fo doing ; feeling numberlefs burthens and taxes laid upon them,

them, chiefly to fupport needlefs offices and places at immenfe falaries : the People are fenfible of it, by their being generally occupied by perfons of loofe lives, without abilities, who make them fine-cures, or, at moft, appoint deputies, at fmall falaries, to tranfact them : they complain their Reprefentatives are debauched from them, that *Tax-Mafters vote Taxes, that the Army vote the Army*; in fhort, *Cuncti pœne patres clamant periffe pudorem.* I muft confefs, I almoft defpair of any good to be done in this detefted age, or of any reformation, fo many having drank of *Circe*'s fell cup, the cup of corruption, that they are, imperceptibly to themfelves, become monfters, and glory in it, that I almoft join in with *Jugurtha*'s reflection when he he left *Rome, Urbem venalem & mature perituram fi Emptorem invenerit.*

Perfons trained up in the principles of Liberty can ill brook this new doctrine, *of being retained in fubjection by an army*; having imbibed other notions in their education, fo ftrong as not to be able to diveft themfelves of them : that he, for one, did deteft and abhor the men that would offer it, and did declare, *Manus hic inimica Tyrannis.* Could, Sir, our forefathers at the Revolution, have conceived that their much-boafted and dear-purchafed Liberty would have ended in a large Standing Army, as a protection for *Bureaux* and *Pactors*, from the remonftrances of their much-injured pofterity, and faddled with a debt of eight millions, would they have called that a *Deliverance?* They would fcarce have thought the alternative a valuable confideration. Though I fhould allow, Sir, there is no intention in fome of our managers to enflave us, it will be but a melancholy reflection when it does happen, towards alleviating the diftreffed, to fay it was not intended. Is it not a fevere imputation upon thofe who have every advantage to make themfelves efteemed by, as the difpofal of all the revenue, pofts, and preferments in the realm, to call out for a Military to fupport their meafures againft the hate of the People ? Does it not

convey

convey fomething as if they were not the beft managers in the world?

Perfons in high ftations, furrounded by flatterers and fyco-phants, are much impofed upon, and impofe upon themfelves, by imagining their actions are not, and ought not to be fcanned by the People; they flatter themfelves they are approved. Much in the manner of a ftory I have heard of a certain Efquire, op-preffive and arbitrary in his neighbourhood, where he bafhawed it away, had good eating and drinking, for the fake of which many perfons reforted to him, who always faid as he faid, com-mended all his faults, and told him they were virtues, and that the whole country admired him; and flattered him continually, for the fake only of what they could get from him.

He not long after put it to the teft, by fallying out into a neighbouring village, where, inftead of pæans and fhouts of joy, he was faluted with dirt and dead dogs, and pelted out of the village with rotten eggs. He came home vaftly difcon-certed and dejected, and accofted his Parfon, who had been one of the forwardeft of his flatterers, *How now, Parfon*, fays he, *did not you tell me how much I was admired, and you fee what has happened?*

Sir, I fhall leave the application to the Houfe, and conclude with imploring Gentlemen, if they have any bowels for their Country, any affection for his Majefty, and for his Family being long amongft us, or any regard for the Liberties of their Pofterity, to reduce the Army, and to leffen thereby our numerous Taxes.

William Thornton, Efq; Nov. 26, 1751.

THE dangers that muft arife from the introduction of foreign troops into the dependencies of the realm, if not illegal, might be very great; for it might eafily be in the power of an ill de-figning Prince, to fill all the exterior parts of the dominions with foreign mercenaries, and take opportunities to make them the means of overturning the Conftitution. No man fhould

forget

forget the natural tendency of ftanding foreign troops; they cannot efteem your Laws; they know not your Conftitution; they cannot refpect it. Recollect the cafe of the Hanoverian foldier at Maidftone, where the commanding Officer told the civil Office, *Releafe the man, or I have eight thoufand men here, and I will beat down your gaol, and take him by force.* Sir, that will be the language of Commanders of foreign troops; they know not the Laws; they cannot refpect them. Difputes will arife in quarters, and they muft be terminated in this manner. But let us turn our eyes to the other countries of Europe, and fee what miferable work the foldiery have made. Sir, they have overturned Europe from its bafis. Look at Sweden, where the King, merely by the means of an army, has cut the throat of Swedifh Liberty, and rules by the fword: and I might here obferve, *à-propos*, that this Adminiftration in England was acceffary to the mifchief, or at leaft attempted to prevent a reparation. I do not affert this upon my own knowledge, but I have been told it upon pretty good authority, when the Emprefs of Ruffia was about to ftir in favour of the old Government of Sweden, we interpofed, and threatened her with the fleet of England, if fhe made any fuch attempt.

Right Hon. T. Townfhend, Nov. 2, 1775.

BRIBERY.

THOUGH this Bill at firſt ſight ſeemed to be a ſelf-deny-
ing Bill, and to ſome particular Members, might perhaps
prove ſo, yet I ſuſpeᴄt the Commons, conſidered as a Houſe of
Parliament, would find in it a very great enlargement of power.
Whatever tends to break the balance between the Powers eſſential to this Conſtitution, muſt, ſooner or later, prove the ruin
of the whole. An independent Houſe of Commons, or an independent Houſe of Lords, is as inconſiſtent with our Conſtitution, as an independent, that is an abſolute King. Whoever
loves the Liberties and Laws of his Country, would no more
deſire to ſee one than the other. Let Bribery be puniſhed, but
not by giving ſo much ſtrength to one Power of this Conſtitution, as ſhall make it able to overbear the reſt.

*Biſhop of Bangor, Jan. 21, 1731; on the Bill for preventing
Bribery in the Election of Members of Parliament.*

MY LORDS, it is now ſo late, and ſo much has been ſaid in.
favour of the Motion, for the ſecond reading of the Penſion
Bill, by Lords much abler than I am, that I ſhall detain you but
a very ſhort while with what I have to ſay upon the ſubjeᴄt. It
has been ſaid by a Noble Duke, that this Bill can be looked on
only as a Bill for preventing a grievance that is foreſeen, and
not as a Bill for remedying a grievance that is already felt; becauſe it is not aſſerted, nor ſo much as inſinuated in the Preamble of the Bill, that any corrupt praᴄtices are now made
uſe of, for gaining an undue influence over the other Houſe.
My Lords, this was the very reaſon for bringing in the Bill.
They could not aſſert, that any ſuch praᴄtices are now made
uſe of, without a proof; and the means for coming at this proof,
is what they want, and what they propoſe to get by this Bill.
They ſuſpeᴄt there are ſuch praᴄtices, but they cannot prove it.

The

The crime is of fuch a fecret nature, that it can very feldom be proved by witneffes; and therefore they want to put it to the trial, at leaft, of being proved by the oath of one of the parties; which is a method often taken in cafes that can admit of no other proof. This is, therefore, no argument of the grievance not being felt; for a man may, very fenfibly, feel a grievance, and yet may not be able to prove it.

That there is a fufpicion of fome fuch practices being now made ufe of, or that they will foon be made ufe of, the many Remonftrances from all parts of the united kingdoms are a fufficient proof. That this fufpicion has crept into the other Houfe, their having fo frequently fent up this Bill, is a manifeft demonftration, and a ftrong argument for its being neceffary to have fome fuch Bill paffed into a law. The other Houfe muft be allowed to be better judges of what paffes, or muft pafs, within their own walls, than we can pretend to be. It is evident, they fufpect that corrupt practices have been, or foon may be made ufe of, for gaining an undue influence over fome of their meafures; and they have calculated this Bill for curing the evil if it is felt, for preventing it if it is only forefeen. That any fuch practices have been actually made ufe of, or are now made ufe of, is what I fhall not pretend to affirm, but I am fure I fhall not affirm the contrary. If any fuch are made ufe of, I will, with confidence, vindicate his Majefty. I am fure he knows nothing of them. I am fure he would difdain to fuffer them; but I cannot pafs fuch a compliment upon his Minifters, nor upon any fet of Minifters that ever was, or ever will be, in this nation: and therefore I think I cannot more faithfully, more effectually ferve his prefent Majefty, as well as his fucceffors, than by putting it out of the power of Minifters to gain any corrupt influence over either Houfe of Parliament. Such an attempt may be neceffary for the fecurity of the Minifter, but never can be neceffary for, muft always be inconfiftent with, the fecurity of his Mafter; and the more neceffary it is for the Minifter's fecurity, the more inconfiftent it will always be with the King's, and the more dangerous to the Liberties of the nation.

To pretend, my Lords, that this Bill diminifhes, or any way encroaches upon the Prerogative, is fomething very ftrange. What Prerogative, my Lords? Has the Crown a Prerogative to bribe, to infringe the law, by fending its Penfioners into the other Houfe? To fay fo, is deftroying the credit, the authority of the Crown, under the pretence of fupporting its Prerogative. If his Majefty knew, that any man received a Penfion from him, or any thing like a Penfion, and yet kept his feat in the other Houfe, he would himfelf declare it, or withdraw his Penfion, becaufe he knows it is againft law. This Bill, therefore, no way diminifhes or encroaches upon the Prerogatives of the Crown, which can never be exercifed but for the public good. It diminifhes only the Prerogatives ufurped by Minifters, which are never exercifed but for its deftruction. The Crown may ftill reward merit in the proper way, that is openly. The Bill is intended, and can operate only againft clandeftine rewards or gratuities given by Minifters. Thefe are fcandalous, and never were, nor will be given but for fcandalous fervices.

True generofity, and true merit, my Lords, delight in funfhine. It is glorious to reward true merit, it is glorious to receive the reward; and therefore, whoever gives or receives the reward, will be fond of doing it publicly, and of declaring it openly, without fear of being impeached of corruption. When *Admiral Vernon* was a Member of the other Houfe, the Majority was generally againft him : they did not then like his face; and I believe, if he were ftill a Member, they would as little like it now : yet, if he fhould receive a reward from the Crown, that Majority would not, I believe, vote that reward to be a bribe. I am fenfible, Majorities have fometimes done very extraordinary things ; but yet I do not believe they would do this, becaufe that Admiral has fo well deferved a reward. He has done with *fix* fhips, about 2000 feamen, and 200 tattered foldiers from Jamaica, what, we are told, could not be

done

done by a larger fquadron, and at leaft 8000 feamen, when our
fhips and failors lay rotting at the *Baftimento's*. When war was
refolved on, he was called from ploughing the ground, to plough
the ocean; and as the fervice of his country required difpatch,
he defired but three days to fettle his family-affairs. In time of
peace, he was never employed: he was even difappointed in
his preferment. The reafon is plain: he was not fit for thofe
fervices that entitle our fea and land Captains to preferment in
time of peace. He had fhewed it, when he was a Member of
the other Houfe; and this, I believe, is the true reafon of his
not being a Member now. But if he fhould be a Member in
the next Parliament, as he probably will, if he lives, the paffing
of this Bill could no way prevent his Majefty from rewarding
him in any manner he may then think fit; nor could his accepting of the reward fubject him to any inconvenience or danger.

This Bill can, therefore, no way affect the Prerogatives of
the Crown, or prevent any man's receiving a juft and well-
deferved reward; which is the only reward the Crown ought,
or has any title, even from Prerogative, to beftow: for this
Prerogative, like all the other Prerogatives of the Crown, is fo
far fubject to the controul of Parliament, that if it be abufed,
the Parliament may enquire into, and punifh the advifers of
that abufe.

It is very remarkable, my Lords, it is even diverting, to fee
fuch a fqueamifhnefs about perjury upon this occafion, amongft
thofe, who upon other occafions, have invented and enacted
multitudes of oaths, to be taken by men who are under great
temptations, from their private intereft, to be guilty of perjury.
Is not this the cafe of almoft every oath that relates to the
collection of the public revenue, or to the exercife of any office?
Is not this perjury one of the chief objections made by the Dif-
fenters againft the Teft and Corporation Act? And fhall we
fhew a lefs concern for the prefervation of our Conftitution,
than for the prefervation of our Church? The reverend Bench
fhould be cautious of making ufe of this argument, for if they

will

will not allow us an oath for the prefervation of the former, it may induce many people to think, they ought not to be allowed an oath for the prefervation of the latter.

By this time, I hope, my Lord, all the inconveniencies pretended to arife from this Bill have vanifhed; and therefore I fhall confider fome of the arguments brought to fhew that it is not neceffary. Here I muft obferve, that moft of the arguments made ufe of for this purpofe, are equally ftrong for a repeal of the laws we have now in being, againft admitting Penfioners to fit and vote in the other Houfe. If it be impoffible to fuppofe, that a Gentleman of great eftate, and antient family, can, by a penfion, be influenced to do what he ought not to do; and if we muft fuppofe that none but fuch Gentlemen can ever get into the other Houfe, I am fure the laws for preventing Penfioners from having feats in that Houfe, are quite unneceffary, and ought to be repealed. Therefore, if thefe arguments prevail with your Lordfhips to put a negative upon the prefent Queftion, I fhall expect to fee that negative followed by a Motion for the repeal of thofe laws. Nay, in a few Seffions, I fhall expect to fee a Bill brought in, for preventing any man's being a Member of the other Houfe, but fuch as have fome place or penfion under the Crown. As an argument for fuch a Bill, it muft be faid, that his Majefty's moft faithful fubjects ought to be chofen Members of Parliament, and that thofe Gentlemen will always be moft faithful to the King that receive the King's money. I fhall grant, my Lords, that fuch Gentlemen will be always the moft faithful, and the moft obedient to the Minifter; but for this very reafon, I fhould be for excluding them from Parliament. The King's real intereft, however much he may be made by his Minifters to miftake it, muft always be the fame with the People's; hut the Minifter's intereft is generally diftinct from, and often contrary to both: therefore, I fhall always be for excluding, as much as poffible, from Parliament, every man who is under the leaft inducement to prefer the intereft of the Minifter,

to

to that of both King and People: and this I take to be the cafe of every Gentleman, let his eftate and family be what they will, that holds a penfion at the will of the Minifter.

Thofe who fay, they depend fo much upon the honour, integrity, and impartiality of men of family and fortune, feem to think our Conftitution can never be diffolved, as long as we have the fhadow of a Parliament. My opinion, my Lord, is fo very different, that if ever our Conftitution be diffolved, if ever an abfolute Monarchy be eftablifhed in this kingdom, I am convinced it will be under that fhadow. Our conftitution confifts in the two Houfes of Parliament being a check upon the Crown, as well as upon one another. If that check fhould ever be removed, if the Crown fhould, by corrupt means, by places, penfions, and bribes, get the abfolute direction of our two Houfes of Parliament, our Conftitution will, from that moment, be deftroyed. There would be no occafion for the Crown to proceed any farther. It would be ridiculous to lay afide the forms of Parliament; for under that fhadow, our King would be more abfolute, and might govern more arbitrarily than he could do without it. A Gentleman of family and fortune would not, perhaps, for the fake of a penfion, agree to lay afide the forms of Government; becaufe, by his venal fervice there, he earns his infamous penfion, and could not expect the continuance of it, if thofe forms were laid afide: but a Gentleman of family and fortune may, for the fake of a penfion, whilft he is in Parliament, approve of the moft blundering meafures, confent to the moft exceffive and ufelefs grants, enact the moft oppreffive laws, pafs the moft villainous accounts, acquit the moft heinous criminals, and condemn the moft innocent perfons, at the defire of that Minifter who pays him his penfion. And if a majority of fuch Houfe of Parliament confifted of fuch men, would it not be ridiculous in us to talk of our Conftitution, or to fay we had any liberty left?

This misfortune, this terrible condition we may be reduced to by corruption: as brave, as free a people as we, the *Romans*,

were

were reduced to it by the fame means; and to prevent fuch a horrid cataftrophe, is the defign of this Houfe.

If people would at all think, if they would confider the confequences of corruption, there would be no occafion, my Lords, for making laws againft it. It would appear fo horrible, that no man would allow it to approach him. The corrupted ought to confider, that they do not fell their vote, or their country only: thefe, perhaps, they may difregard; but they fell likewife themfelves: they become the bond-flaves of the corrupter who corrupts them, not for their fakes, but for his own. No man ever corrupted another, for the fake of doing him a fervice. And, therefore, if people would but confider, they would always reject the offer with difdain. But this is not to be expected. The hiftories of all countries, the hiftory even of our own country fhews, it is not to be depended on. The proffered bribe, people think, will fatisfy the immediate cravings of fome infamous appetite; and this makes them fwallow the alluring bait, though the liberties of their country, the happinefs of their pofterity, and even their own liberty, evidently depend upon their refufing it. This makes it neceffary, in every free State, to contrive, if poffible, effectual laws againft corruption: and as the laws we now have for excluding Penfioners from the other Houfe, are allowed to be ineffectual, we ought to make a trial, at leaft, of the remedy now propofed: for though it fhould prove ineffectual, it will be attended with this advantage, that it will put us upon contriving fome other remedy that may be effectual; and the fooner fuch a remedy is contrived and applied, the lefs danger we fhall be expofed to of falling into that fatal diftemper, from which no free State, where it has once become general, has ever yet recovered.

Earl of Chefterfield, Feb. 22, 1740,

C I V I L

I Agree with the Hon. Member who spoke first, (Sir Robert Walpole) that on his Majesty's happy Accession to the Throne, there ought to be no other contention amongst us, than who should most contribute to his service, than who should express their duty and loyalty in the most respectful and the most extensive manner. But then I hope he will agree with me, that this is to be done with some regard to those we represent : that this is to be done, consistent with the trust reposed in us; consistent with that frugality which this House is bound to use, whenever the Crown is pleased to call upon it, to exercise its great power of giving money.

Now, notwithstanding what has been urged, I think we shall so far depart from the rule of frugality, as we exceed the revenue granted to his late Majesty, whether that exceeding shall a-mount yearly to 93,000 l. as computed at the highest by the Hon. Member, or to above 130,000 l. as I have seen it more truly computed by another. For I remember very well, that the yearly sum of 700,000 l. though now thought too little, was not obtained for his late Majesty, without a long and solemn debate ; and it was allowed by every one that contended for it, to be an ample Royal revenue. Nor was it asked inconsiderately, and on a sudden ; it was asked on mature deliberation, after the Queen's Civil List branches were found deficient ; it was asked after many computations had been made of every charge requisite to support the honour and dignity of the Crown, and to maintain the present Royal Family ; it was asked, after duly weighing what provision would be sufficient to answer all the ordinary and extraordinary occasions of the Civil Government ; what would be sufficient to answer all proper augmentations of salaries, all reasonable and charitable pensions, all secret services at home and abroad, necessary to carry on a just

L 4   and

and wife Adminiſtration. It was aſked by that Hon. Member himſelf and others, who were entering into great employments, who were going to taſte of the Royal bounty, and who therefore could not poſſibly be ſuſpected to have any deſign of cramping his Majeſty, by a too contracted and narrow revenue.

Nor does the late alteration in the Royal Family call for any increaſe of expence. For if the eſtabliſhment for the Queen ſhould be enlarged, whoſe diſtinguiſhed character and many princely virtues, taken notice of in your Addreſs, entitle her to all degrees of grandeur, which any former Queen Conſort ever enjoyed; I ſay, if her Majeſty's eſtabliſhment ſhould be enlarged, I preſume the eſtabliſhment for Prince Frederick will be much inferior to that ſettled on his preſent Majeſty when Prince of Wales. Beſides, our ardent wiſhes for his Majeſty's conſtant reſidence in theſe kingdoms, and his Royal intentions of making us a great and happy people, give us hopes, that many perſonal, many particular expences in the late reign, eſpecially thoſe for frequent journies to Hanover, will be diſcontinued and entirely ceaſe.

Nor is it any objection to the reaſoning of that time, when the 700,000 l. was granted to the late King, or to the computation then made, that this ſum is ſaid to have been found, by the experience of paſt time, to be not anſwerable to the neceſſities of the Civil Government.

For this experience could not be found in the Queen's reign, becauſe her Civil Liſt branches ſeldom amounted to 600,000 l. commonly to about 550,000 l. and ſometimes to very little above 500,000 l. as appears by accounts formerly laid before this Houſe: and I will not ſuppoſe thoſe accounts which were brought from the Treaſury to be otherwiſe than true, in regard to my Hon. Friend.—I aſk pardon, I ſhould have ſaid the Hon. Member, for there is no friendſhip betwixt us. But he muſt give me leave to obſerve, that when he aſſerts her Civil Liſt Branches amounted to about 700,000 l. yearly, he can only

mean

mean the grofs, and not the neat produce; which is a very un-
candid and fallacious way of arguing.

Though her revenues were fo low, yet fhe called upon her Parliament but once in her reign of above thirteen years, to pay
the debts contracted in her Civil Government; and it is a juftice due to the memory of that excellent Princefs, to remind
Gentlemen of the unparalleled inftances of her piety and generofity which occafioned thofe debts. She gave the firft-fruits
and tenths, arifing now, as the Hon. Member who made this
Motion, fays, to 19,000 l. a year, for the augmentation of the
maintenance of the poor Clergy; fhe gave 5000 l. a year out of
the Poft-office to the Duke of Marlborough; fhe fuffered 700 l.
a week to be likewife charged on the Poft-office for the public
fervice, and by that conceffion loft a vaft fum, the additional
duty then producing only 8000 l. a year; fhe gave feveral hundred thoufand pounds for building the Caftle of Blenheim; fhe
allowed Prince Charles of Denmark 4000 l. a year; fhe fuftained great loffes by the Tin Contract; fhe fupported the poor
Palatines; fhe gave 100,000 l. to the ufe of the war.—Thefe,
with many other Royal bounties, which efcape my prefent remembrance, were the reafons that brought her under the neceffity of afking for 500,000 l. But fhe was fo fenfible of the inconvenience, and fo determined never to apply to her Parliament again in the like manner, that fhe ordered a confiderable
reduction to be made of her Civil Government expences. I
have feen a fcheme of this reduction, as it was actually fettled a
little before her death, and intended to commence the Lady-
day following. It would be tedious to go through all the particular articles of it, and I will only name three or four. The
Cofferer's-office payments were reduced from 85,000 l. to
75,000 l. the allowances for Foreign Minifters from 75,000 l.
to 30,000 l. Penfions and Bounties from upwards of 87,490 l.
to 60,000 l. Secret Services from 27,000 l. to 20,000 l. a fum
furprizingly fmall, when compared with the late difburfements
on that head. In fhort, the whole yearly expences were defigned

figned to be reduced to 459,941 l. and that would have been done without eclipsing the glory of the Crown, which, fome Gentlemen fo roundly affirm, cannot now be maintained under almoft a double appointment.

From hence it appears plainly, that this argument of the experience of paft times can have no reference to the Queen's reign. It muft therefore be applied, though put in the plural number, to the late Adminiftration only : and I confefs, if the fame management was to be continued, if the fame Minifters were to be again employed, a million a year would not be fufficient to carry on the exorbitant expences, fo often, and fo juftly complained of in this Houfe. For it is notorious, it is frefh in all our memories, that befides the yearly 700,000 l. there have been many occafional taxes, many exceffive fums raifed, and they have been all funk in that bottomlefs gulf of Secret Service. Firft, the memorable 250,000 l. was raifed, in defiance of the ancient parliamentary methods, to fecure us from the apprehenfions of a Swedifh invafion. Then the two Infurance-offices were erected in as regular a manner, by a Bill brought into this Houfe, at the latter end of a Seffion, and after the Committee of Supply had been clofed, upon the Hon. Member's return into power ; and thofe bubbles paid near 300,000 l. for their charters. Then a new fcene of affairs opening in Sweden, changed our enmity into an alliance, and there was a fubfidy of 72,000 l. implicitly granted, to make good fome fecret bargain and engagement with that Crown. At that time near 24,000 l. were given for burning two Merchant fhips arrived from infected places ; but the goods, as well as the fhips, were paid for by the Houfe, that they might, without injury to the Owners, be deftroyed for the public fafety ; yet moft of them were privately conveyed into counties adjacent to the port where the fhips lay, and fold there. Then foon after a fum of 500,000 l. was demanded and granted for the payment of the Civil Lift Debts ; on which occafion his late Majefty declared in his Meffage, " That he was refolved to caufe a retrench-

ment to be made of his expences for the future." But notwithstanding that resolution, in less than four years, the necef-
sities of the Government having rendered the promifed re-
trenchment impracticable, there was a new demand, and a new
grant of 500,000 l. more, to difcharge new incumbrances. I
might mention, too, the Spanifh fhips which were taken in the
famous Mediterranean fea-fight, and, as we have reafon to believe, fold for a confiderable fum of money. Nor is it poffible
to forget the 125,000 l. which we could only be told the laft
Seffion, in a general unexplained article, was fecretly difpofed
of for the public utility, for the confervation of the peace of Europe, and for the fecurity of the commerce and navigation of
Great-Britain.

After all thefe and other extraordinary fupplies, I am informed there yet remains a debt in the Civil Government of
above 600,000 l. If fo, furely there muft have been a moft
egregious neglect of duty, to fay no worfe; there muft have
been a ftrange fpirit of extravagance fomewhere, or fuch immenfe fums could never have been fo foon, fo infenfibly fquandered away : and it is amazing this extravagance fhould happen under the conduct of perfons, pretending to furpafs all their
predeceffors in the knowledge and care of the public revenue.
But we are not to wonder that the world has been free in its
cenfures, fince none of thefe fums have been accounted for, fince
they have been employed in fervices not fit to be owned.
None but thofe who were in the fecret, and who had the difpofal of them, can refute the reflections that are made without
doors, not only on the Miniftry, but even on both Houfes of
Parliament.—I muft fay no more—But I heartily wifh, that
time, the great difcoverer of hidden truths and concealed ini-
quities, may produce a lift of all fuch, if any fuch there were,
who have been perverted from their public duty by private penfions; who have been the hired flaves, and the corrupt inftruments of a profane and vain-glorious Adminiftration. If
there have been none fuch, then the whole weight, then the
whole

whole guilt of the late mifmanagement lies on the Minifters themfelves.

But it feems to be matter of univerfal joy to the nation, that the cafe is like to be altered; we hope we are arrived at a day of better œconomy; we hope fuch practices will be fo far from being imitated, that they will be detefted and abhorred: nor can any one entertain the leaft doubt of this, when he confiders that a Prince is afcending the Throne, who will chufe a knowing, faithful, and frugal Miniftry; who will not permit his domeftic or foreign affairs to be negotiated by bribery and corruption, for want of fufficiency and fkill in politics; whofe wifdom will enable him, and whofe goodnefs will incline him, not only to infpect the management of the Civil Lift branches, but in juftice to his Parliaments, and in compaffion to his people, to direct and require a due and exact difpofition of all the other public funds, according to their refpective appropriations.

Now, in confequence of this moft juft notion of his Majefty's fruguality, which, amongft other his innumerable virtues, endears him fo much to his fubjects, I hope I may, without offence, propofe the addition of fome words to the queftion, that may reftrain it to 700,000 l. and in this I as much confult the fervice of his Majefty, and the honour and dignity of the Crown, as thofe who are for granting the funds without any reftrictions. For, in my humble opinion, the voting a greater than was fettled on his late Majefty, is only voting an indemnity; is voting at leaft in favour of Minifters, whofe conduct, as I have already hinted, if laid before you, and duly examined, would perhaps rather deferve your cenfure than approbation.

Befides, the furplus of thefe branches is appropriated to the Sinking Fund; and that, I thought had been a facred depofitum, referved for the gradual difcharge of the national debt. I thought it would be looked upon as a fort of facrilege, to have diverted the leaft part of it, on any pretence whatfoever, from its original ufes: and it is as furprizing to me, that the Honour-

3   able

able Perfon fhould be for deftroying his own darling projeƈt, and that he fhould be for pulling down the boafted monument of his glory, as it may be to others,—that I am for fupporting any fcheme of his, which might have tranfmitted his name with advantage to pofterity.

If his Majefty was rightly apprized of thefe circumftances, he would doubtlefs rather be content with a clear annual revenue of 700,000 l. than fuffer his firft demand of money, by any precipitate proof of our zeal, to carry the leaft appearance of being burthenfome to his people, who have long laboured under the preffure of grievous and exorbitant taxes; for he has been gracioufly pleafed to fignify from the Throne his fixed refolution, " By all poffible means to merit their love and affeƈtion, " which he fhall always look upon as the beft fupport and fecu- " rity of his Crown."

Mr. Shippen, July 3, 1727, on Sir Robert Walpole's Motion for fettling on the King the entire revenues of the Civil Lift.

I MUST declare it to be my opinion, that the creditors of the public have, in a manner, a right to that facred fund, called the Sinking Fund ; it is in its nature a fecurity to them : firft, for the payment of the intereft coming yearly due to them, and next for the payment of their principal fums. The whole people of England have a right to have it duly applied; becaufe it is by fuch application only, that we can get free of thofe many and grievous taxes, which lie fo heavy upon the poor, and are fuch a clog to the trade and the manufaƈtures of this nation: and therefore the applying that fund to any other ufe, is robbing the public creditors of their right, and doing an injuftice to the whole people of England.

The prefent circumftances of this motion are, my Lords, in fome manner deplorable. By the many taxes we now pay, the neceffaries and conveniencies of life are rendered fo dear, that it is impoffible for our tradefmen or manufaƈturers to live fo cheap, or to fell the produce of their country at fo fmall a price

as

as our neighbours do: from hence it is, my Lords, that our neighbours are every day encroaching upon us, and our trade is daily decaying. If a journeyman in any manufacture whatever, can live better in France or Germany on fix-pence a day than he can live in England on a shilling, we may depend on it, that moft of our tradefmen will find their way thither, if they are not prevented either by our own good politics, or by fome very bad policy amongft our neighbours: and if a mafter tradefman can get the fame work done in France for fix-pence, which would coft him a shilling in England, he certainly can underfell the Englifh tradefman in all the foreign markets in the world. The only method, therefore, to preferve our trade, is to take off thefe taxes, which now lie fo heavy upon the poor tradefmen and labourers; and this the whole people of England know, can be done no other way but by a due application of the Sinking Fund. How fhocking then muft it be to the whole nation, to fee that fund plundered of fo large a fum at once? The whole nation muft from thence conclude, that they muft for ever groan under thefe taxes and burthens, which they now find almoft infupportable, and which muft foon become abfolutely fo, by the decay cf our trade and our manufactures.

This fund, my Lords, has therefore been clandeftinely defrauded of feveral fmall fums, at different times, which, indeed, together, amount to a pretty large fum: but by the Bill which we have ordered to be committed, (for granting to his Majefty a certain fum out of the Sinking Fund) it is to be openly and avowedly plundered of 500,000 l. at once. After fuch a direct mifapplication of that fund, can any public creditor depend upon his ever being paid his principal fum? Can any public creditor ever think himfelf fecure, even of that yearly intereft or annuity which is due to him? By this Bill, he fees one half of the Sinking Fund applied to the current fervice of the year: this he fees done, and this, my Lords, he fees done at a time of the moft profound peace and tranquillity: how then can he be certain,

tain, but that the whole Sinking Fund may be next year applied to the fame purpofes? He muft then fee himfelf deprived of all hopes of ever receiving his principal fum; and if the funds now appropriated to the payment of the yearly intereft or annuities, growing due to the public creditors, fhould hereafter prove deficient, where could they have recourfe for the payment even of thofe annuities? The Sinking Fund being otherwife applied, their annuities, or at leaft fome part of them, muft remain unpaid; and at laft, perhaps, the whole might ceafe. Such a fufpicion may, even by this mifapplication, arife among the creditors of the public; and if fuch fhould arife, it would be the moft terrible fhock that ever happened to the public credit of this nation. To prevent, therefore, any fuch fufpicion, it will be abfolutely neceffary for your Lordfhips to come to fome refolution for quieting the minds of the people, and for affuring them, that no fuch mifapplication fhall for the future be admitted of on any pretence whatever.

Lord Carteret, May 30, 1733.

I wonder to hear it affirmed by any Noble Lord in this Houfe, that the public creditors have any manner of right in the Sinking Fund: they certainly have no right to any part of it: they have a right only to receive their yearly intereft when it comes due; for the payment of which there are other funds appropriated: and therefore as long as they are regularly paid their intereft, they have nothing to fear, they have nothing to complain of. It is well known that the Sinking Fund was from its very firft original, fubject to be difpofed of by Parliament; and the Parliament has it ftill in their power to apply it to the paying off a part of the public debt, or to whatever other public ufe they fhall think moft proper; and in this year, there is as much of it applied towards the paying off the public debts as is either neceffary or convenient.

By the fame Bill, my Lords, there is a million to be applied towards the paying off a part of the public debts of the nation,

which

which is more than the creditors of the public either defire or expect. The circumftances of this nation are now fo happy, and the public credit fo well eftablifhed, that none of the public creditors defire to have their money : on the contrary, my Lords, we fee that thofe funds bear the higheft price, and are the moft fought after, which are expected to be the longeft in being paid off. Under fuch circumftances we have an oppor-tunity to look about us, and to apply a part of that fund where we find it is moft wanted : this is what is propofed by this Bill. It muft be granted, my Lords, that the landed Gentlemen have. of all others borne for many years the greateft fhare of the public charge ; they are, therefore, the firft that ought to be relieved ; and for this reafon, 500,000 l. part of the Sinking Fund, is to be applied to the current fervice of the prefent year, in order to relieve them of a part of that burden they have long laboured under. Since then by this Bill the landed Gentlemen are to be relieved, and the fervice of the year pro-vided for without contracting any new debt, or laying any new burden on the people, it muft be allowed to be a public benefit. It is, my Lords, a good defign; fuch a defign as can give no man an alarm ; it can raife no jealoufies or fears, and is, there-fore, highly deferving your Lordfhips approbation and fupport.

Duke of Newcaftle, May 30, 1733.

THE Meffage that has been read, will, I dare fay, meet with no obftruction in this Houfe. It is with pleafure, Sir, that every good fubject fees the Royal Line fo ftrong, as to fecure a long duration of happinefs to thefe kingdoms, in the perfons of his Majefty's defcendants : and the attachment of his Royal Houfe to the liberties of this nation, give us all reafon to hope, that fucceeding Princes will tread in the paths of his prefent Majefty, who has been hitherto fo careful of all his fubjects rights, and fo watchful over their prefervation.

Sir, his Majefty has been fo tender of afking for any thing on account of his own family, that they are now, in cafe of

his

his demife, in a more precarious fituation than the children of any Gentlemen of fortune in England. In fuch an event, Sir, which heaven avert! no Gentleman can, from the hiftory of our conftitution, take upon him to fay, in what manner they have a right to be provided for. I believe a future Parliament will reflect with gratitude upon the bleffings of his prefent Majefty's reign, and make a fuitable provifion for his Royal progeny; but I imagine no Gentleman in this Houfe, would chufe to leave the provifion of his younger children upon a precarious footing. Parliaments, like other bodies, are changeable; and it would be an unpardonable neglect in his Majefty, as a father, fhould he leave fo numerous an iffue to the uncertainty of a parliamentary provifion to be made after his demife.

The other only method, by which his Majefty's younger children in fuch a cafe could be provided for, is by the Prince upon the Throne. But, Sir, tho' I have, and I believe every Gentleman has, the greateft opinion of the virtues of the Royal Perfon who is the Heir of the Crown, yet we are to confider, that his Royal Highnefs is bleffed with a young progeny; and that, as no man can anfwer for events, if the two Royal lives fhould fall before the children of his Royal Highnefs are of age, the Government devolves upon a Regency: and give me leave, Sir, to fay, that there is no precedent in this nation, nor any pofitive law now in being, that can determine, as the Royal Family muft in fuch a cafe ftand, to what perfon the Regency devolves. This confideration is of itfelf fufficient to juftify the application now made by his Majefty to this Houfe; it is no more than any private Gentleman would do, to put his younger children above a precarious dependence: and I dare fay, that no Gentleman will think, that his Majefty ought to be put under difabilities, which every one here, who is a father, would look upon as hard and unreafonable.

I hope Gentlemen are fully convinced, how becoming it is in his Majefty, as a father, to make fuch an application; and how becoming it is in us, as a Houfe of Commons, to anfwer

it in the moſt effectual manner: the only conſideration, therefore,
that Gentlemen can now have, is with regard to the *quantum*
that is demanded by this Meſſage. As to that, Sir, I will
venture to ſay, that when we grant it, it is the ſmalleſt proviſion that ever was granted for the Crown of Britain; nay,
the whole of the proviſion for four Royal Perſonages, does not
amount to one half of what former Parliaments have thought
but a moderate proviſion for one. King James, Sir, when
Duke of York, had 100,000l. ſettled upon him by Act of Parliament; and that, I think, is the only parliamentary proviſion
for younger children that can ſerve as a precedent on this occaſion, becauſe it is the only one ſince the Reſtoration; for
before that time the Crown had a great property in lands, and
could, without a parliamentary concurrence, provide for its
younger children. King Charles the IId had a lawful iſſue
of his own body to provide for; the children of King James
were married, and their ſettlements made before he came to
the Crown; King William had no children; Queen Anne had
none that lived till after ſhe came to be Queen; and the
daughters of his late Majeſty were married before his acceſſion
to the Throne of Britain. Upon the whole, therefore, I believe there never was a demand made by the Crown more
reaſonable and moderate than this is. It is for a proviſion to
younger children, which cannot be made without conſent of
Parliament; and a proviſion ſo moderate, that I dare ſay, no
other objections to it will be made in this Houſe, but that it
is too little. Therefore I humbly move, That leave be given
to bring in a Bill, to enable his Majeſty to ſettle an annuity
of 15,000l. *per annum* upon his Royal Higneſs the Duke of
Cumberland, and his heirs; and alſo one other annuity of
24,000l. *per, annum* upon the Princeſſes Amelia, Carolina,
Mary, and Louiſa.

Sir Robert Walpole, May 3, 1739.

SIR,

SIR, we ought to look back to what former Princes and Parliaments have done. I will take the confideration only from the glorious æra of the Revolution, and I will ftate it fairly and fully. The Civil Lift was not granted to King William for life till the year 1698, when 700,000 l. a year was fettled on him. The diftractions of his Government, and of all Europe at that period, are well known. His moft generous views for the public were thwarted at home, during the greater part of his Reign, by the Tories. Queen Anne had the fame annuity fettled on her. She gave yearly 100,000 l. for carrying on the war, a war againft France, befides 200,000 l. at leaft towards the building of Blenheim-Houfe, and above 100,000 l. for the fupport of the poor Palatines. It is on the Journals of May 13, 1715, and in the following. " Refolved, " That the fum of 700,000 l. per annum was fettled upon his " late Majefty King William during life, for the fupport of his " Majefty's houfhold, and other his neceffary occafions ; and, " at the time of his Majefty's demife, after the deduction of " 3700 l. a week, that was applied to the public ufes, was the " produce of the Civil Lift Revenues, that were continued " and fettled upon her late Majefty Queen Anne during her ' life." The deduction for public fervices at 3700 l. a week, or 192,400 l. a year, from that part of the Civil Lift Revenue called the hereditary and temporary Excife, was firft made in the laft year of King William. Notwithftanding this deducion, the Civil Lift Funds produced in that very year 709,420 l. In the firft of Queen Anne, the fame funds with the fame deductions were fettled on her for life, and declared to be for raifing 700,000 l. a year for the fupport of her houfhold, and he dignity of her Government. In the ninth of her Reign he old Poft-Office Act was repealed, and a new General Poft-Office with higher rates were eftablifhed ; in confideration of which, another deduction was made from the Civil Lift Revenue of 700 l. a week, or 36,400 l. a year, and both thefe deductions have ever fince been continued.

M 2 George

George the Ift had the fame Revenue fettled upon him at
Queen Anne; but if 300,000 l. paid him by the Royal Ex-
change and London Affurance Companies, and a million
granted in 1726 towards paying his debts, are included, his
income will appear to have been nearly 800,000l. *per annum*.
In the firft fpeech to his Parliament he took notice, " That
" it was his happinefs to fee a Prince of Wales, who may, in
" due time, fucceed to the Throne, and to fee him bleffed
" with many children." Yet the eftablifhment of the Civil
Lift, at the beginning of that Reign, was only fettled at
700,000l. a year. It was not till after the great expences con-
fequent on the rebellion of the Earl of Mar, and the other per-
jured Scots, who, although they had taken the oaths of allegiance to his Government, traitoroufly waged open and im-
pious war againft a mild and juft Sovereign, that the Parliament paid the King's debts. In the Reign of George the Ift,
the Prince of Wales had an Eftablifhment of 100,000l. *per
annum*.

George the IId had a very numerous family, and 800,000l.
was at firft fettled upon him, with whatever furplus might
arife from the duties and allowances compofing the Civil Lift
Revenue. In 1726, that part of the hereditary and temporary
Excife, which confifted of Duties on Spirituous Liquors, was
taken from the Civil Lift, in confideration of which 70,000l.
was transferred to it from the Aggregate Fund. The income
of George the IId, including 115,000l. granted in 1729, and
456,733l. in 1747, towards making good the deficiencies which
had arifen in the Civil Lift Duties, was 810,749l. *per annum*
for thirty-three years. His late Majefty likewife had in his
reign a Scottifh Rebellion, carried on by many of the fame
traitors who had been pardoned by his father. The expence
of that Rebellion to the King and Kingdom was enormous;
for it was not confined to the extremities of the Ifland, but
raged in the heart of the Kingdom, and the rebels advanced to
within a hundred miles of the capital. Such an event, Sir,
not

not unforeseen, because foretold, was a just ground for the
Parliament's discharging a debt, contracted by securing to us
every thing dear to men and Englishmen.

The establishment of the present King, at the yearly rent-
charge to the nation of 800,000l. was a measure, at the time,
equally pleasing both to the Prince and People. The Minister
boasted, that there was not a possibility of any future dispute
about the hereditary Revenues, or concerning accounts sus-
pected to be false, wilfully erroneous, or deceitful, kept back
or anticipated, to serve a particular purpose. I am aware, Sir,
that the Civil List Revenues have been increasing for many
years. The mean annual produce for the five last years of
George the IId was 829,150l. and for the first six years of his
present Majesty it would have been, had the establishment in
the late reign continued 894,000l. In 1775 it would have
been 1,019,450l. Near 90,000l. *per annum* of this great increase has been produced by an increase in the Post-Office revenue, occasioned chiefly by the late alteration in the manner
of franking, and by the falling of the cross posts to the public by the death of Mr. Allen: but these profits would probably, at least certainly ought to have been reserved to the
public, had the establishment in the late reign been continued.
At the foot of one of the accounts on our table, it is stated;
" The amount of 800,000l. granted to his Majesty, from
" Oct. 25, 1760, to Jan. 5, 1777, is 12,965,517l. 4s. 9d¼.
" The produce as above exceeds the annuity by 2,381,241l.
" 9s. 1d¼. But Parliament granted to pay off the Civil List
" debt on Jan. 5, 1769, out of the supplies for the year 1769,
" 513,511l. which being deducted, shews the gain to the pub-
" lic to be 1,867,730l. 9s. 1d¼." The bargain concluded
for the public, was of an annuity to the King of a clear
800,000l. subject to no deductions or contingencies for his life,
on a solemn promise of that being made to bear all the expences of the Civil List and the Royal Houshold. It was a
fair compact of finance between the King and the subject, rati-

M 3   fied

fied by both parties. The moſt explicit aſſurances were given by the Chancellor of the Exchequer, in the King's name, that no more ſhould be aſked; and that now his Majeſty could never be under the diſagreeable neceſſity of importuning this Houſe with meſſages of perſonal concern. I have, Sir, carefully examined the accounts laid before the Houſe by his Majeſty's command, the eight folio books, and the other papers; and I will venture to ſay, they are as looſe, unſatisfactory, perplexed, and unintelligible, as thoſe delivered in by the Noble Lord with the blue ribbon in 1770, a year after the former demand to pay the debts on the Civil Liſt; and more looſe, unſatisfactory, perplexed, and unintelligible, no accounts can be.

Mr. Wilkes, April 16, 1777.

OUR funded debt is two hundred and thirty millions, and our unfunded debt will amount to thirty-eight millions, without the bottom of the war expences being wound up, beſides nine millions Navy Bills, and other debts, that will make the whole amount to the enormous ſum of two hundred and ninety millions; the yearly Intereſt of which would take fourteen millions to diſcharge: now our national eſtate, including Malt and Land Tax, and the whole of the Sinking Fund, amounts only to thirteen millions two hundred thouſand pounds; ſo that there will remain eight hundred thouſand pounds to be provided annually to make good the intereſt. This is a very ſerious ſituation, and ſuch as muſt give every friend to his country great pain to obſerve; but at the ſame time it is highly neceſſary, that ſome means or other ſhould be ſuggeſted and taken, in order to extricate us from the difficulties in which our preſent circumſtances involve us. One way of lightening our burthens certainly is, by reducing our Peace Eſtabliſhments even lower than they ſtood at the beginning of the war. To ſuch a propoſition I have not the ſmalleſt objection; but ſtill ſomething more muſt be done to give the country effectual relief, which can only ariſe from paying off a part of the national

tional debt. I wifh, therefore, to call the attention of the Houfe to this point, and to fhew them how much might be done by the application of a fingle million yearly. According to a calculation made by that accurate calculator Dr. Price, it appears, that by the laying by of a million annually, and fa-credly and religioufly applying it to pay off a part of the national debt, provided the three per cents. are changed to four per cents. (which are much more eafily paid off than the three per cents.) two hundred and fixty-feven millions might be paid off in fixty years; fo that his prefent Majefty (if his life-fhould laft to about the fame length that many of his anceftors had lived to) will in his life-time have the comfort of feeing his people relieved from all the burthens and expences brought upon them by the American war; and the Heir Apparent, whofe reign it is to be hoped will be a long one, will live to fee the whole of the debt cleared. According to the calculations of Baron Mazeres, it appears, that if the plan of laying by a million a year was adopted and purfued for twenty years, and the country then under the neceffity of defifting from it, that thofe twenty millions, with the money provided to pay the in-tereft of that part of the national debt, that fhould be paid off from time to time, appropriated to the fame purpofe, would in fifty-feven years difcharge the greateft part of the debt. Mr. Sinclair has very fenfibly and clearly fhewn in his book what might be done, by putting in practice fuch a fcheme as I have mentioned; and, in order to carry the plan into effect, Com-miffioners ought to be fpecially appointed.

Mr. Dempfter, June 23, 1784.

COM-

COMMERCE and REVENUE.

AS I had the honour to move for the House to refolve itfelf into this Committee, I think it incumbent upon me to open to you what was then intended to be propofed, as the fubject of your confideration. We are now in a Committee for confidering of the moft proper methods, for the better fecurity and improvement of the duties and revenues already charged upon and payable from tobacco and wines : this can be done in no way fo proper or effectual, as that of preventing for the future thofe frauds, by which the public revenues have been fo much injured in times paft. I know, that whoever attempts to remedy frauds, attempts a thing that muft be very difagreeable to all thofe who have been guilty of them, or who expect a benefit by fuch in time to come. This, Sir, I am fully fenfible of, and from this have fprung all thofe clamours, which have been raifed without doors, againft what I am now to propofe to you. The fmugglers, the fraudulent dealers, and thofe who have for many years been enriching themfelves by cheating their country, forefaw, that if the fcheme I am now to propofe took effect, their profitable trade would be at an end; this gave them the alarm, and from them I am perfuaded it is, that all thofe clamours have originally proceeded.

In this it is certain, that they have been moft ftrenuoufly affifted and fupported by another fet of people, who, from motives much worfe, and of much more dangerous confequence to their country, are fond of improving every opportunity that offers, for ftirring up the people of Great-Britain to mutiny and fedition. But, Sir, notwithftanding all the clamours that fuch wicked and deceitful men have been able to raife, as the fcheme I have to propofe will be a great improvement to the public revenue, an improvement of 2 or 300,000l. *per annum*, and perhaps more, and as it will likewife be of great advantage

to

to the fair trader, I thought it my duty, not only as being in the ftation I am in, but alfo as being a Member of this Houfe, to lay it before you; for no fuch clamours fhall ever deter me from doing what I think is my duty, or from propofing any thing that I am convinced will be of fuch fignal benefit to the revenue, and to the trade of my country.

It has been moft induftrioufly fpread abroad, that the fcheme I am now to propofe, was a fcheme for a General Excife; but I do aver no fuch fcheme ever entered into my head, nor, for what I know, into the head of any man I am acquainted with. My thoughts were always confined folely to thofe two branches of the revenue, arifing from the duties on wine and tobacco: and it was the frequent and repeated advices I had of the notorious frauds committed in thofe branches of the revenue, and the clamours even of fome of the Merchants themfelves, that made me turn my thoughts particularly towards confidering thofe two branches, in order to find out, if poffible, fome remedy for the growing evil. What I am now going to propofe will, I believe, if agreed to, be an effectual remedy; but if I now fail in what I am to propofe, it will be the laft attempt of this kind that I fhall ever make: I believe it will be the laft that will ever be made, either by me, or by any that fhall fucceed me in the ftation I am now in.

At prefent, I fhall lay before you only the cafe as it now ftands, with refpect to the tobacco trade, and the revenue arifing therefrom. And here it will be neceffary firft to confider the condition of our planters of tobacco in America. If we can believe them, if we can give any credit to what they themfelves fay, we muft conclude that they are reduced almoft to the laft extremity; they are reduced even almoft to a ftate of defpair, by the many frauds that have been committed in that trade, by the heavy duties which the importers of tobacco are obliged to pay upon importation, and by the ill ufage they have met with from their factors and correfpondents here in England; who, from being their Servants, are now become their Lords and Mafters.

Masters. These poor people have sent home many representations of the bad state of their affairs, and have lately sent over a Gentleman with a Remonstrance, setting forth their grievances, and praying for some speedy relief. This they may obtain by means of the scheme I intend now to propose; and I believe it is from this scheme only that they can expect any relief.

The next thing we are to consider, is the state of the tobacco-trade, with regard to the fair trader. The man who deals honourably and fairly with the public, as well as with private men; the man who honestly pays all those duties which the public is justly entitled to, finds himself prevented and fore-stalled, almost in every market within the island, by the smuggler and the fraudulent dealer: and even as to our foreign trade in tobacco, those who have no regard to honour, to religion, or to the welfare of their country, but are every day contriving ways and means for cheating the public by perjuries and false entries, are the greatest gainers: and it will always be so, unless we can fall upon some way of putting it out of their power to carry on any such frauds for the future.

And lastly, we ought to consider the great loss sustained by the public, by means of the frauds committed in the tobacco-trade, and the addition that must certainly be made to the public revenue, if those frauds can be prevented in time to come. By this addition we may be enabled to relieve the nation from some of those taxes, which it has laboured under so many years; whereas, as the case now stands, the innocent and the honest part of the nation are charged with taxes, which they would be free from, if the fraudulent dealers and the smugglers could be any way obliged to pay that, which is justly due by them to the public. This will, I am convinced, be the effect of the scheme I am to propose to you: and whoever, therefore, views it in its proper light, must see the planters, the fair traders, and the public, ranged on one side in favour of it; and none but the unfair traders and the tobacco-factors on the other.

I shall

I ſhall beg leave to mention to you ſome of thoſe frauds which have come to my knowledge : the evidence I have had of them is to me very convincing ; but in ſuch caſes, Gentlemen ought always to conſider what evidence it is impoſſible to bring, what evidence it is, by the nature of the thing, unreaſonable to expect.

A particular inſtance of fraud came lately to my knowledge by mere accident. One Midford, who had been a conſiderable tobacco-merchant in the city, happened to fail, at a time when he owed a large ſum of money upon bond to the Crown; whereupon an extent was iſſued out immediately againſt him, and thereby the Government got poſſeſſion of all his books, by which the fraud he had been guilty of was diſcovered : for it appeared, as may be ſeen by one of his books I have in my hand, that upon the column where the falſe quantities, which had been entered at the importation, by colluſion between him and the Officer, by which he paid or bonded the duty payable upon importation, a ſlip of paper had been ſo artfully paſted on that it could not be diſcovered ; and upon this ſlip of paper were written the real quantities which were entered, becauſe he was obliged to produce the ſame book when that tobacco was entered for exportation : but then, upon exportation, the tobacco was entered and weighed according to the quantities marked upon this ſlip of paper ſo artfully paſted on, as I have mentioned, by which he got a drawback, or his bonds returned, to near double the value of what he had actually paid duty for upon importation. Yet this Midford was as honeſt a man, and as fair a trader, as any in the city of London. I deſire not to be miſunderſtood ; I mean, that before he failed, before theſe frauds came to be diſcovered, he was always reckoned as honeſt a man, and as fair a trader, as any in the city of London, or in any part of the nation.

After this, he mentioned the ſeveral frauds following : That of re-landing the tobacco after it was ſhipped off for exportation ; that of ſocking of tobacco, which was a cant-word uſed for

ſtealing

ftealing and fmuggling it out of the fhips, after their arrival in the river, before they were unloaded at the cuftom-houfe; that of ftripping the ftalks, and afterwards fplitting and prefling them by an engine contrived for that purpofe, and then exporting them; that of giving bonds for the duty payable upon importation, whereby the Government had loft feveral large fums by the failure of payment of fuch bonds; that of the rich moneyed men making prompt payments, by which the public was obliged to allow them ten *per cent.* difcount as to the duties; and by entering the tobacco foon after for exportation, they drew back the whole duties; fo that Government actually loft ten *per cent.* upon all the tobacco that had been fo entered.

Thefe frauds are notorious, moft of them are known to the whole world; and as the Laws of the Cuftoms have been found ineffectual for preventing of fuch frauds, therefore, it is propofed to add the Laws of Excife to the Laws of the Cuftoms, and by means of both it is probable, I may fay certain, that all fuch frauds will be prevented in time to come.

By the feveral fubfidies and impofts now payable upon tobacco, by feveral Acts of Parliament made for that purpofe, it appears, that the duties now payable upon tobacco on importation, amount to 6¾d. per pound weight; all which muft be paid down in ready money, by the Merchant, upon importation thereof, with the allowance of ten *per cent.* upon prompt payment; or otherwife there muft be bonds given, with fufficient fureties for payment of the money; which is often a great lofs to the public, and is always a great inconvenience to the Merchant importer: whereas, by what I am to propofe, the whole duties to be paid for the future, will amount to no more than 4¾d. per pound weight, and this duty not to be paid till the tobacco comes to be fold for home confumption; fo that if the Merchant exports his tobacco, he will be quite free from all payment of duty, or giving bond, or finding out proper fureties for joining in fuch bond, he will have nothing to do, but to re-load his tobacco on board a fhip for exportation,

without

without being at the trouble to attend for having his bonds cancelled, or for taking out debentures for the drawbacks; all which, I conceive, muſt be a great eaſe to the fair trader; and to every ſuch trader the preventing of frauds muſt be a great advantage ; becauſe it will put all the tobacco traders in Britain upon the ſame footing : which is but juſt and equal, and what ought certainly to be accompliſhed, if it be poſſible.

Now, in order to make this eaſe effectual to the fair trader, and to contribute to his advantage, by preventing as much as poſſible any frauds in time to come, I propoſe, as I have ſaid, to join the Laws of Exciſe to thoſe of the Cuſtoms, and to leave the one penny, or rather three farthings *per* pound, called the farther ſubſidy, to be ſtill charged at the Cuſtom-houſe, upon the importation of any tobacco ; which three farthings ſhall be payable to his Majeſty's Civil Liſt as heretofore : and I propoſe, that all tobacco for the future, after being weighed at the Cuſtom-houſe, and charged with the ſaid three farthings *per* pound, ſhall be lodged in a warehouſe or warehouſes, to be appointed by the Commiſſioners of Exciſe for that purpoſe; of which warehouſe the Merchant importer ſhall have one lock and key, and the warehouſe-keeper to be appointed by the ſaid Commiſſioners ſhall have another ; in order that the tobacco may lie ſafe in that warehouſe, till the Merchant finds a market for it, either for exportation or for home-conſumption : thus, if his market be for exportation, he may apply to his ware-houſe-keeper, and take out as much for that purpoſe as he has occaſion for ; which, when weighed at the Cuſtom-houſe, ſhall be diſcharged of three farthings *per* pound, with which it was charged upon importation ; ſo that the Merchant may then export it without any further trouble : but if his market be for home-conſumption, that he ſhall then pay the three farthings charged upon it at the Cuſtom-houſe upon importation ; and that then, upon calling his warehouſe-keeper, he may deliver it to the buyer, on paying an inland-duty of 4d. *per* pound weight, to the proper officer appointed to receive the ſame.

And

And whereas all the penalties and forfeitures to become due, by the laws now in being, for regulating the collecting of the duties on tobacco, or at leaft all that part of them which is not given to the informers, now belonging to the Crown ; I propofe that all fuch penalties and forfeitures, fo far as they formerly belonged to the Crown, fhall for the future belong to the public, and be applicable to the fame ufes to which the faid duties fhall be made applicable by Parliament : and for that purpofe, I have his Majefty's commands to acquaint this Houfe, that he, out of his great regard for the public good, with pleafure confents that they fhall be fo applied : which is a condefcenfion in his Majefty, that I hope every Gentleman in this Houfe is fully, fenfible of, and will fully acknowledge.

I know there has been an objection made ; I expect to hear it again made in this Houfe, againft what I now propofe. The objection is this ; that a great many of his Majefty's fubjects will be liable to be tried in a multitude of cafes, by the Commiffioners of Excife, from whom there is no appeal, but to Commiffioners of Appeal, or to Juftices of the Peace in the country, all named by the King, and removeable at pleafure ; from whom the appellants cannot expect to meet with juftice or redrefs. I am far from thinking there is any ground for this complaint ; I am far from thinking that any man ever had juft reafon to fay that he was wronged, or unjuftly dealt with, either by the Commiffioners of Appeal, or by the Juftices of Peace at their quarter-feffions : but, in order to obviate any objection of this nature, I propofe that all appeals in this cafe, as well as in all other cafes relating to the Excife, fhall for the future be heard and determined by two or three of the Judges, to be named by his Majefty, out of the twelve Judges belonging to Weftminfter-hall ; and that in the country, all appeals, from the firft fentence of his Majefty's Juftices of Peace, fhall be to the Judge of Affize upon the next circuit which fhall come into that county ; who fhall in all cafes proceed to hear and determine fuch appeals in the moft fummary way, without
formality

formality of proceedings in courts of law or equity. From fuch Judges, and from fuch a manner of proceeding, every man muft expect to meet with the utmoft difpatch, and with the moft impartial juftice: and therefore I muft think, that what I now propofe can be no inconvenience to thofe, who may thereby be fubjected to the Laws of Excife; but that if there was formerly any ground of complaint, it may be a great relief to thofe who are already fubjected to fuch laws.

This is the fcheme which has been reprefented in fuch a dreadful and terrible light: this is the monfter, that many-headed monfter, which was to devour the people, and to commit fuch ravages over the whole nation: how juftly it has been reprefented in fuch a light, I fhall leave to this Committee, and to the whole world without doors to judge; I have faid, I will fay it again, that whatever apprehenfions and terrors people may have been brought under, from falfe and malicious reprefentations of what they neither did nor could poffibly know or underftand, I am firmly perfuaded, when they do come to know and fully to underftand the fcheme which I have now had the honour to open to you, they will view it in another light; and that if it has the good fortune to be approved of by Parliament, and comes to take effect, the people will foon feel the happy confequences thereof; and when they feel thofe good effects, they will no longer think thofe people their friends who have fo grofly impofed on their underftanding.

I look upon it as a moft innocent fcheme; I am convinced it can be hurtful to none but fmugglers and unfair traders; I am certain it will be of great benefit and advantage to the public revenue; and if I had thought otherwife of it, I never would have ventured to have propofed it in this place: therefore I fhall now beg leave to move that it may be refolved, That it is the opinion of this Committee, that the fubfidy and additional duty upon tobacco, of the Britifh Plantations, granted by an Act of the 12th of King Charles IId, and the impoft thereon, granted by an Act of the firft of King James IId,

and

and alſo the one-third ſubſidy thereon, granted by an Act of the ſecond of Queen Anne, amounting in the whole to 5¼d. per pound, for ſeveral terms of years in the ſaid reſpective Acts mentioned, and which have ſince been continued and made perpetual, ſubject to redemption by Parliament, ſhall from and after the 24th day of June, 1733, ceaſe and determine.

Sir Robert Walpole, March 14, 1733.

WHEN I firſt heard of this ſcheme I was in the country, and there I muſt ſay, that it had been repreſented in ſuch a light, as created a general diſlike to it, and raiſed great appre-henſions in the minds of moſt people. It was repreſented as a ſcheme for introducing a general Exciſe ; ſuch a ſcheme I own I would not allow myſelf to think was contrived or approved of by any Gentleman in Adminiſtration. I did imagine that all thoſe in the Adminiſtration were very well convinced, that a general Exciſe was what the People of England would never quietly ſubmit to ; and therefore did not believe, that any of them ever would countenance a ſcheme which had the leaſt tendency that way. But now after having heard it opened, and fully explained by the Honourable Gentleman (Sir Robert Walpole) on the floor, I cannot but think that it is a wide ſtep towards eſtabliſhing a general Exciſe, and therefore I muſt be excuſed aſſenting to it.

How far it relates to trade, with which it certainly has a very cloſe connection, I ſhall leave to be explained by others more converſant in thoſe affairs ; nor will I take upon me to ſay how far it may be a remedy for the frauds mentioned hy the Honour-able Gentleman ; but there is another concern which I always ſhall, while I have the honour to ſit in this Houſe, have a par-ticular eye to, and that is, the Liberty of my Country. The danger with which this ſcheme ſeems to threaten many of my fellow-ſubjects, is alone of ſufficient force to make me give my negative to the Queſtion. Let Gentlemen but reflect, let them but caſt their eyes back on the ſeveral laws that have been made

5   ſince

since the Revolution, they will there find, that there has been already more power vested in the Crown, than may be thought altogether consistent with the Constitution of a free Country; and therefore I hope this House will never think of adding to that power, which there may be some ground to suspect is already too far extended.

The Laws of Excise have always been looked upon as most grievous to the subject. All those already subjected to such Laws, are, in my opinion, so far deprived of their Liberty; and since by this scheme, a great many more of his Majesty's faithful subjects are to be subjected to those arbitrary Laws, let the advantages accruing to the public be ever so great or many, they will be purchased at too dear a rate, if they are purchased at the expence of the Liberty of the meanest of his Majesty's subjects; for even the meanest man in the nation, has as natural and good a right to his Liberty, as the greatest man in this, or any other kingdom.

Let us but take a view of the neighbouring nations in Europe; they were all once free; the people of every one of them had once as many Liberties and Privileges to boast of as we have now; but at present they are most of them reduced to a state of Slavery; they have no Liberty, no Property, no Law, nor any thing they can depend on. Let us examine their histories, let us enquire into the methods by which they are deprived of their Liberties, and we shall find a very near resemblance to the schemes now proposed to us. Almost in every country in the world, the Liberties of the People have been destroyed, under pretence of preserving or rescuing the People from some great evil, to which it was pretended they were exposed. This is the very case now before us; in order to enable the Crown to prevent some little frauds, pretended to have been committed in the ancient method of collecting the public revenue, it is proposed to us to put such a power in the hands of the Crown, as may enable some future Prince to enslave the whole nation. This is really the light in which this

fcheme appears to me; but to the Honourable Gentleman who
propofed it to us, I am perfuaded it appears in a quite different
light, otherwife I am certain he would never have propofed it
to this Committee. However, fince the generality of the nation have already fhewn a great diflike to it, I hope the Honourable Gentleman may be prevailed on to delay it till another Seffion of Parliament: in fuch a delay there can be no
danger, there can be no great lofs to the Public, more efpecially fince the money to be thereby raifed, is not fo much as
propofed to be applied to the current fervice of the prefent year.
If it be delayed till another Seffion of Parliament, Gentlemen
will then have time to confider it fully, and to confult with
their Conftituents about it; by that time it may poffibly appear in a quite different light both to me and many other Gentlemen without doors as well as within; and then, if upon examination it appears to be a good thing, as fome Gentlemen
now feem to believe, it will, without doubt, be approved of by
the generality of thofe without, as well as by the majority of
thofe within.

But I hope thofe Gentlemen who have now fo good an opinion of the fcheme, will not think of thrufting it down people's
throats, when they fee that the generality of the nation have an
opinion of it quite different from what they have; fuch a Refolution, fuch an attempt, might produce confequences which I
tremble to think of: and this is another motive which is of
great weight to me, I have the honour to know his Majefty,
his Royal Perfon I have formerly had the honour to approach,
and know him to be a Prince of fo much goodnefs, that were
this fcheme reprefented to him in this light, he never would
approve of it; to him it will always be a fufficient reafon
againft any propofition, that the generality of the people have
fhewn their diflike to it. I love his Majefty, I have a fincere
and a dutiful refpect for him, and all the Royal Family; and
therefore I fhall always be afraid of any thing that may alienate
the affections of many of his Majefty's faithful fubjects, which
8   I be-

I believe would be the certain confequence of the eftablifhment of this fcheme; for which reafons, if the Queftion be now pufhed, I fhall moft heartily give my negative to it.

Sir Paul Methuen, March 14, 1733.

THE profperity of this nation, Sir, or at leaft our fecurity, depends upon the tranquillity of our neighbours: while they are at peace, they will always confume more of our manufactures than when they are involved in blood and confufion; and confequently we fhall always, in times of peace, have a greater demand for the manufactures of our country than in time of war. Befides, while they continue at peace, the Balance of Power can be in no danger; but the events of war no ·nation can depend on; and therefore this nation, amongft the reft, may be deeply affected by the extraordinary fuccefs of any one Power in Europe. Let us not therefore grudge a trifling expence, when it may evidently contribute towards reftoring peace among our neighbours, upon which our own profperity and fecurity does and always muft depend.

Our houfe is not yet on fire, but our neighbour's is all on a flame; and then certainly it is time for us to prepare the engines neceffary for preferving our own. Thefe are a powerful fleet, and a fufficient body of regular well-difciplined troops, ready to march at the firft word of command. This, Sir, will give weight to his Majefty's Councils, it will make all the parties concerned give a due regard and attention to what may be propofed by his Majefty's Minifters for reftoring the peace of Europe; for a Minifter, whofe equipage confifts of a large body of good troops, will always be better hearkened to, than one whofe equipage confifts only of a great number of fine pages and ufelefs footmen.

Sir Robert Walpole, Feb. 14, 1735.

As this day feems to be a day of paradoxes, amongft the reft, we have been told one with refpect to our trade. We are

N 2　　　　　　　　　　　　told,

told, Sir, that the profperity of this nation depends upon the tranquillity of our neighbours; and that in times of peace, there is always a greater demand for the manufactures and produce of this country than in time of war. This, Sir, is fo far from being a true maxim in trade, that the direct contrary is true. The chief part of the produce of this country, confifts in the neceffaries, and not the luxuries of life; and confequently our neighbours will always confume as much of fuch fort of things in time of war as in time of peace. But the difference is, that when their heads are not diftracted, nor their hands diverted, by any foreign or domeftic war, they have time to apply themfelves to tillage; they have time to apply themfelves to manufactures of all kinds; they have leifure to think of, and to improve all the arts of peace; and by fo doing, they furnifh themfelves at home with a great many of thofe neceffaries which, in time of war, they are obliged to purchafe of us. This is not only evident in theory, but is confirmed by experience; for our trade has fuffered more by the domeftic improvements made by our neighbours, during the laft long tranquillity in Europe, than it has done by any other means; except the heavy duties we have laid upon ourfelves, and the great trouble, and many fees, and many perquifites we have fubjected our Merchants to, both in importing and exporting their goods and merchandize.

Mr. Pulteney, Feb. 14, 1735.

OUR great King Edward III. fhewed fuch a regard for our trade and navigation, that upon a complaint from our Merchants of their having been plundered by the Spanifh pirates or guarda coftas of thofe days, he immediately fitted out a fleet and went in perfon to revenge the depredations that had been committed upon his fubjects; by which he reftored the freedom of our commerce, and added a naval triumph, to the many triumphs he had before obtained at land. The protection of trade and navigation has always been one of the chief concerns of all great Kings and all wife nations. Even the Romans, who could never be faid to be a trading people, fhewed a great regard for it, as appears from the reprocf Cicero gave them in his days, for neglecting to fupprefs the pirates, and to affert the honour of their flag.

Mr. Pulteney, March 30, 1738.

OUR travellers, Sir, who make but very fuperficial inquiries into the manners or cuftoms of any country they pafs through, may perhaps imagine the people of France or Holland, are more heavily or more oppreffedly taxed, than the people of this kingdom, becaufe they hear the people complain there as they do here; but any Gentleman who underftands thefe things, and has made a proper inquiry, may foon be convinced of the contrary ; and as for the other countries of Europe, they have not, it's true, fuch numbers of rich Merchants, mafters of ma-nufacturers, and mafter tradefmen, as we have in this country, which is the reafon that many of their poor live in idlenefs, or ftarve for mere want, becaufe there are few or no rich Mafters or Merchants in the country, that have money to em-ploy them ; but in all countries, where the poor have any em-ployment, they are pretty nearly equally poor ; they neither get, nor expect more than a comfortable fubfiftence by their daily labour : and if you enhance the means of that fubfiftence by taxes on the neceffaries and conveniencies of life, their Mafters muft increafe their wages ; fo that all taxes fall at laft upon the Mafters, foreign or domeftic, who muft pay for that increafe of wages in the price of goods they purchafe : but the difference is, that a tax laid directly upon the Mafter, only prevents his growing rich fo faft, or makes him live lefs luxu-rioufly, but does not enhance the price of your manufactures : whereas a tax laid upon thofe things, that are neceffary for the fupport of the poor, enhances the price of labour, and confe-quently raifes the price of all your manufactures both for do-meftic and foreign fale, which at laft ruins your trade. There-

N 3

fore, if the poor of this kingdom be more heavily taxed than the poor of any other country of Europe, it is what ought to be remedied as foon as poffible ; it is what will give that country a great advantage over us, if they fhould ever begin to apply themfelves to trade, which every country of Europe is now aiming at as much as they can.

Sir John Barnard, March 21, 1737.

D E F E N C E.

DEFENCE.

' I STAND up to agree in fome part with the Honourable Gentleman who fpoke laft : if we are at prefent in any unhappy fituation, and if it be but thought, by any Gentleman in this Houfe, that that fituation is any ways owing to the mifmanagement of thofe in Adminiftration, in my opinion, whoever thinks fo, ought to move for this Houfe's going into fuch an inquiry; they ought to move for the Houfe's going into a Committee on the State of the Nation, and upon the foot of fuch an inquiry, I will willingly join iffue with the Honourable Gentleman, or any other Gentleman in this Houfe. Whenever the Houfe fhall refolve upon going into fuch a Committee, I promife, that fo far as lies in my power, nothing fhall be refufed that is thought proper or neceffary for giving the Houfe all the information that can be wifhed or defired. But as that time is not yet come, I muft think that the Motion now under confideration is very irregular, and feems calculated rather for giving Gentlemen an opportunity of declaiming againft thofe, who have the honour of ferving the Crown, than for procuring any proper information to the Houfe, or any advantage to the country.

' It is ufual for fome people to make Motions, rather to fix unpopular things on others, than to have any information for themfelves : they make Motions in order to make a figure in the Votes, which are fent to all parts of the nation, and to ferve fome particular ends of their own : when a negative is put upon any fuch Motion, they are then ready to cry out, " we would have relieved you, we would have extricated you " from all the difficulties you labour under, but we were by " power denied the means of doing it." This is a piece of management ; it is a fort of parliamentary play, which has always been practifed by thofe who oppofe the meafures of Ad-

N 4   miniftration.

miniftration. I remember it as long as I remember Parliaments, and have by my own experience been acquainted with
it : I can remember Motions made with no other view but to
have a negative put upon them ; and particularly at the beginning of a Seffion, the language amongft fuch Gentlemen
has always been, " We muft give them no reft, but make
" Motion after Motion ; if they agree in any Motion we make,
" it will diftrefs them ; and if they put a negative upon every
" one, it will render them odious amongft the People."

' This, I fay, has always been the conftant practice of thofe
who are refolved, at any rate, to oppofe the Adminiftration :
but I muft take notice, that to fay that any Motion in Parliament is refufed by power, is, in my opinion, a very unparliamentary way of fpeaking : when any Motion is made, every
Gentleman is at liberty to debate with freedom upon it, and to
agree or difagree as he thinks reafonable : if it be rejected, it
muft be by a Majority of the Houfe, and becomes an act of
this Houfe ; and to fay, that what is the act of the Houfe, is
an act of power, is not, I think, fpeaking in the language of
Parliament.

Sir Robert Walpole, Jan. 23, 1734.

My honourable friend was pleafed to inveigh very feverely
againft the luxury and vice that reigns too generally amongft
us. I know not from what this luxury and vice proceeds ;
but proceed from what it will, I am fure it does not proceed
from any example fet by the Royal Family : for I am perfuaded that every Gentleman who hears me, is fenfible that no
nation was ever bleft with a Royal Family that has given fuch
eminent inftances of frugality and temperance, as the Family
that is now upon the Throne. If a People, Sir, grown wanton with liberty and riches, fhall degenerate into luxury, is a
Prince or his Minifters to be blamed for that ? Or if the
People is tainted with difcontent and diffatisfaction, are we to
endeavour to cure it by giving up the only means of reftraining

ing them? Yet this, Sir, is the very-thing for which some
Gentlemen have argued so strenuously since the opening of this
debate. It has been allowed on all hands, that had it not been
for our standing forces, the nation must have, ere this time,
run into confusion from that spirit of dissatisfaction that has
broke loose among the People. But, say some Gentlemen,
that spirit is occasioned from the oppression of the Government.
But they have not been pleased to give us any instance of such
oppression; they have given us no instance of an invasion upon
the liberty and property of any subject; they have not given us
one instance of any encroachment of the military upon the
civil power, or of one attack that has been made by the Administration to subvert the freedom of Parliament. There is
nothing more common, Sir, than to raise a clamour upon the
topics of bribery, corruption, and venality; and nothing more
easy than to make the People believe, that when an Administration continues long in the same hands, it can only be by
these means. But this is a misfortune that has attended the
best Administrations in all ages and in all countries. The very
success that Minister meets with, is improved by his enemies
to his prejudice. If a Majority in this House concur with his
measures, it must be the effects of corruption. If he has the
favour of the Prince, he owes it to flattery and misrepresenting
the state of the nation. Does the kingdom under his Administration enjoy a profound peace and extended commerce,
this is attributed to the Minister's sacrificing something still
more valuable than these advantages in order to procure them.
So that, Sir, the very well-being of a state, gives a handle to
clamour against the Minister: whereas, in reality, his success
in the Parliament may be owing to the justness of his measures; the favour he is in with his Prince, to his integrity;
and the increase of the national wealth and power, to his vigilance and the firmness of his resolutions. Sir, I shall make
no particular application of what I have said here; only one
thing

thing I will be bold to affirm, that had the clamours that have been raifed in Great-Britain thefe eighteen years paft againft the Adminiftration been well-founded, we muft before this time have been the moft miferable, the moft beggarly, and the moft abject People under the fun.

Sir Robert Walpole, Feb. 3, 1738.

I THINK a man is an honeft man, who votes according to what his confcience tells him the prefent fituation of things requires; and an honeft man, Sir, if he fees the circumftances which induced him to vote in favour of a Refolution laft year altered, or if he finds that he himfelf has been miftaken in the apprehenfion of thefe circumftances; I fay, Sir, an honeft man will, in either of thefe cafes, vote this Seffion directly contrary to what he voted before: if ever I voted for a ftanding army, Sir, in time of peace, it was when my confcience told me, that the prefervation of our liberties required it. But, Sir, though at that time, perhaps, I was convinced that our keeping up a ftanding army for one year was neceffary, it does not follow that I act inconfiftently, if I don't vote for a perpetuity of that army. Therefore, though a Gentleman has voted for every Queftion, for every job of the Miniftry; though his whole life has been but one continued vote on their fides; yet he ought neither to be afhamed nor afraid to oppofe them, as foon as his own judgment, or the fituation of things is altered. This is acting upon no other principles, Sir, but thofe of an honeft man, and a lover of his country: and, as the diftinction between Whigs and Tories is now in effect abolifhed, I hope foon to fee our People know no other denominations of party amongft us befides thofe of Court and Country. The Honourable Gentleman talks of the eftablifhment of the Government, and of the Adminiftration; but, Sir, I know of no Eftablifhment, I know of no Government, I know of no Adminiftration that ought to be kept up, but for the prefervation of the

Liberties

Liberties of the People: for it is not two-pence matter to me, whether the Prince's name under whom I am to be enflaved, is Thomas, James, or Richard; I am fure I fhall never be enflaved under a George.

William Pulteney, Efq; Feb. 3, 1738.

THOSE employed in the Adminiftration of affairs, are always in the moft ticklifh fituation. If they propofe to make provifions againft danger, by which provifions the People muft be put to an expence, they then are charged with raifing imaginary dangers, in order from thence to take an opportunity to load the People with new Taxes: and their misfortune is, that the more careful they have been in time paft, the argument grows every day more ftrongly againft them; becaufe people begin at laft to believe, that the dangers which were never felt were imaginary, though in reality they were prevented only by the provifions that were made againft them. However many people may come at laft to be confirmed in this erroneous opinion, by which the Minifters may be at laft refufed thofe provifions that are actually neceffary; and, if by fuch refufal, any fignal misfortune fhould befal the nation, the Minifters would be fure to be loaded with the blame of it, though they had done all that was in their power to warn us of the danger.

I cannot really comprehend, Sir, what fort of information it is that Gentlemen want. Would they have his Majefty fend to tell us, that there is a bloody war carried on by France, Spain, and Sardinia, againft the Emperor? Surely they do not expect that his Majefty fhould fend us a particular Meffage, in order to acquaint us with a piece of news that is known to the whole world!

Sir Robert Walpole, Feb. 14, 1735.

I WAS a little furprized to hear it faid by the Honourable Gentleman who fpoke laft, that this Motion's being oppofed

by

by Minifters and Placemen is a ftrong argument in its favour. In my opinion, this is a fort of begging the Queftion. Before we can fuppofe this to be an argument in favour of the Motion for excluding Placemen, we muft fuppofe, that Minifters and Placemen oppofe it, not becaufe they think it wrong, but becaufe that they are Minifters and Placemen, which is the very Queftion now in debate. I do not believe, that ever any any Minifter or Placeman oppofed, or fupported a Queftion in this Houfe, contrary to his private fentiments, and only becaufe he was a Minifter or Placeman. I am fure their conduct of late years has given us no room to think fo; nor can we ever have room to think fo, as long as none but Gentlemen of credit and honour are employed in the Adminiftration, or in any place of honour and profit under the Crown. If mere upftarts, or perfons of no fortune or credit were employed, and by illegal methods brought into this Houfe, for by fair means they could not, there might be fome room for making fuch a fuppofition; and then there would be fome caufe for bringing in fuch a Bill as is now propofed: but when I look round me, and confider the particular circumftances of thefe Gentlemen now here, who have the honour to be at the fame time in the fervice of the Crown, I muft look upon the danger now pretended to be fo real and imminent, to be as chimerical a danger as the moft luxuriant fancy can invent.

I fhall agree with the Honourable Gentlemen who feem fo fond of this Bill, that if the Crown could gain an abfolute and uncontroulable power over all, or a majority of the elections in the kingdom, every Parliament thus chofen by the power would be under the direction of the Crown, and in this cafe our Conftitution would be at an end; but this I think impoffible. Whilft the Crown purfues right meafures, whilft none but Gentlemen of good credit and fortune are employed in the Adminiftration, or in any fuperior Poft or Office under the Adminiftration, the Crown will certainly have a great influence both in Parliament and at Elections: but this proceeds from

the

the wifdom and uprightnefs of its meafures, and from the
weight of thofe that are employed; and it would certainly
ceafe as foon as the Crown began to purfue contrary meafures; becaufe we muft fuppofe the Adminiftration would then
certainly be deferted, and oppofed by all; or moft Gentlemen
of any fortune or credit in their country, would foon unite in
meafures in making a facrifice of themfelves, as well as their
country, which is a fuppofition that cannot, I think, be made
nor pretended by any man whofe head is found and heart
fincere.

In all Queftions, Sir, *which do not admit of demonftration,*
there muft be a variety of opinions; and as Queftions of a
political nature are lefs capable of demonftration than any
other, it is natural to fee a difference of fentiments in every
country like this, where the People have not only a power of
judging, but a liberty to talk and write againft the meafures
purfued by Government: this is natural, and even neceffary in
every country where the People are free: and as every man is
fond of his own opinion, and fully convinced of his having
reafon on his fide, he is apt to imagine, that thofe who differ
from him muft be governed by fome prejudice, or by fome
felfifh confideration. From hence it is, that all thofe who dif-
approve of the Meafures of the Government conclude, that
the approbation of thofe who differ from them, proceeds from
the influence of fome lucrative Poft they are in poffeffion or
expectation of; and on the other hand, thofe that approve of
and fupport the meafures purfued by the Government, are apt
to conclude, that the oppofition is entirely owing to party
prejudice, or to malice and refentment. For my part, I fhall
always endeavour to keep in the middle courfe, and to believe
that both are in the wrong: and therefore I fhall always be
againft any alteration in our Conftitution, when I think that
the alteration propofed is founded upon one or other of thefe
miftakes. I fhould be as much againft reftraining the Liberties
of the People, in order to prevent that influence which is

fuppofed to proceed from party-prejudice, malice, and refentment, as I fhall be againft reftraining the power or free choice
of the Crown, in order to prevent that influence which is fuppofed to proceed from the difpofal of places or preferments.
There may, perhaps, I believe, there 'always will be a little of
each in the nation, but never can be of any dangerous confequence to our conftitution: on the contrary, they ferve as a
balance to each other; fo that by removing either without removing the other at the fame time, the conftitution will run a
great rifk of being overturned.

There are many caufes, Sir, which naturally raife a party
againft the beft and wifeft Adminiftration. In this life it is
impoffible for us to be completely happy. All men feel fome
wants, preffures, or misfortunes; and very few are willing to
impute them to their own folly, or to any miftake in their own
conduct. To fuch men, the Adminiftration is in politics, what
the Devil is in religion; it is the author of all their mifdeeds,
and the caufe of all their fufferings: this naturally breeds in
them a bad opinion of the Adminiftration, and then, of courfe,
they not only condemn, but oppofe all its meafures. This muft
raife a great many enemies to the Adminiftration in every
country; and their number will be confiderably increafed by
thofe that are difappointed of the honours and preferments they
expected, and juftly, as they thought, deferved; as well as by
thofe that wifh for a change in the Adminiftration, for no other
reafon but becaufe they hope for a fhare in the next. In all
countries it is honourable to have a fhare in the Government
of one's country: in rich countries, it is profitable as well as
honourable; and as there are but a very few, in any country,
that can have a fhare of the Government, and ftill fewer that
can have fuch a fhare as, they think, they deferve, there muft
be many candidates for every title of honour, or poft of profit,
that is to be difpofed of. Of thefe candidates, one only can be
chofen, and all the reft will, of courfe, think they have had injuftice done them; for few men are fo modeft, as to think fuch

a dif-

a difappointment owing to their own want of merit, or to the
fuperior merit of their rival; and from thence they will begin
to entertain a fecret animofity, nay, perhaps, they will declare
an open enmity to thofe at the head of the Adminiftration.

By thefe two forts of men united together, there will always
be a confiderable party, in every country, ready to condemn
and vilify the wifeft meafures that can be purfued by the Adminiftration: and, as in every free country, there are different
parties, as in this country there are at prefent, and, I believe,
always will be different parties, the parties that are by their
profeffion and principles oppofite to the party in power, will be
ready to find fault with every thing done by the Adminiftration.
In this country, I fay, Sir, there are, and, I believe, always will
be different parties. There are at prefent, and will be, as long
as our prefent happy eftablifhment endures, three different parties in this kingdom: the Jacobites of one fide, the Republicans
of the other, which I may call the two extremes; and the party
for fupporting our prefent happy eftablifhment, which may be
juftly called the proper mean between thefe two extremes.

Thus, Sir, we fee what a numerous party our Adminiftration
muft always have to ftruggle with. All thefe forts of men, the
difcontented, the difappointed, the Jacobites, and the Republicans, will always be ready to condemn and oppofe the meafures
of the Adminiftration, let them be never fo wife, let them be
never fo juft; and by their arguments, they will often be able
to prevail with fome well-meaning and unthinking men, or at
leaft to ftagger them in their opinions. With regard to Parliaments, and the choice of Members of Parliaments, our Adminiftration has no defence againft this formidable union of parties;
but by the wifdom of their meafures, to engage moft Gentlemen
of intereft and fortune in their intereft. Whilft the Adminiftration purfues right meafures, fuch Gentlemen will be ready to
join with them; and by this means the Adminiftration will always have a prevailing influence, both in Parliament, and at
elections: for when a majority of thofe who have the beft fortunes,

tunes, and greateft intereft in their refpective counties, are friends to the Adminiftration, it is not at all furprifing that an Adminiftration, by means of fuch friends, fhould have a prevailing influence at elections, as well as in Parliament. But fuch friends, or at leaft a great number of fuch, no Adminiftration can have, that purfues meafures inconfiftent with the good of the community in general.

I fhall grant, Sir, that a title of honour, or a lucrative poft or employment, may be of fome fervice in prevailing with a Gentleman to judge favourable of the Government's meafures in all cafes, where he is wavering in his opinion ; but a bad Government can never, by this way, gain many friends : even a good Government can never gain near fo many friends, as it will lofe by caufelefs difcontents and juft difappointments : and if you fhould take away from the Crown the chief advantage it can reap by the difpofal of pofts and employments, not only a good Adminiftration, but even the Crown itfelf, may fink under the weight of party-prejudice, fupported by caufelefs difcontents and juft difappointment. Therefore, to fupport the Crown againft the difadvantages and oppofition which the wifeft and beft Adminiftration muft always have to ftruggle with, I think you ought to leave it in the power of the Crown to difpofe of all pofts and employments in the fame manner they have been hitherto, without any bad effects, difpofed of.

Sir Robert Walpole, Jan. 29, 1739.

COMMON fame may be a good foundation for a parliamentary inquiry ; but that it always ought to be efteemed fuch, is what I cannot agree to. A parliamentary inquiry, Sir, muft always be attended with many and great inconveniencies. In the firft place, it muft always raife a great ferment in the nation ; and when it relates to foreign affairs, it generally difobliges fome of our allies, or difturbs fome of the negociations that may then be on foot for the benefit of our trade, or for preferving the tranquillity of Europe. In the next place, it poffeffes the thoughts

4   of

of our Minifters fo much, as every inquiry muft relate to fome part of their conduct, that they have no time to mind any thing elfe; fo that all our foreign affairs, and all projects for domeftic utility, muft be at a ftand during that inquiry. And in the third place, it takes up a great deal of the time of this Houfe, which never ought to be employed but in matters of the utmoft importance to the nation, or to fome particular perfons, who can have relief no way but by Act of Parliament.

For this reafon, Sir, common fame ought not to be made the foundation of a parliamentary inquiry, unlefs it be grounded upon fome proofs, or at leaft upon very ftrong prefumptions, that fomething very weak or very wicked has been tranfacted; and that by fuch an inquiry the nation may meet with a proper redrefs, without being thereby expofed to a greater evil. If otherwife, Sir, if we were to inquire into every public tranfac- tion, of which a bad report might be artfully raifed, we fhould every Seffion have fuch a multitude of inquiries, that we could never do any other bufinefs: for it would always be in the power of the diffaffected or difappointed to invert facts, and by afferting thefe facts openly and boldly, they might raife a gene- rally bad report againft every meafure an Adminiftration could engage in. This is an engine which has been often played againft Minifters in all ages, and in all countries; and in this age and country it may now be played with greater fafety than ever it was in any other country; for by our old laws, even in this country, it was moft feverely punifhed. By a law of the great and wife King Alfred, the author and fpreader of falfe ru- mours among the people was to have his tongue cut out, if he could not redeem it by paying the value then put by the law upon his head. By a law of Edward the Ift, called Weftmin- fter the Firft, the fpreaders of falfe reports, whereby difcord might arife between the King and his people, or the great men of the realm, were to be imprifoned till they produced their author; confequently, if they could produce no author, they were to be held as the inventors, and to be punifhed according to common law, by fine and imprifonment; and this very law was revived and re-enacted in the reign of Edward the IIId.

Thus, Sir, we fee, that even in this country, we had very fevere laws made againft this crime, and that by fome of the beft and wifeft of our Kings: and in Scotland, before the Union, this very crime was a fpecies of high-treafon, which they called Leifing-making; and upon which, though by a moft extraordinary ftretch, the Reprefentative of one of the greateft families in that kingdom, was tried and attainted of high treafon, fome time before the Revolution, as is well known by feveral Gentlemen that hear me. But why fhould I fay we had very fevere laws againft this crime? We have them ftill; for they ftand as yet unrepealed, though by the lenity of this Government none of them have of late years been carried into execution. If they were, I believe few of our Pamphleteers, Journalifts, or Coffee-houfe Politicians, could long efcape punifhment: and if this were the cafe, fome Gentlemen of this Houfe would not have fo often an occafion to talk of common fame, or general reports, which are often artfully raifed, and induftrioufly fpread, on purpofe to give a handle for difturbing the Government, and diftreffing the Adminiftration, by fetting on foot a parliamentary inquiry.

Right Hon. Henry Pelham, Jan. 31, 1749.

WHAT do their Lordfhips infinuate, that I have been the author of the prefent meafures again *America?* and it is I that direct them? I fhould be proud to own them if it were, becaufe I think them wife, politic, and equitable: but furely they will permit me to repeat again, that I have been a nominal Cabinet Minifter part of the laft reign, and the whole of the prefent; that I was an efficient Cabinet Minifter during part of both periods; but that fince the time before alluded to in this debate, I have had no concern or participation whatever in his Majefty's Councils. Threats are thrown out, and inquiries predicted: I heartily wifh they may be fpeedy: I am prepared for them, and
put

put their intended authors to the moſt utter defiance. It has been urged againſt me as a crime to-day, that I have courted popularity. I never did *court* it, but I have always ſtudied to *deſerve* it. Popularity will always fly the purſuers; ſhe muſt follow. I do not mean to ſay that I deſpiſe it; on the contrary, I ſincerely wiſh for it, if not purchaſed at too dear a price, at the expence of my *conſcience* and my *duty*. If a faithful diſcharge of one, and execution of the other, be the means of procuring it, I hope I ſhall always be a warm candidate for popular fame. I have hitherto, to the beſt of my abilities, acted on that plan, and I hope I ſhall perſevere to the end. I have ſeen much of Courts, Parliaments, and Cabinets, and have been a frequent witneſs to the means uſed to acquire popularity, and the baſe and mean purpoſes to which that popularity has been afterwards employed. I have been in Cabinets, where the great ſtruggle has not been to advance the public intereſt; not by coalition and mutual aſſiſtance to ſtrengthen the hands of Government, but by cabals, jealouſy, and mutual diſtruſt, to thwart each others deſigns, and ſo circumvent each other, in order to obtain power and pre-eminence. I have been no leſs careful to ob-ſerve the effects of popularity, where it has been courted and gained for particular purpoſes; but when every engagement was abandoned which led to its attainment, when the keeping of them become no longer neceſſary to the views of ſelf-intereſt and ambition, I am threatened! I dare the authors of thoſe threats to put any one of them in execution. I am ready to meet their charges, and am prepared for the event; either to cover my adverſaries with ſhame and diſgrace, or in the fall, riſque the remnant of a life nearly drawing to an end, and con-ſequently not worth being ſolicitous about.

Lord Mansfield, Feb. 7, 1775.

I **EVER** eſteemed the India alliances, at beſt, a neceſſary evil. I ever believed their ſervices to be overvalued; ſometimes inſignificant, often barbarous, always capricious; and that the

O 2   employ-

employment of them was only juftifiable, when, by being united to a regular army, they could be kept under controul, and made fubfervient to a general fyftem.

Upon this principle I heartily concurred with that gallant and humane General, Sir Guy Carleton, in the year 1776, to decline the offers and folicitations of the Indians to be then employed feparately: the impoffibility of compleating the preparations for paffing the regular troops over the Lakes, made it impoffible to employ them conjunctively.

In that year, Sir, it was my lot, by delegation from Sir Guy Carleton, who was then at Quebec, to prefide at one of the greateft councils with the Indians that had been held at Mont-real: many Gentleman here knew, that the ceremony pre-ceding the taking up the hatchet, is, to offer to the reprefen-tative of the power they mean to ferve the pipe of war. It was preffed upon me by the Chiefs prefent; and it was in my power, by a fingle whif of tobacco, to have given flame and explofion to a dozen nations. I never felt greater fatisfaction than in being able to fulfil the inftructions I was charged with, for reftraining the impetuous paffions of thefe people: it was a fecondary fatisfaction, at my return to England in the winter, to juftify the conduct of Sir Guy Carleton in this refpect; though the juftification was very unpopular, amongft thofe— I mean not to particularize Minifters, or Minifters of Minifters —but amongft thofe men, who in their zeal againft the Colo-nifts, had adopted the reafoning, that " *partial feverity was* " *general mercy,*" provided by carrying terrors it conduced to finifhing the war. How juft foever this principle may be, my mind is not of a texture for carrying it into effect; and I re-turned into Canada the following fpring, when I fucceeded to the command, determined to be the *foldier*, not the *executioner* of the State.

I found care had been already taken by General Carleton, upon the fame principles of humanity which always direct his conduct, to officer the Indians with Gentlemen felected from the

the Britiſh troops, upon a diſtinction of their temper and judgment, as well as upon that of their valour, and in much greater
number than ever was deſtined to that ſervice before. To theſe
precautions I added that of a favourite prieſt, who had more
controul over the paſſions of the Indians than all their Chiefs
put together ; and I truſt the expence put upon Government
to engage that Gentleman's aſſiſtance through the courſe of the
campaign, will not be eſteemed an improper article in my
accounts.   —

Sir, with theſe aſſurances, I was able to enforce obedience to
the injunctions of my ſpeech at the great council, upon aſſem-
bling the army, which has been made public. Barbarity was
prevented ; ſo much ſo, that in one inſtance, two wounded
provincial Officers were brought off in the midſt of fire, upon
the backs of Indians ; and a Captain and his whole detachment,
placed in ambuſcade, were brought priſoners to my camp by
Indians, without a man hurt : though it is evident they were
placed for the ſpecial purpoſe of deſtroying me, upon a recon-
noitering party, and I was at that time very popular with the
Indians.

I could produce many more inſtances of the kind, to ſhew
that every poſſible exertion of humanity was uſed ; and that
the caſe of Miſs *Mecree* excepted, which was accident, not
premeditated cruelty. My deſign was to excite obedience, firſt
by encouragement, and next by the *dread*, not the *commiſſion* of
ſeverity ;—" *to ſpeak daggers, but uſe none.*"

General Burgoyne, May 26, 1778.

THE Honourable Gentleman (Alderman Sawbridge) has
attacked me, on my activity to require reverſions and emoluments. In anſwer to this, it is a very natural thing for people
without doors, and people who do not inquire into the truth of
aſſertions thrown out in Parliament, to be led away with an idea
that the attacks made upon me on that ſcore are well founded.
Let Gentlemen, however, as I have been called upon to ſpeak

O 3   to

to the charge, only fee the fmall degree of truth that belongs
to it. I have been in a moft laborious and very expenfive office
for twelve years, without afking for a fingle emolument, either
for myfelf or my family : the laft year his Majefty was gracioufly
pleafed to fend for me, and prefent me with the place I now
hold, the Wardenfhip of the Cinque Ports. I accepted it, but
it is well known, that I refufed to accept it with the lucrative
falary which the Noble Perfon who held it before me received
for it ; the falary which I receive, and exprefsly at my own defire receive, is that lower falary which had been paid previous
to the office having been beftowed on my predeceffor. I really
do not know what the income of it is exactly, becaufe I have
not inquired what it is, but I believe it to be about a thoufand
a year. I have, however, told his Majefty that I am ready to
refign it, whenever I am called upon for that purpofe ; and that
readinefs I fhall continue to adhere to. Another charge too
of rapacioufnefs, which has been mentioned on a former occafion, is, that I have procured a reverfionfhip, for the lives of
two of my fons, in the Cuftoms. The charge is not true
that I fought the reverfionfhip, though it is true that I accepted
it. Let Gentlemen confider this reverfionfhip, it is the very
fame that had been given to Mr. Pelham on his firft coming
into government, and being appointed to the very office which
I now hold. It will be worth a thoufand a year, and is granted
on the lives of two of my younger fons. The third benefit my
family has received, is a place which lately fell vacant, in the
gift of the Treafury, and is of fo trifling a value, that feveral
of my predeceffors in office have thought it beneath the accept-
ance of any part of their family ; becaufe they looked much
higher, and to far greater emoluments. The place is worth
500 l. a year, and as I thought it fufficient for my fon, he has,
with the confent of my brethren at the Board, been appointed
to it. This is all the benefit that I and my family have reaped,
in confequence of my holding the office I now poffefs. I repeat it, that I have not afked for, or fought after, any one of
my

my employments. I am ready to refign the Wardenfhip of the
Cinque Ports; and when I go out of office, (which I affure
the Honourable Gentleman I am and long have been as defirous
of quitting, as he can poffibly be of having me difmiffed) after
my twelve years laborious fervice, my family will reft in pof--
feffion of fifteen hundred a year. This, every Gentleman muft
know, however greater the merits of my predeceffors in office
may have been (and that they were much greater, no man is
more ready to allow than myfelf) is infinitely and out of all
comparifon lefs than any one of them have received. I truft
Gentlemen will not think I have fhewn a very avaricious difpofition, or have been eager to grafp at reverfions or emoluments, as has been fo often afferted, when it is recollected,
that the whole I am poffeffed of is fifteen hundred pounds a
year for my children, and that mine is a pretty numerous
family. [At thefe words his Lordfhip ftruck his breaft, and
burft into a flood of tears, from the cafual recollection that one
of his fons lay dead at that moment. The Houfe touched at
the circumftance, called for the queftion, but his Lordfhip
recovering himfelf defired leave to go on.] No part of my conduct, while I have been in office, warrants the charge of
avarice: naked I came into the world, and naked I fhall go
out of the world: I was not a rich man when I was appointed
Chancellor of the Exchequer, nor fhall I go out of office a
rich man: and I defy any one to prove, that I have, in the
fmalleft inftance, acted with a view to aggrandize myfelf, or
any one that belongs to me; or that enriching myfelf, or thofe
that belong to me, has ever been my favourite object.

, *Lord North, June* 21, 1779.

A MINISTER ought not to be a Minifter, after he is fufpected; he fhould be like *Cæfar*'s wife, not only free from
guilt, but even from fufpicion. If the Houfe fhould withdraw
their confidence from me, it would be my duty, without waiting for an Addrefs for my removal, to wait upon my Sovereign,

O 4 and

and delivering up to him the Seal of my office, fay—" Sir, I
" have long ferved you with diligence, with zeal, and with
" fidelity, but fuccefs has not crowned my endeavours: your
" Parliament have withdrawn from me their confidence, and
" all my declarations to them are fufpected; therefore, Sir, let
" me refign to you thofe employments, which I ought not to
" keep longer than I can be ferviceable to your Majefty and
" your fubjects; and beg you will beftow them upon fome
" other, who, with greater fuccefs, though not with greater
" zeal or fidelity, may give more fatisfaction to your Majefty
" and your Parliament."

Lord North, Feb. 27, 1782.

I AM forry to differ in many points from my Honourable
Friend who fpoke laft, who undoubtedly may be faid to be independent, as far as a perfon ftanding fingular in his opinion
is independent of every perfon who has argued on either fide
of the queftion.   My Honourable Friend has conceived that a
Right Honourable Gentleman on the floor (Mr. Fox) intends
to cram the India Bill, under another name, down the throats
of the Houfe of Lords.   The Honourable Gentleman is miftaken in calling him the Right Honourable Secretary, for forry
I am to fay, that to the misfortune of this country, it is a
name which no longer belongs to him.   But I will call him
by a name which I truft will ever belong to him, a name
which it is my pride to boaft of fince I knew him beft; I will
henceforth call him by the name of my Right Honourable
Friend! by that word I mean in future to defcribe him, and I
hope that by that name he will be in future known in the
Houfe.   Our intimate connection was founded in principles of
honour; when the great points on which we differed were no
more, we thought we might act together with cordiality and
without inconfiftency.   We were not miftaken; we tried the
experiment and it fucceeded; no meannefs, no difhonour, no
jealoufy difcovered itfelf; all was inviolable adherence to
                                                        honour

honour and good faith on one part; all was confidence on the
other. No mean conceffions were made on either fide. I
appeal to my Right Honourable Friend, if ever I facrificed any
one opinion which I formerly ferioufly held upon principle,
unlefs where reafon and argument might have pointed out the
propriety of it : and in juftice to my Right Honourable Friend I
muft declare, that he never facrificed to me any principle
which he ever held when in oppofition to my government.
The neceffity of the State called for that Coalition, which has
been fo often called a curfed Coalition; nay, the very circumftances of the prefent day demonftrate that neceffity; for
where could an Adminiftration be formed without a Coalition?
There were at prefent but two Cabinet Minifters; and if
Coalition was a curfed thing, then this Miniftry of two men
is a curfed Miniftry, for it is formed in a Coalition of two perfons who differed formerly on effential points. The difference, however, of the two Coalitions is this: The Coalition
between my Right Honourable Friend and myfelf, was a Coalition of whole parties blended into one, for the purpofe of
forming a ftable and permanent Government : whereas the
Coalition between the prefent Firft Lord of the Treafury and
the Lord Prefident [Earl Gower] is a Coalition of fhreds, of
ends and remnants ; a Coalition of fmall parts of parties, but
not of the parties themfelves. Why then is it the fafhion to
call the one a curfed Coalition, and yet take no notice of the
other ? I cannot tell, unlefs it is that one is fufficiently ftrong
to form a ftrong Government, while the former cannot mufter
more as yet than two Cabinet Minifters. The experience of
time has juftified the Coalition, and' rendered it a bleffing to
the country. When Parliament put an end to my Adminiftration by the Addrefs againft the American war, it was fucceeded
by another which appeared to be ftrong ; but it carried in its
own bofom the feeds of its own weaknefs, in the difunion
which appeared in feveral parts of it ; which foon fhewed itfelf
by their fplitting afunder, and a feceffion of a part of it from
the

the Cabinet: the next Adminiftration was but weak, becaufe it was ill connected; and it had loft the fupport of thofe who formerly acted with it: the members of it therefore fell off one after another, till lofing the confidence of the Houfe, the poor remnant of it was obliged to yield to the voice of Parliament and retire. From this experience it appeared neceffary, for the good of the State, that a permanent Government fhould be formed, and it was clear that it could not poffibly be formed; unlefs a Coalition fhould take place among thofe, who though once enemies upon points which could no longer come into debate, might act together very cordially in every other refpect: fuch a Coalition was formed; but then it was charged with having feized upon Government: this is indeed a charge that I do not underftand, for the public waited for fix weeks for a Miniftry; and every means were tried for a new one, without the affiftance of the Coalition; but failing in every atempt, the Minifters all quitted the Cabinet before the Coalition were fent for. The Cabinet was then empty; fo that if we feized upon it, it was by marching in after the garrifon which ought to have defended it had fled; and who as they were going out, cried, " What a terrible curfed thing " is this Coalition, that is driving us from our fituations." But if we became poffeffed of Government, we are at worft charged with having carried it by ftorm, bravely, in the face of the enemy, not by fap; we carried on our advances regularly and above ground, in view of the foe; not by mining in the dark, and blowing up the fort before the garrifon knew there was an intention to attack it. It has been faid on a former day, that a ftarling ought to be brought, placed in this Houfe, and taught to fpeak the words, " Coalition! Coalition! curfed " Coalition!" Now, for my part, I think, that while there is in this Houfe an Honourable Gentleman who never fails, let what will be the fubject of debate, to take an opportunity to curfe the Coalition, I think there will be no occafion for the ftarling: and while he continues to fpeak by rote, and without

any

any fixed idea, I think what he fays will make juft as much impreflion as if the ftarling himfelf was to utter his words. [Here the Houfe could fcarcely give the Noble Lord an opportunity to proceed, they fell into fo violent a fit of laughter.] As to the Coalition, and the abufe which was fo often thrown upon it, they always bring to my mind two perfons for whom I felt no inconfiderable fhare of concern; thefe were two men who were fhut up in the Eddyftone Light-houfe to mind the fire. They were both of different principles, and therefore though they were fhut in from all intercourfe with the reft of mankind, and though they might by their converfation have amufed one another, yet they never exchanged a word with each other for fix weeks; and they had rather let the fire go out, and fee all the navy of England dafhed to pieces under them, than that one fhould confent to give up the moft trivial point to the other.—[Here the Houfe was a confiderable time in another fit of laughter.] The enemies of the Coalition would have had my Honourable Friend and me refemble the two men in the Light-houfe; but we have acted more wifely for the public good; we confidered the fafety of the public our principal care and duty; and in order to fave the fhip of State from running afhore or dafhing againft the rocks, we all agreed, at all events, that the fire in the Light-houfe fhould not be extinguifhed; but that let who would ftir it, it was to be kept in: thus what fome affected to call a curfe, was in reality a blefling to the nation. I will not charge the Right Honourable Gentleman at prefent at the head of his Majefty's affairs with being an enemy to Coalitions; on the contrary he likes them fo well, that he has formed one himfelf with the Noble Lord who fits with him in the Cabinet. The Right Honourable Gentleman has endeavoured to imitate our Coalition, but he has bungled the bufinefs; for, as I faid before, he has coalefced with the remnant of parties, and not with the parties themfelves: therefore I may apply to them the expeffion of tho Roman Orator, *Placuiffe, fed non tetigiffe.* But to return from

my

my digreffion, my Honourable Friend behind me (Governor
Johnftone) fays, that my Right Honourable Friend means to
cram down the throats of the Houfe of Lords, a Bill which
they had already rejeƈted : but furely he cannot be in earneft,
for he knows my Right Honourable Friend is no longer in a
fituation to cram any thing down their throats ; and the Honourable Member over the way (Mr. Banks) fays, that a Bill
totally different from that which was rejeƈted, in as much as it
is free from all thofe objeƈtions which are faid to have made fo
many enemies to the Bill that is loft, is to be prefented by the
new Minifter : and therefore as one perfon has it not in his
power to prefent the fame Bill again, and another perfon will
prefent a totally different one, there is no danger that the old
Bill will be crammed down the throats of the Houfe of Lords ;
and confequently there is no danger that the event fhould take
place, which in my Honourable Friend's opinion, would juftify
a diffolution of the prefent Parliament. My Honourable Friend
has been miftaken in another point: he fays, that my Right
Honourable Friend faid, before he refigned, that he would
bring in again the fame Bill. This is, indeed, a capital miftake ; for my Right Honourable Friend did not refign, he was
turned out ; I was turned out ; we were all turned out : not
the merit of having voted againft the Bill, could preferve the
Lord Prefident of the Council from the mortification of being
turned out with all his friends. As to the affurances given to
the Committee on the part of the Right Honourable Gentleman now at the head of his Majefty's affairs, that no diffolution
or prorogation will take place through his advice, I am very
well inclined to fay, that in his honour and integrity I have a
great reliance ; but what fecurity can he give that fecret influence in Lords of the Bedchamber will not defeat his intentions, and produce a diffolution not only without his advice
but even contrary to it ?—I value highly the charaƈter of that
Right Honourable Gentleman ; and though he is my political
enemy, ftill I always feel myfelf difpofed to treat him with more
                                                    refpeƈt

refpe&t than I ever experienced from him : but highly as I value
that chara&ter, I cannot truft to it upon the prefent occafion,
becaufe the events to which that chara&ter is pledged, may not
be within the controul of the Right Honourable Member. At
prefent there are only two Minifters in the Cabinet ; but when
the number is compleated, who can anfwer to the Houfe of
Commons that a diffolution may not be propofed in the Cabinet, the Right Honourable Gentleman out-voted, and the
queftion carried ? This is upon the fuppofition that the event
will depend upon the Cabinet; but the difficulty will be ftill
greater, if the Committee will refle&t on the power of fecret
influence, which can put an end to the ftrongeft Adminiftration, as has been experienced within thefe few days. I therefore muft declare, that as the Addrefs is couched in the
ftrongeft terms of refpe&t, duty, affe&tion and loyalty to his
Majefty, I think it ought to be carried, as the only effe&tual
means of preventing thofe calamities which would flow from
a diffolution of Parliament in the prefent critical fituation of
affairs.

Lord North, Dec. 22, 1783.

THE laft Houfe of Commons a&ted contrary to the opinion
of thofe whom they reprefented, and attempted to fubvert the
Conftitution, by an infra&tion of Charters, which, if effe&t-
ed, would at once have convulfed the empire, and thrown every
thing into anarchy and confufion. But his Majefty, like a
parent, anxious for the fafety and profperity of his children,
has liftened to the voice of his people, and exercifed his undoubted Prerogative by a diffolution of Parliament. This
meafure immediately overturns the dangerous plans of an abandoned fa&tion, who have already ftretched their power to an
alarming length, and panted for univerfal dominion. They
attempted to feize on the effe&ts, trade, and territory of the
Eaft-India Company, whofe Charter had always been confider-

5   ed

ed as fufficiently binding to anfwer the emergency of any time :
but his Majefty, befides difcomfiting the dark manœuvres of
thofe enemies of the Conftitution, has made an excellent choice
of another Miniftry, whofe zeal and patriotifm juftifies the prudence of his meafures, and proves how dearly he has the intereft of his people at heart. I cannot but prefage the happieft
effects from the late diffolution of Parliament ; and flatter myfelf, that the new Houfe of Commons will gratify the wifhes of
the people. In the prefent Minifter, the fondeft hopes of the
people are repofed ; he is a perfon whofe character merits public patronage—he has confecrated that period of early life,
which by others has been commonly fquandered away in idle
frolic, in youthful diffipation, to profitable ftudy, and to the
fervice of his country.—He is not one of thofe characters, who,
having diffipated their fortune, ruined their conftitution, and
proftituted their powers, have entered thefe walls for the purpofe of political traffic, for the purpofe of repairing their finances, or from motives of ambition and aggrandifement. He
has not come to offer the dregs of his being to the fervice of
his country ; he has confecrated to it the firft-fruits of exiftence.
There is therefore every thing in his character to conciliate the
confidence of the people ; notwithftanding the calumnies which
have been raifed and propagated againft him, this he has for-
tunately obtained. I congratulate the Houfe on the event. It
is a prefage aufpicious to the interefts of the country, as it tends
to enfure the prefervation and continuance of their privileges,
which have been attempted to be violated. My Right Honourable Friend has been accufed of being the champion of one
branch of the Legiflature, in oppofition to the other ; of the
ariftocratical influence of the kingdom, in oppofition to the
interefts of the Houfe of Commons ; but the nation knows,
that thefe affertions are unfounded. My Right Honourable
Friend is not the champion of the Houfe of Peers ; he is not
the champion of the Prerogative ; he is not the champion of

the Houſe of Commons, but the CHAMPION of the CON-
STITUTION!

Mr. Hamilton, May 24, 1784.

MANY of thoſe connected with Adminiſtration, are perpetually holding out the idea that I have been the cauſe of all the
calamities of the country by promoting the American war.
Sir, I deny that to be true; I found the American war when
I came into Adminiſtration; I did not create it, it was the
war of the country, and approved of by the people at large.
Sir, had Parliament been reformed, they would not have ex-
preſſed more clearly than the unreformed Parliament did, the
opinion of their conſtituents on that ſubject. But, Sir, I deſire once for all, that Gentlemen will deſiſt from thoſe unfounded aſſertions, that I was the author of thoſe calamities.
If they are of that opinion, let them come forward with a
charge; I am ready to meet it; I call for it; nay, Sir, I demand it as a right. Sir, there can be no reaſon for withhold-
ing it now. If I was protected before, I am not protected now.
Sir, the Miniſter has every thing that can enable him to carry
on the proſecution againſt me; he has a Houſe of Commons to
accuſe, he has a Houſe of Lords to judge; he is maſter of all
the written evidence againſt me. And as to parole teſtimony,
thoſe who were my friends, thoſe who were in my ſecrets,
thoſe whom I received into my utmoſt confidence, from whom
I concealed nothing, are now the friends of the Right Honourable Gentleman, Sir; and I dare ſay their love of juſtice and
regard for the public, will make them fit and uſeful witneſſes
upon ſuch an occaſion. Yet, Sir, with all theſe advantages
on the part of the Miniſter, of accuſer, judge, written and
parole teſtimony, I do not ſhrink from, but court the inquiry:
but this I muſt inſiſt upon, that if the matter is not inquired
into, it ſhall not be argued upon as if proved.

Lord North, June 17, 1784.

THE

.The conduct of the Chancellor of the Exchequer has been attacked without any reason whatsoever; for that Gentleman has acted with the greatest candour respecting the new Taxes. The complaints of the poorest individual have been listened to with the utmost attention and tenderness; and at present there is without doors a deputation from the Hatters, whose case has been attended to with the same regard as that of the first Peer in the land. The Right Honourable Chancellor of the Exchequer has conducted himself with great philanthropy and candour; for he has, with a liberality which will ever do him honour, relinquished the Tax upon Coals, because he found that it was particularly obnoxious to the People. Considering these facts, therefore, it can hardly be insinuated, in the most distant manner, that the complaints of the People have not been attended to: and to my knowledge there are many others, whose cases are at present in contemplation. It must be evident to every Gentleman of this House, that the exigencies of the State must be provided for; and I imagine, that all will confess, the Right Honourable Gentleman alluded to has acted with great caution and circumspection in respect to the new Taxes; and has discharged the trust reposed in him with fidelity to his Sovereign and his Country. There are several other Taxes, besides that on coals, which, I could inform the House, he intends to abandon, and substitute other Duties in their place, equally productive, I hope, but more consonant to the disposition of the People. The propriety, however, of the alterations alluded to, will, on a future day, come before the House, when Gentlemen may assent or object to the measures; but I assure the House, that it is the intention of the present Administration, to conduct themselves with that propriety and decorum which will put malevolence at defiance; and while they discharge their duty with honour and fidelity to their country, they will at the same time take care, that their operations and resolutions will give vigour and energy to their measures.   *Mr. Rose, July* 15, 1784.

WITH

WITH refpect to the fatal confequences to be expected from
the increafe of Indian wealth and influence in this Houfe, and
in this Country, I will quickly remove the apprehenfions of
the Houfe and the Public, by oppofing a few fimple facts to
unmeaning and unfounded affertions. Much has been faid of
the influence of Mr. Haftings in this Houfe and in this nation.
I folemnly deny the fact, if it is meant to convey an infinuation of corrupt or improper influence: Mr. Haftings is as un-
connected with the prefent as with the late Minifters. All I
afk on the part of Mr. Haftings is juftice, and I want neither
favour nor protection from any man. Much alfo has been
faid of the influence of Eaft-Indians in general in this Houfe.
On a former occafion I partly refuted a calumny of this kind,
by the beft poffible mode, by an appeal to facts. I now hold
in my hand a paper which contains an exact lift of all the civil
fervants of the Company, appointed to Bengal in the laft
twenty-two years; and I hope that, with the remarks, will be
received as part of my fpeech. They are in number five hundred and eight—of thefe, thirty-feven only have returned to
England; one hundred and fifty are dead, and three hundred
and twenty-one now, I hope, are alive there. Every Gentleman knows that Bengal is the place for acquiring fortunes;
and if the Houfe will perufe the whole of this paper, calmly
and coolly, they will be convinced that there is not the fmalleft
foundation to apprehend thofe dreadful confequences which
the Right Honourable Gentleman dreads, from the vaft wealth
and influence of Mr. Haftings, and other Eaft-India Gentlemen.—I fhall beg the affiftance of the Honourable Gentleman,
[Mr. Francis, who nodded affent] to refute the ridiculous
ftories that are propagated. I know that they have not the
fmalleft foundation in truth. The following paper is authentic.

A Lift of the Gentlemen appointed in the Civil Service of the Eaft-India Company in Bengal, from 1762 to 1784; fpecifying the number that have returned to England, who died in the country, or are now refident there.

Number appointed.	Year.	Returned home.	In Bengal.	Dead.
28	1762	7	4	17
14	1763	5	5	4
16	1764	3	6	7
34	1765	5	8	21
20	1766	3	5	12
3	1767	1	—	2
35	1768	5	16	14
48	1769	5	22	22
24	1770	—	14	10
33	1771	3	17	13
41	1772	—	26	15
16	1773-4	—	14	2
28	1775	—	24	4
5	1776	—	3	2
22	1777	—	20	2
24	1778	—	22	2
25	1779	1	23	1
26	1780	—	26	—
28	1781.	—	28	—
1	1782	—	1	—
35	1783	—	35	—
508		37	321	150

Names

Names of the Gentlemen who have been appointed to Bengal in the two and twenty years, and have returned to England.

John Bathoe	Robert Colville
Ifaac Sage	William Benfley
Alexander Higginfon	John Shakefpear
B. G. Wright	Edward Parry
Edward Baber	L. Darell
Charles Gering	Richard Sumner
William Harwood	Frederick Stuart
Alexander Campbell	Charles Coxe
Evan Law	Edward Smith
Edward Golding	Richard Griffith
William Lufhington	J. P. Auriol
C. W. B. Roufe	J. Fydell
G. Ducarrell	J. Baugh
W. B. Martin	C. Fleetwood.
Thomas Hinchman	J. Cator
Gideon Johnftone	H. S. Chandler
Thomas Pattle	George Lucas
W. Thackray	Richard Fligham
John Hogarth	

There is not a more miftaken idea, than that which has been fo induftrioufly circulated and believed, of the rapid and enormous fortunes made by the Company's fervants in Bengal. This lift is warranted to be accurate, and it proves, that of five hundred and eight civil fervants, appointed in the laft twenty-two years, thirty-feven only have returned to this country; one hundred and fifty are gone from whence they can never return; and, according to every probable calculation, not thirty-feven of the three hundred and twenty-one now in Bengal, will return in the next ten years, with fortunes acquired in India: of the thirty-feven who have returned, not a

man

man has brought home an enormous fortune; many of them lefs than twenty thoufand pounds, fome of them not a fhilling; nor has one fortune, to my knowledge, been rapidly acquired; and of the whole number, two only are Members of this Houfe.

The fortunes that have been acquired by military Gentle-men, who have gone out, or been appointed Cadets or Officers in Bengal, in the laft twenty-two years, are ftill more incon-fiderable. In that time, above one thoufand two hundred Officers have been appointed in Bengal, but not thirty of the one thoufand two hundred have returned with any fortunes at all; and two, Captain Wathenton and myfelf, have the ho-nour to fit in this Houfe. Of this number, I know only five who have brought home above twenty thoufand pounds; and many have returned with lefs than five thoufand pounds. About thirty Officers have fince returned, being difabled by wounds or ill health, and have now a very bare fubfiftence from Lord Clive's military fund.

That large fortunes have been acquired in Bengal no man will doubt; but the time is long fince paft. At the firft re-volution, in 1756, upon the Englifh acquiring power in Ben-gal, and in confequence of the battle of Plaffey, fome very enormous fortunes were made.

Again, in the firft acquifition of the Duannee, when the entire government of a great kingdom devolved upon a very few Englifh Gentlemen, rapid and enormous fortunes were made by two or three of them; nor was it poffible it fhould be otherwife.

Our Commanders in Chief too, in thofe days, General Smith and Sir Robert Barker, acquired very large fortunes from the power and influence they enjoyed, by being conftantly at Allanabad with the King, or in the Vizier's country.

Again by the Treaty of 1775, with the prefent Vizier, the entire management of Oude fell (as Mr. Haftings foretold it would) into the hands of the refident at his Court. This

was

was naturally the fource of great influence, and great emolument, to two Englifh Gentlemen not yet returned to England.

It is a circumftance worthy of remark, that of all the civil
fervants that have gone out in the laft twelve years, that is,
fince Mr. Haftings became Governor, only one has returned,
and that Gentleman never profited fix-pence by his appointment; for he quitted Bengal either before it arrived, or a very
few months after, with an unblemifhed reputation. He returned with his relation Mr. Francis.

It is equally worthy of remark, that not a fingle Gentleman
who has been in the Governor-General's family, civil or military, has returned to England with any fortune, myfelf excepted; and I certainly did not acquire a fortune in Mr.
Haftings's family: I brought with me, or left behind me, about
feven thoufand pounds, being all that I acquired in fixteen
years.

If fuch is the ftate of fortunes acquired by Gentlemen appointed to Bengal for thefe laft two and twenty years, it will
be found upon inveftigation, that the fortunes acquired at Ma-
dras and Bombay, by Gentlemen of the fame ftanding, are
ftill more inconfiderable. They are fewer in number, and I
do not fuppofe that thirty Gentlemen, who went out in or near
1762, have returned to England from both Prefidencies. This,
however, is capable of proof; but as Bengal has been called
the garden of Eden, I confine myfelf to that fpot. Enormous
as were the fortunes acquired in Bengal at the battle of Plaffey, by which an empire was conquered for Great-Britain. And
at our acquifition of the Duannee, they did not amount to fo
much as was acquired by individuals here, by one of the Noble
Lord's Loans, during the late calamitous and unfortunate war.
I fhall be truly happy, if it fhould be my good fortune, by preferving that facred regard to truth, from which I have never
yet deviated, to remove from the minds of the Public thofe
prejudices that have been inftilled into them by the bold affertions of men, who have faid, and unfaid, juft as it anfwered

P 3   their

their political purpofes; and who, when they were in the pleni-
tude of power, never dared to do what they ought to have
done, if they really thought Mr. Haftings a delinquent; that
is, to have brought in a Bill for his removal, upon fome one
fpecific charge.   Inftead of this, what is it they did?—Their
leader accufed him of crimes, for which, if he had been guilty,
his life would have been too poor a facrifice; he then declared,
he meant nothing perfonal againft him; and in the end, this
Mr. Haftings, this notorious delinquent, was offered a full and
free pardon for all his offences, provided his friends would ta-
citly fubmit to fee the Company, his benefactors and prefervers,
deprived of their rights, and plundered of their property.

Major Scott, July 16, 1784.

ELOQUENCE.

I Believe moft Gentlemen, as well as myfelf, whofe expectations were raifed when the Hon. Gentleman (Sir Robert
Walpole) ftood up, have met with a very great difappointment.
That Gentleman, from whom we had reafon to expect fomething that would have been of weight in the prefent debate, has
not only told us, that we are to have no reafon for what we are
defired this day to agree to, but has given us very little hopes
of having, at any other time, that information, which one would
think a Britifh Parliament might expect. Are we to vote powerful fleets and numerous armies; are we to lay new and great
burthens on the people, and all this without being told any reafons for what we are defired to do ? What fatisfaction can we
give our conftituents, if they fhould afk us, why we have augmented our ftanding army, which muft always be dangerous to
the liberties of our country ? Why we have confented to the increafing the public charge, which is already heavier than the
people can bear ? Really to this moft material and reafonable
queftion, I know as yet of no other anfwer we can give, but
only that his Majefty has told us in his Speech, that there is a
war broke out in Europe, in which we have no manner of concern; and his Minifters have told us, that we ought to be afraid
of the armies and fleets raifed and fitted out by our neighbours,
becaufe they are under an abfolute neceffity of employing all
the armies they can raife, and all the fleets they can fit out, in
thofe parts of Europe which are moft remote from us. We
have zeal, Sir, I hope we have all a great deal of affection and
zeal for his Majefty's Perfon and Government; but do not let
us allow his Majefty's Minifters, or even his Majefty himfelf, to
expect fuch a blind zeal from his Parliament: it is inconfiftent
with the dignity of Parliament; and I am fure that Parliaments,
thirty or forty years ago, would hardly have been perfuaded

to

to have fhewn fo much complaifance to the Minifters of the Crown.

What has been obferved by fome Gentlemen, I own, Sir, weighs greatly with me. From the demand now before us we have reafon to conclude, that 13,000 men may be the number intended to be always kept up within this ifland, even in times of the greateft peace and tranquillity ; and that the augmentation now required, is done with a view only, that when fuch times fhall again come, thofe in the Adminiftration may have an opportunity to pretend great merit, in reducing the 13,000 men now propofed to be added. We all know what fears and jealoufies the people have entertained at the continuing this army, during the laft years of perfect peace and tranquillity both at home and abroad : and if that meafure fhould be again attempted when thofe days of peace return, every man muft then conclude, that the army is kept up, not for defending us againft our foreign enemies, but for the fafety of thofe who have rendered themfelves odious among the people, and for defending them againft the refentment of an injured and a plundered nation. If this fhould ever happen to be our unfortunate condition, the people will certainly make a ftruggle for the prefervation of their ancient conftitution. This will certainly be the cafe ; I know it muft be the cafe ; and when it is, I hope thofe who fhall bring us under fuch hard circumftances will find, that even this army of 13,000 will not be able to ftand againft the people of England. I have a great opinion of many Gentlemen who have commands in the army ; and if fuch a cafe fhould happen, while they have any command, I make no doubt but they would behave as their predeceffors did at the Revolution ; I dare fay, that moft of them would foon be found of the people's fide of the queftion.

If we are, Sir, to have any fhare in the war, the addition of 13,000 men is but a bauble ; and if we are to have no fhare, why fhould we bring any additional expence upon the people ? The Hon. Gentleman would not fay pofitively that we were engaged,

gaged, or not engaged, or that we were, or were not to be engaged, but that we might be engaged relatively and confequentially: and this refined quibbling, Sir, is, it feems, all the
fatisfaction, all the reafons he will vouchfafe to give Gentlemen,
for agreeing to the demand now made upon them. Is an Englifh Houfe of Commons to take this as a reafon for breaking in
upon their conftitution, and for loading their conftituents with
taxes ? Surely, Sir, let our condition be never fo bad, and I believe it is bad enough, if the advice of Parliament is wanted on
that occafion, if their affiftance be defired, they ought to have
a full information of the prefent circumftances of the nation,
and they ought to have fufficient reafons for the demand that is
made. But it feems we are, for the future, to have no other
reafon given us for complying with any demand that comes
from the Crown, but only becaufe it is afked: and if any Gentleman fcruples to take that as a fufficient reafon, he is, it feems,
always to be told, that his not agreeing readily to the demand,
will be looked upon as a want of refpect to the Crown: but,
for God's fake, let us have likewife fome regard to ourfelves
and to our fellow-fubjects, without which I am fure we have
no bufinefs here, nor can the nation ever reap any benefit from
our meeting in this place.

Mr. William Pulteney, Jan. 23, 1734:

GOVERNMENT, Sir, is an evil, which the perverfe nature of
fome has obliged all to fubmit to. Mankind, for the fake of
preferving their lives, and the fruits of their labour, againft the
invafions of the wicked and rapacious, have been obliged to
form themfelves into focieties, and to promife obedience to the
Civil Magiftrate: but that which was intended for protecting
the people of the fociety, is often made ufe of for their oppreffion; and inftead of being a bridle upon the inclinations of the
wicked, it often ferves to ftrengthen their hands, by tying up
thofe of the innocent. To prevent this fatal effect, many forts
of Governments have been invented by men, all of which may

be

be refolved into thefe three, to wit, the Monarchical, the Arifto-cratical, or the Democratical: for every form of Government muft either be a Monarchy, an Ariftocracy, or a Democracy; or it muft be a mixture of fome two of thefe, or of all the three.

By experience, Sir, it has been found, that when the fupreme Power is lodged either in a fole Monarch, or in a fet of Nobles, it often deviates into tyranny; and that when it is lodged in the people in general, there is no poffibility of preventing it from running into anarchy; and the next ftep which follows is commonly a Monarchical, or Ariftocratical Tyranny; efpecially if the people of the fociety be numerous, and their dominions extenfive. For this reafon, many various forts of mixtures have been contrived by Lawgivers: but of all the mixtures that ever were contrived, that of an equal mixture of the three is, I be-lieve, the beft and moft lafting. How our anceftors, the Ger-mans, hit upon this mixture; whether it proceeded from their experience, or from their natural fagacity, I fhall not pretend to determine; but it is certain, that from the earlieft accounts we have of them, this appears to have been the form of Govern-ment generally eftablifhed among them. The fupreme Power among them was always lodged in an Affembly of their King or General, their Nobles or Chiefs of Families, and their People or Soldiers in general. In this Affembly all matters of great im-portance were confidered and determined; the King and Nobles propofed and refolved, and the People confented or difapproved. The powers and privileges of thefe three branches of their Le-giflature, were not, perhaps, fo diftinctly afcertained as they are by the prefent form of our Conftitution; or if they were, no certain account of them has been handed down to us: but it is plain that the fame fpirit, upon which our prefent Conftitution is founded, was the prevailing fpirit in their form of Govern-ment; and this fpirit may be traced from the beginning of our hiftory to this very day.

The fpirit I mean, Sir, is, to have in our form of Government fuch an equal mixture of the Monarchical, Ariftocratical, and

Democra-

Democratical forms of Government, that each may prove a proper counterpoife to the other, in fuch a manner, as that all thefe three conftituent Powers may continue equal and independent. If they do, any one of them may, and always will, be a guard for our Conftitution and for our People, againft the violence and oppreffion of both, or either of the other two. If our King fhould refolve to make himfelf abfolute, or if he and his Minifters fhould begin to opprefs the People, both this and the other Houfe would certainly join together in oppofing fuch fchemes: if the other Houfe fhould begin to fet themfelves up as fovereign and arbitrary mafters of our Government, the King and this Houfe would certainly join againft them: and if this Houfe, as perhaps has been the cafe, fhould begin to fet ourfelves up as mafters, the King and the Houfe of Lords would as certainly join againft us, and probably, by means of a diffolution and new election, be able to prevent any fatal confequences. Again, if any two of thefe branches of our Legiflature fhould join together in any fcheme for oppreffing the People, they could not carry their fcheme effectually into execution without the concurrence of the third: but, on the contrary, that third branch of our Legiflature, with the affiftance of the People, would probably be able, not only to difappoint, but to punifh the authors of fuch a fcheme.

Therefore, Sir, while our Conftitution remains entire, while the three conftituent parts of our form of Government remain equal and independent, our People can never be oppreffed, nor can a barefaced arbitrary power ever be eftablifhed. From hence one may fee, that from our Conftitution, confidered in itfelf, without any undue influence, we can have nothing to apprehend; the only danger we are expofed to is, that of its diffolution: and for this reafon we ought to confider carefully, and guard watchfully againft all thofe methods by which it may be overturned. The only methods by which our Conftitution can be overturned, and confequently the only evils we have to guard againft is, left any one of the branches of our Legiflature fhould

get

get the abfolute direction of the other two; and left any one, by a diffolution or difcontinuance of the other two, fhould be able to affume to itfelf an abfolute and arbitrary power. As the power of calling, proroguing, and diffolving the Parliament is lodged intirely in the Crown; as the execution of our Laws is now more fully and extenfively lodged in the Crown, than it was by the ancient form of our Conftitution; and as his Majefty is provided with a very large revenue for life, I cannot think there is the leaft danger, that either Houfe of Parliament will become able to prefcribe to the other and to the King: therefore we are at prefent in no danger of either Houfe of Parliament ever getting the abfolute direction of the other two branches of our Legiflature, as was once the cafe of this nation.

But, Sir, that the Crown may be able to get the abfolute direction of both Houfes of Parliament, and may confequently make both intirely dependant upon the King, or rather upon the King's Minifters, for the time being, I muft think we are at prefent in fome danger: nay, I muft fay, I think we are in fuch danger, that I am afraid nothing preferves us from it but his Majefty's known wifdom, juftice, and moderation. I have, I confefs, fuch a bad opinion of mankind, that I believe the generality of them will facrifice the public good for their private advantage, often for a very trifling private advantage; efpecially when they can do it, without bringing immediately infamy and reproach upon themfelves. This, I am forry to fay it, is my opinion of the generality of mankind: and confidering what vaft fums of money, and what a vaft number of lucrative pofts and employments, of all forts and fizes, the Crown has to beftow yearly, and what extenfive powers have been put into the hands of the Crown, by the many Penal Laws lately enacted, I am much afraid, that if his Majefty would allow his Minifters to apply them towards managing and purchafing votes at elections, or even in Parliament, it would foon come to be in the power of the Crown to direct both Houfes of Parliament: for if the voting at elections, or in Parliament, from corrupt confiderations,

tions, fhould once come to be frequent, the frequency of the crime would extenuate the guilt, and the multitude of criminals would fmother that reproach, which now fo defervedly attends fuch an infamous practice.

Lord Noel Sometfet, Feb. 3, 1738.

I AM unable to offer any thing that has not been faid by the Honourable Gentleman (Mr. Lyttelton) who made you the Motion for an Addrefs of Congratulation to the King, on account of the nuptials of the Prince of Wales with the Princefs of Saxe-Gotha, in a manner much more fuitable to the dignity and importance of this great occafion. But, Sir, as I am really affected with the profpect of the bleffings to be derived to my country from this fo defirable, and fo long-defired meafure, the marriage of his Royal Highnefs the Prince of Wales, I cannot forbear troubling you with a few words, to exprefs my joy, and to mingle my humble offering, inconfiderable as it is, with this great oblation of thanks and congratulation to his Majefty.

How great foever the joy of the public may be, and very great it certainly is, in receiving this benefit from his Majefty, it muft be inferior to that high fatisfaction which he himfelf enjoys in beftowing it : and if I may be allowed to fuppofe, that to a royal mind any thing can tranfcend the pleafure of gratifying the impatient wifhes of a loyal people, it can only be the paternal delight of tenderly indulging the moft dutiful application, and moft humble requeft of a fubmiffive obedient fon. I mention, Sir, his Royal Highnefs's having afked a marriage; becaufe fomething is in juftice due to him, for having afked what we are fo ftrongly bound by all the ties of duty and of gratitude, to return to his Majefty our moft humble acknowledgments for having granted.

The marriage of a Prince of Wales, Sir, has at all times been a matter of the higheft importance to the public welfare, to prefent, and to future generations : but at no time has it

8   ever

ever been a more important, a more dear confideration, than
at this day; if a character at once amiable and refpectable,
can embellifh and even dignify the elevated rank of a Prince
of Wales. Were it not a fort of prefumption to follow fo
great a Perfon through his hours of retirement, to view
him in the milder light of domeftic life, we fhould find him
bufied in the noble exercife of humanity, benevolence, and of
every focial virtue. But, Sir, how pleafing, how captivating
foever fuch a fcene may be, yet, as it is a private one, I fear I
fhould offend the delicacy of that virtue I fo ardently defire to
do juftice to, fhould I offer it to the confideration of this Houfe.
But, Sir, filial duty to his Royal Parents, a generous love for
Liberty, and a juft reverence for the Britifh Conftitution,
thefe are public virtues, and cannot efcape the applaufe and
benedictions of the Public. They are virtues, Sir, which render his Royal Highnefs not only a notable ornament, but a firm
fupport, if any could poffibly be neceffary, of that Throne fo
greatly filled by his Royal Father.

I have been led to fay thus much of his Royal Highnefs's
character, becaufe it is the confideration of that character
which, above all things, enforces the juftice and goodnefs of
his Majefty in the meafure now before you; a meafure which
the nation thought could never come too foon, becaufe it brings
with it the promife of an additional ftrength to the Proteftant
fucceffion in his Majefty's illuftrious and Royal Houfe. The
fpirit of Liberty dictated that fucceffion, the fame fpirit now
rejoices in the profpect of its being perpetuated to the lateft
pofterity: it rejoices in the wife and happy choice, which his
Majefty has been pleafed to make of a Princefs fo amiably
diftinguifhed in herfelf, fo illuftrious in the merit of her family;
the glory of whofe great anceftor it is, to have facrificed himfelf to the nobleft caufe for which a Prince can draw his fword,
the caufe of Liberty and the Proteftant Religion. Such, Sir,
is the marriage, for which our moft humble acknowledgments
are due to his Majefty; and may it afford the comfort of feeing

5   the

the Royal Family (numerous as I thank God it is) still growing and rifing up in a third generation: a Family, Sir, which
I moft fincerely wifh may be as immortal as thofe Liberties and
that Conftitution which it came to maintain.

Mr. William Pitt, April 14, 1736.

THOUGH charity obliges us to believe, that all men are
fincere, till the contrary evidently appears; and though decency
often obliges us to avoid telling them they are not fo, yet one
cannot help a fufpicion arifing in one's breaft, when we find
Lords profeffing their readinefs to join in an inquiry, or in
exerting our birth-right of being the great Counfellors of the
Crown, and yet upon all occafions oppofing it; and in fupport
of their oppofition offering fuch arguments, as, if they were
admitted, would render it impoffible for this Houfe ever to inquire into the conduct of paft meafures, or offer any advice in
relation to future. The Noble Lord (Lord Ifla) fays, we
ought never to offer our advice in affairs relative to peace or
war; that is to fay, in any foreign affairs whatfoever, unlefs
called upon by the King to do fo. My Lords, I know nothing
elfe we can have occafion to offer our advice in, unlefs it be,
whether the King fhall go to the play or the opera, whether he
fhall fhew mercy to a thief, or order him to be hanged, or
fomething of equal importance; for in all domeftic affairs of
great importance, our King, thank God! is limited by the
laws, and ought not to tranfgrefs them, even though this Houfe
fhould advife him to do fo. And as to our being called upon,
we know from experience, that though this Houfe be the hereditary great Council of the Crown, yet our advice is very feldom afked in a ferious manner. Kings, my Lords, are generally for confulting with fuch as are of their own chufing, and
thefe are often fuch as have no dignity, privilege, or right, by
their birth. We know the greateft empire that ever was on
earth, was once governed by the fole advice of a freed flave; and
one of the greateft empires now in being, by the advice of a
.   Cabinet

Cabinet Council of Eunuchs, and fuch as they fhall chufe for their Privy Council; therefore, if we never offer our advice but when it is ferioufly afked by the Crown, I am afraid we fhall very feldom exert that privilege, which is our birthright.

How this Houfe has of late years come to be fo much fufpected of blabbing, I do not know; but it is *a very new doctrine* to fay, that nothing can be communicated to this Houfe, without making it public. The very firft inftance of our being refufed any papers we thought neceffary for our information, for fear it fhould thereby be made public, was in the year 1721 : fince that time, indeed, it has been commonly and frequently practifed; and yet whatever fecrets our Minifters may have had fince that time, I do not think the nation had ever any fewer in any equal period of time.

Earl of Chefterfield, Dec. 1, 1740.

I am forry to obferve, that it is now become a common topic of debate here, as well as in our converfation without doors, that public praife ought to be defpifed, and the opinion of the giddy multitude altogether difregarded. This, my Lords, is a moft terrible fymptom, if Mr. Addifon be right in his obfervation; for in one of his Spectators I remember he obferves, *We then only defpife commendation, when we ceafe to deferve it.* As I am acquainted with the Noble Lord (Lord Ifla) who fpoke laft, I am convinced he will never ceafe to deferve commendation; but I was really in pain, when I heard him endeavouring to perfuade your Lordfhips to defpife the opinions, the fufpicions, and the clamours of the people without doors : I fay I was in pain, left fome of thofe who are not acquainted with his Lordfhip, fhould think of this obfervation, which I am fure is very unjuft, when applied to him. The defire of fame, the defire of applaufe, is one of the moft exalted, and one of the moft ufeful affections of the human mind. It is fo clofely connected with our nature, that I believe no man can intirely

rid

rid himself of it; and therefore no man will pretend to defpife the reproaches or the fuspicions of his countrymen, but he that is confcious of their being juft. A man of fteady refolution will not allow himfelf to be carried away with every new opinion that prevails among the people, nor will he do what is wrong, in order to gain a popular applaufe; but furely he will not allow his character to lie under fufpicion amongft his countrymen, if he can by any means clear it up. The multitude may fometimes be artfully led into a wrong way of thinking, or they may be induced to clamour without reafon; but it is not the part of a good citizen to defpife that opinion, or that clamour; it is his duty to endeavour to fet the people right, and if the opinion or clamour be againft himfelf, for the fake of his own character, as well as in duty to the public, he ought to take the moft proper and the moft fpeedy method for his juftification.

This, my Lords, is the duty of every private man, and much more is it the duty of a Magiftrate or Minifter. Even in abfolute governments the Minifters ought to take all proper methods for gaining the affections and efteem of the people, and confequently for removing every fufpicion and clamour that may happen to arife againft them : but in a free government, this is not only the duty of the Minifters and Magiftrates, but they are under an abfolute neceffity to do fo, if they have a mind to continue in their office : for the diftinguifhing and fole fign of a people's being free, is that of their being governed by thofe laws and thofe men they approve of. If a law comes to be thought inconvenient or oppreffive, by the majority of a free people, it will be repealed; if a Magiftrate or Minifter comes to be hated or defpifed by the majority of a free people, he will be removed; and therefore, if in any country a law ftands unrepealed for fome time after it begins to be difapproved by a majority of the people, or if a Magiftrate or Minifter continues in office for fome time after he begins to be generally hated or defpifed, that government is not a free government, that People have no pretence to call themfelves a free people. For this reafon, I am furprized to hear it faid, that our Minifters defpife the clamours of the people, or that they do not defire your Lordfhips affiftance for allaying thofe clamours. My Lords, if they defpife thofe clamours, if they do not defire to take the moft proper and the moft fpeedy method for allaying them, which is by an impartial parliamentary inquiry, I will affirm they have, or at leaft they think they have, found out another method of governing, another method of preferving their power, than that which is the only method in a free country, I mean the efteem and affections of the generality of the people; and if they have any fuch thoughts, I hope they will foon find themfelves difappointed.

Earl of Halifax, Dec. 1, 1740.

I am not only againft fome particular Claufes of this Bill, but againft the whole contexture of it; and though, my Lords, Bills of this nature have been canvaffed in both Houfes by men of far greater abilities and experience than I can pretend to, yet I fhould think myfelf highly blameable, if I did not, as far as in me lies, oppofe a Bill which ftrikes directly at the root of the conftitution, and is an infringement both of the liberties of the people, and the prerogative of the Crown. In the fequel of what I fhall offer to your Lordfhips, I think, I can plainly make out this affertion; but fhould I be miftaken, my Lords, I will venture to fay, my head, not my heart, will be in fault.

To weigh the merits of this Bill, it will be neceffary to take it from its birth, confider its parents, and how and upon what occafions it has appeared. My Lords, this bleffed plant was fown by party and faction; it was nurfed by fury and difcontent; lofs of *Englifh* liberty was its fruit. It was the firft ftep by which *Oliver Cromwell*, and fome few others, mounted up above the liberty of mankind. It was framed to divide and deftroy the bulwark of our conftitution, the Parliament: and furely, my Lords, it would be very extraordinary, if Parliaments again

fhould

fhould cherifh this cankerworm, which fince its birth never has dared to appear, but when a diftempered air hovered round us, and, like fudden and intenfe darknefs, was the forerunner of a ftorm.

My Lords, the very preamble of this Bill fets up a ftandard of divifion between the Crown and the people; it declares their intereft feparate, and of confequence they muft draw feparately; which is a doctrine quite different from what I have been taught from my cradle. I am fure, it is a moft melancholy doctrine; for a State divided againft itfelf can never ftand long.

But, my Lords, to be more particular, let us confider (fhould this become an Act) what effect it would have, firft by excluding all but fome few of the moft important places from the Houfe of Commons, and afterwards by excluding the army.

Firft then, with regard to thofe places of importance which it does not exclude, and thofe leffer which it excludes, I fhall only beg leave of your Lordfhips to put a few queftions; if then we exclude all but thofe of the greateft truft, and where the very being of public affairs is centered, how fhall we in the next age find men capable of filling them? For by taking away the leffer, we take away the proper fteps to the greater: how are thofe who are young and inexperienced, to acquire a knowledge in bufinefs, fo as to be able to tranfact affairs, on the well or ill conducting of which depends the public good, or the mifery of this whole nation? My Lords, how fhall we find men fit for thefe important pofts? It is an undeniable fact, that bufinefs makes men of bufinefs; the greateft natural capacity a man was ever bleffed with, can never teach him the intricate road, form, and *routine* of public officers; practice muft do it, and practice alone. If then the means of practice be cut off, how muft young men arrive at this knowledge? It muft be by infpiration, or by one fingle way elfe, which is, by the great men of the prefent age turning School-mafters, keeping a fchool for foreign and domeftic politics. I am apprehenfive they will not eafily be induced to turn pedagogues; not to mention that they themfelves may not, perhaps, wifh to have the market overftocked. What then muft be the confequence? Young men of fortune and rank cannot accept of places, when by accepting them they are to be deemed unfit for ferving their country in Parliament, and to have the ignominious mark of flavery fet on them; and without accepting which, they cannot arrive at a knowledge of bufinefs fit to be trufted with the public affairs. What will be the effect? Men of no fortune, no rank in the State, who have firft drudged through the lower and mean offices, muft have thofe of the greateft truft and profit, as being the only perfons capable of filling them : and it is too much to be ·feared, that the complaifance of fuch (who owe all they poffefs to the Crown) will be boundlefs, and that the King will have bad Counfellors, and the nation be ill ferved.

My Lords, with regard to the Officers of the Army, I think the fame argument is ftill ftronger, as the misfortunes which will flow from it are of a more immediate and a more dangerous confequence, and the danger without remedy. This Bill will exclude all young men of fortune from the army, for the fame reafon it will from all civil employments. Your Gentry, your Nobility, deprived of all laudable ambitious views, will fink, like *Italians*, into a flothful idlenefs. But, my Lords, I muft beg leave to remind you of this nation's being faved from flavery, by having men of property in the army : for God's fake, do not let us ruin that great barrier of our liberty. It may be faid, we do not ftand in need of an army; we are an ifland, have a moft powerful fleet, fo that an army is both ufe-lefs and dangerous. I fhall not enter into all that may be faid in anfwer to that complicated affertion ; but only beg leave to put a cafe, and it is a cafe, as the affairs of *Europe* ftand, muft happen once in twenty years; and I hope our liberty will be upon a founder foundation than to be hazarded every twenty years : within that fpace of time, you muft, in all probability, raife a confiderable army, either to defend your own poffeffions, or preferve the balance of power in *Europe*; which are equally

and

and abfolutely neceffary. When this army has done what you raifed them for, you will think it neceffay likewife to difband them, and eafe yourfelf and the people of fo coftly a burden; but your Lordfhips, perhaps, will find the difbanding them more difficult than the raifing them. I am apt to believe, that a Vote of either Houfe, how rhetorically foever it may be expreffed, will not perfuade them it is for their intereft to lofe their bread, when by keeping together, you and all you have is entirely at their mercy: and, my Lords, at fuch a feafon, fhould a Prince, lefs a father of his people than his prefent Majefty, fhould a Prince of more ambition than honeft intentions, fill the Throne, it would be in his power, with fuch an army, to become as abfolute as the King of *France*. My Lords, by what I have offered to you, it plainly appears to me, that nothing can keep and confirm your liberties but having the Officers, at leaft, men of property, who have a ftake in the country, and whofe intereft is the fame with ours. It was by an army of hirelings, debtors, renegados, and fuch like, that *Rome* at laft fell a victim to the ambition of one man.

It may, perhaps, be faid in excufe for this Bill, that men of too fmall fortunes have employments and feats in Parliament; have you not an Act of Qualification? If that is not obferved, why will you imagine this will? I fhould think it would not; for tho' it is an extraordinary thing to fay fo, it would be contrary to the intereft of the Crown, contrary to the intereft of every particular, and contrary to the intereft of the nation in general. But if the fum limited in the Qualification Bill is not already fufficient, increafe it: that is the only way which will anfwer what is in vain expected from this Bill. But, my Lords, to conclude, what a compliment would it be to his Majefty, to fay, you are not fit to be trufted with what your anceftors have always hitherto enjoyed, the power of difpofing of places and judging of merit? We will, by a public Act, fhew we miftruft you: what a compliment will it be to thofe the people chufe, to fay, we will not truft your integrity, becaufe the people chufe you their Repre-

Q 3

fentatives ? Is this the means to endear a people to their Prince,
a Prince to his people, or mankind to one another ?

Lord Raymond, April 6, 1742.

I SHOULD imagine, my Lords, that when a King of the
Houfe of *Hanover* furveys his navies, reviews his troops, or
examines his revenue, beholds the fplendour of his Court, or
contemplates the extent of his dominions, he cannot but fometimes, however unwillingly, compare his prefent ftate with
that of his anceftors; and that when he gives audience to the
Ambaffadors of Princes, who, perhaps, never heard of *Hanover*,
and directs the payment of fums, dearly purchafed, and reflects,
as furely he fometimes will, that all thefe honours and riches,
this reverence from foreign powers, and his domeftic fplendour, are the gratuitous and voluntary gifts of the mighty
people of *Great-Britain*; he fhould find his heart overflowing
with unlimited gratitude, and fhould be ready to facrifice to the
happinefs of his benefactors, not only every petty intereft, or
accidental inclination, but even his repofe, his fafety, or his
life : that he fhould be ready to eafe them of every burthen
before they complained, and to aid them with all his power,
before they requefted his affiftance ; that he fhould confider his
Britifh kingdom a kind of nurfery for troops, to be employed
without harraffing his more valuable fubjects.

It might be at leaft hoped, my Lords, that the Princes of
the Houfe of *Hanover* might have the fame regard to this nation, as to Kings from whom they never received any benefit,
and whom they ought in reality always to have confidered as
enemies, yet even from fuch levy-money was not always required, or, if required, was not always received.

There was once a time, my Lords, before any of this race
wore the Crown of *Great-Britain*, when the great *French*
Monarch, Lewis XIV. being under a neceffity of hiring auxi-
liary troops, applied to the Duke of *Hanover*, as a Prince whofe
neceffities would naturally incline him to fet the lives of his

fubjects

fubjects at a cheap rate : the Duke, pleafed with an opportunity
of trafficking with fo wealthy a Monarch, readily promifed a
fupply of troops, and demanded levy-money to be paid him,
that he might be enabled to raife them; but *Hanoverian* reputation was not then raifed fo high, as that the *French* King
fhould truft him with his money. *Lewis* fufpected, and made
no fcruple of declaring his fufpicion, that the demand of levy-
money was only a pretence to obtain a fum which would never
afterwards be repaid, and for which no troops would be obtained ; and therefore with his ufual prudence infifted, that the
troops fhould firft march and then be paid. Thus for fome
time the Treaty was at a ftand ; but the King being equally
in want of men as the Duke of money, and perceiving, perhaps, that it was really impracticable for fo indigent a Prince
to raife troops without fome pecuniary affiftance, offered him
at length a fmall fum, which was gladly accepted, though
much below the original demand. The troops were engaged
in the fervice of *France* ; and the Duke of *Hanover* thought
himfelf happy, in being able to amufe himfelf at his leifure
with the rattle of the money.

Such, my Lords, were the conditions on which the troops of
Hanover were furnifhed in former times ; and furely what could
then be produced by the love of money, or the awe of a fuperior
power, might now be expected as the effect of gratitude and
kindnefs.

Earl of Sandwich, Feb. 1, 1742.

I KNOW not how fuccefsfully I may repeat affertions in this
Houfe, for which I have been formerly cenfured and committed to the Tower, and which few other Members have hitherto
maintained ; but I rife with confidence, that I fhall be at leaft
acknowledged to act confiftently with myfelf in feconding the
noble perfon, (Lord Somerfet) who has made the Motion now
before you, for addreffing his Majefty, not to engage thefe
kingdoms in a war for the prefervation of his foreign domi-

nions : and I am convinced, that many who differ from me in opinion, would be glad to boaft of refembling my fteadinefs of conduct.

But fteadinefs, Sir, is the effect only of integrity; he that fpeaks always what he thinks, and endeavours by diligent inquiry to think aright before he ventures to declare his fentiments; he that follows in his fearches no leader but reafon, nor expects any reward from them but the advantage of difcovering truth, and the pleafure of communicating it, will not eafily change his opinion; becaufe it will feldom be eafy to fhew, that he who has honeftly inquired after truth has failed to attain it.

For my part, I am neither afhamed nor afraid to affirm, that thirty years have made no change in any of my political opinions; I am now grown old in this Houfe, but that experience which is the confequence of age, has only confirmed the principles with which I entered it many years ago: time has verified the predictions which I formerly uttered, and I have feen my conjectures ripened into knowledge.

I fhould be therefore without excufe, if either terror could affright, or the hope of advantage allure me from the declaration of my opinions; opinions which I was not deterred from afferting, when the profpect of a longer life than I can now expect might have added to the temptations of ambition, or aggravated the terrors of poverty and difgrace; opinions, for which I would willingly have fuffered the fevereft cenfures, even when I had enforced them only in compliance with reafon, without the infallible certainty of experience.

Of truth it has always been obferved, Sir, that every day adds to its eftablifhment, and that falfhoods, however fpecious, however fupported by power, or eftablifhed by confederacies, are unable to ftand before the ftroke of time: againft the inconveniencies and vexations of long life may be fet the pleafure of difcovering truth, perhaps the only pleafure that age affords. Nor is it a flight fatisfaction to a man not utterly infatuated

or

or depraved, to find opportunities of rectifying his notions, and regulating his conduct by new lights.

But much greater is the happinefs of that man, to whom every day brings a new proof of the reafonablenefs of his for-mer determinations, and who finds, by the moft unerring tefts, that his life has been fpent in promoting doctrines beneficial to mankind. This, Sir, is the happinefs which I now enjoy, and for which thofe who never fhall attain it, muft look for an equivalent in lucrative employments, honorary titles, pompous equipages, and fplendid palaces.

Thefe, Sir, are the advantages which are to be gained by a feafonable variation of principles, and by a ready compliance with the prevailing fafhion of opinions; advantages, indeed, which I cannot envy when they are purchafed at fo high a price, but of which age and obfervation has too frequently fhewn me the unbounded influence; and to which I cannot deny, that I have afcribed the inftability of conduct and incon-fiftency of affertions, which I have difcovered in many men, whofe abilities I have no reafon to depreciate, and of whom I cannot believe they would eafily diftinguifh truth, were not falfhood recommended to them by the glittering ornaments of wealth and power.

If there are in this new Parliament any men devoted to their private intereft, and who prefer the gratification of their paf-fions, to the fafety and happinefs of their country; who can riot without remorfe in the plunder of their Conftituents; who can forget the anguifh of guilt in the noife of a feaft, the pomp of a drawing room, or the arms of a ftrumpet, and think expenfive wickednefs, and the gaieties of folly, equiva-lent to the fair fame of fidelity, and the peace of virtue, to them I fhall fpeak to no purpofe: for I am far from imagining any language in my power can gain thofe to truth, who have refigned their hearts to avarice or ambition, or to prevail upon men to change opinions, which they have indeed never believed, though they are hired to affert them. For there is a

degree

degree of wickednefs, which no reproof or argument can re-
claim, as there is a degree of ftupidity which no inftruction
can enlighten.

If my country, Sir, has been fo unfortunate as once more
to commit her intereft to thofe who propofe to themfelves no
advantage from their truft but that of felling it, I may, perhaps, fall once more under cenfure for declaring my opinion,
and be once more treated as a criminal for afferting what they
who punifh me cannot deny; for maintaining the inconfiftency
of *Hanoverian* maxims with the happinefs of this kingdom,
and for preferving the caution which was fo ftrongly inculcated
by the patriots that drew up the act of fettlement, and gave
the prefent Royal Family their title to the Throne.

Thefe men, Sir, whofe wifdom cannot be difputed, and
whofe zeal for his Majefty's fervice and family was equal to
their knowledge, thought it requifite to provide fome fecurity
againft the prejudices of birth and education. They were far
from imagining, that they were calling to the Throne a race
of beings exalted above the frailties of humanity, or exempted
by any peculiar privileges from error or from ignorance.

They knew that every man was habitually, if not naturally
fond of his own nation; and that he was inclined to enrich it
and defend it at the expence of another, even, perhaps, of that
to which he is indebted for much higher degrees of greatnefs,
wealth, and power; for every thing which makes one ftate of
life preferable to another, (and which, therefore, if reafon
could prevail over prejudice, and every action were regulated
by ftrict juftice) might claim more regard than that corner of
the earth in which he only happened to be born.

They knew, Sir, that confidence was not always returned,
that we muft willingly truft thofe whom we have longeft
known, and carefs thofe with moft fondnefs, whofe inclinations
we find by experience to correfpond with our own, without
regard to particular circumftances which may entitle others to
greater regard, or higher degrees of credit, or of kindnefs.

Againft

Againſt theſe prejudices, which their ſagacity enabled them to foreſee, their integrity incited them to ſecure to us, by proviſions which every man then thought equitable and wiſe, becauſe no man was then hired to eſpouſe a contrary opinion.

To obviate the diſpoſition which a foreign race of Princes might have to truſt their original ſubjects, it was enacted, That none of them ſhould be capable of any place of truſt or profit in theſe kingdoms. And to hinder our Monarchs from transferring the revenues of *Great-Britain* to Hanover, and enriching it with the commerce of our traders and the labours of our huſbandmen; from raiſing taxes to augment the ſplendour of a petty Court, and increaſing the garriſons of their mountains, by miſapplying that money which this nation ſhould raiſe for its own defence, it was provided, That the King of Great-Britain ſhould never return to his native dominions, but reſide always in this kingdom, without any other care than that of gaining the affections of his Britiſh ſubjects, preſerving their rights, and increaſing their power.

Mr. Shippen, Oct. 14, 1741.

ALL that can be ſaid, Sir, againſt forfeitures for treaſon, muſt proceed from miſtaking or miſrepreſenting the nature of puniſhments, and the ends for which they have been introduced into ſociety. Puniſhment is ſaid to be *malum paſſionis, quod infligitur ob malum actionis*; and therefore, in its own nature, it muſt be confined to the perſon of the criminal; for whoever pretends to inflict a puniſhment upon an innocent perſon, cannot properly be ſaid to puniſh: on the contrary, he deſerves to be puniſhed, becauſe in ſo doing he commits a crime, or a *malum actionis*, and for that reaſon ought to have a *malum actionis* inflicted upon him: however, there are many misfortunes, loſſes, and inconveniencies, which innocent men are ſubject to by the nature of things, and may be expoſed to by the laws of ſociety, for the preſervation and welfare of the ſociety. As there are many diſeaſes that deſcend from the parent to the child,

child, it is a misfortune for a child to be born of parents afflicted with such diseases: it is a misfortune for a child to be
born of parents that are poor and indigent; but these misfortunes are not to be called punishments, because they are, by the
nature of things, inflicted upon innocent persons. There are
others, as I have said, which innocent men may be exposed
to by the laws of society: such were the confinements which
leprous or unclean persons were exposed to by the Jewish law;
and such are those confinements which people are subjected to by
our law, who are infected, or under suspicion of being infected with the plague: such, likewise, are the misfortunes
which attend children who are born of slaves, in countries
where *slavery* is established: such were the incapacities of children born of *Plebeians*, in the ancient Roman Commonwealth,
who could not intermarry with the *Patricians*, nor be advanced
to any of the chief posts in the Government: and such are
the misfortunes attending children born in this country of parents who happen to be convicted of High-Treason; because,
by their attainder, they are divested of every thing that belonged to them; and therefore the children are in the same
state, as if they had been born of poor and indigent parents.
But none of these misfortunes can be said to be punishments,
nor were ever called so, by those who understand any thing of
the laws of nature or nations.

Both the learned *Grotius* and the learned *Puffendorff* are clear
upon this subject. The former, in treating of what he calls
the communication of punishments, in order to show, that an
innocent man ought not to be made to suffer for the crime of
the guilty, distinguishes between that damage or loss, which a
man may suffer directly, and that which he may suffer consequentially. A man suffers directly, he says, when any thing is
taken directly from him, which properly belonged to him; and
he suffers consequentially, when he loses what he has a conditional right to, by the failure of the condition upon which he
was to have it; and forfeitures he expresly mentions as a damage

or

or lofs of this laft fort; becaufe children have but a conditional right to their father's eftate, that is, provided the father dies poffeffed of it. For this reafon, that learned Gentleman fays, that forfeiture is no punifhment upon the children, but only a damage which they fuffer, not directly, but confequentially, by the crime of the father, which prevented the exifting of that condition upon which they were to have had his eftate; and after having thus diftinguifhed, he concludes, that no man who is perfectly innocent can be punifhed for the crime of any other man.

The learned *Puffendorff* again treats this fubject in the fame manner, and almoft in the very fame words. He diftinguifhes between a damage fuffered directly and confequentially. " The " firft is, fays he, when a man is deprived of that he has al- " ready a proper right to; the fecond, when that condition is " intercepted, without which he could not enjoy fuch a right. " Thus, when the eftate the parents were poffeffed of is for- " feited, the children alfo feel the lofs of it: but, however, " this is not à punifhment properly, with refpect to the chil- " dren, becaufe they cannot come to the inheritance of their " father's eftate, unlefs the father preferves it for them till he " dies; and therefore the confifcation, or forfeiture, only in- " tercepts the condition, without which, the children can have " no right to the father's eftate."

To the opinion of thefe two learned moderns, Sir, I fhall add the opinion of a very famous man among the ancients, I mean *Marcus Tullius Cicero*; who, in one of his letters to *Brutus*, approves of the forfeiture of *Lepidus*, and fays, it was as juft to reduce his children to a ftate of want and mifery, as it was in the Athenians to reduce the children of *Themiftocles* to that wretched ftate; to which he adds, that this was an ancient and general cuftom in all commonwealths: from whence, I think, I may infer, that the forfeiture of traitors was a law which prevailed among the *Romans*, long before the eftablifhment of their empire: and that this law was eftablifhed

among

among the Jews, even in King *David's* time, is evident from the ftory of *Mephibofheth* and his fervant *Ziba*; for from thence we find, that the eftate of Saul had been forfeited, but was reftored to *Mephibofheth*, for his father Jonathan's fake; and was again taken from him by a new forfeiture, on a falfe fuggeftion of *Ziba's*.

Having thus fhewn, Sir, that the forfeiture of a guilty father cannot be looked on as a punifhment upon the innocent children, it can no way be faid to be inconfiftent with religion, efpecially that precept delivered to the Jews, which forbids punifhing the father for the fon's iniquity, or the fon for the father's. That law was certainly meant againft fubjecting either the one or the other, directly to any lofs, damage, or inconvenience, for the crime of the other, and not againft that confequential damage which is brought upon the fon by the forfeiture of the father: and, as I have fhewn that forfeitures have been approved of by the moft learned Lawyers, both ancient and modern, and were eftablifhed in the *Jewifh*, *Grecian*, and *Roman Commonwealths*, no Gentleman can, I think, have the confidence to aver, that they were, or are, inconfiftent with natural juftice, or the liberties of a free People.

The next thing I am to fhew, Sir, is, that they are confonant to the laws of this kingdom, both ancient and modern. Here, indeed, I am at fome lofs what Gentlemen may mean by our ancient Laws; and therefore, that I may not be accufed of any neglect, I fhall go as far back as I can. I think I may be very fure, that no man can tell what our Laws were, or whether we had any, before the Romans came amongft us. If Gentlemen mean, by our ancient Laws, the Laws which prevailed amongft us whilft we were fubject to the *Romans*, then certainly the Law of Forfeiture for treafon was eftablifhed, becaufe it was then a part of the *Roman* Law. If we come to the Laws of the Saxons, and fay, that thefe were the ancient Laws of the kingdom, I think the point may be as pofitively determined in favour of Forfeitures; for that the feudal cuftoms prevailed

2   amongft

amongſt the *Saxons*, as well as among their other northern
neighbours, is, in my opinion, clear to a demonſtration : and it
is certain, that by the Feudal Law, the forfeiture of the eſtate
was the certain conſequence of any breach of fealty in the tenant
or vaſſal. If we refer to the fragments ſtill remaining of the
Saxon Laws that were eſtabliſhed in this kingdom, the point
will be as clear in my favour. It is very true, that from theſe
fragments it appears, that fines, or mulcts, were the puniſhments inflicted upon moſt crimes ; but ſtill there were ſome that
were puniſhable with death, or forfeiture of eſtate, and ſometimes with both. By a Law of King *Ina*'s it is expreſsly enacted, that whoever fights in the King's palace ſhall loſe his inheritance : *Hæreditatem perdat*, are the words of the Law. And,
by a Law of the famous King Alfred's, it is enacted in theſe
words, *Si quis vitæ Regis inſidietur, per ſe, vel per ultores mercede
conductos, vel ſervos ſuos, vita privetur & omnibus quæ poſſidit.*

Thus, Sir, it is evident, that the forfeitures were in uſe
amongſt the Saxons, and that they have been conſtantly in uſe
ſince the conqueſt, not only in treaſons, but in felonies, ſo far as
relates to goods and chattels, no man can deny ; therefore they
muſt be allowed to be conſonant to our laws, both modern and
ancient : and that they are not inconſiſtent with the freedom of
our Conſtitution, experience itſelf muſt bear witneſs ; for we
have hitherto preſerved our Conſtitution entire, and I doubt
much if we ſhould be able to do the ſame, ſhould forfeitures of
all kinds be aboliſhed : for it is certain, that nothing can be of
more dangerous conſequences to the liberties of a free people,
than frequent civil wars. The firſt civil war that happened
among the Romans, was that which they called the *Sociale Bel-
lum*, or the war begun by the ſeveral people and cities in Italy,
whom the Romans, that is to ſay, the citizens of Rome,
would not admit to an equal ſhare in the Government with
themſelves. How long did they preſerve their liberties after
the commencement of the civil war? Not much above ſixty
years ; for this war began about the year 660 after the building

ing of their city, which was their æra; and Auguſtus Cæſar, after the battle of *Actium*, was confirmed in the abſolute Government of that vaſt empire in the year 725 of the ſame æra. And even in this kingdom, a civil war has more than once put an end to the freedom of our Conſtitution; for the civil war between the Houſes of York and Lancaſter, eſtabliſhed what I may very properly call an abſolute Government in the perſon of Henry the VIIIth; and the civil war between Charles the Iſt and his Parliament, eſtabliſhed an abſolute Government in the perſon of *Oliver Cromwell.* It is true, as our Conſtitution is more perfect, and better contrived than that of the Roman ever was, it has hitherto always recovered itſelf; but conſidering the change in the manners of our People, if it ſhould hereafter be overturned by a civil war, I am afraid it will never recover: therefore there is nothing we ought to guard more cautiouſly againſt than a civil war. The execution of a traitor is a fleeting example which is ſoon forgot; but the misfortunes of his poſterity is a permanent example, which many have continually before their eyes: and as this permanent example certainly contributes to the preventing of civil wars, it muſt, in my opinion, contribute to the ſecurity of the happy Conſtitution we now live under.

Whether we ſhould ever allow the puniſhments which produce theſe permanent examples to be aboliſhed, is a queſtion, Sir, that I ſhall not take upon me to determine, nor is there any neceſſity for my giving my opinion upon it at preſent; but this I am very ſure of, that we ſhould not allow theſe puniſhments to be aboliſhed, during the life of either of the Pretender's ſons; becauſe while they live, there will always be too many amongſt us infected with an itch of rebellion; and all Politicians, as well as Lawyers agree, that the greater likelihood there is that a crime of any particular ſort will be committed, the more ſevere ought the puniſhment to be; for the terror of the puniſhment ought, if poſſible, to be made ſuperior to the itch of committing the crime; and as that itch,

or

or inclination, will be ftronger and more general during the lives of the Pretender's two fons, than we can fuppofe it to be afterwards, we muft have, during that period, more fevere punifhments upon treafon, than may be afterwards neceffary to be continued. I am therefore ftrongly in favour of the Bill, for preventing all correfpondence between his Majefty's fub-jects and the Pretender's fons.

Sir Dudley Ryder, Attorney-General, May 3, 1744.

THE Honourable Gentleman (Sir Dudley Ryder) who fpoke firft in the debate, and diftinguifhed himfelf fo greatly by his long and laboured fpeech, has laid down thefe two propofitions, upon which he has built his whole argument, *That this claufe is confiftent with natural juftice*; and, *that it is confiftent with our ancient and modern conftitution.* Yet, notwithftanding all that he has faid, I muft take the liberty to maintain the contrary.

As to natural juftice, no one principle can ftrike the mind of man more ftrongly, at the very firft view, than that the innocent ought not to fuffer for the guilty; and *that every man fhould fuffer only for his own fault.* Can there be a man fo abfurd in this, or any other affembly in the world, as to deny this propofition?—To deny this, is to violate the fundamental laws of all fo-ciety, to be ignorant of the true nature of punifhments, and of the only title men have to inflict any feverities upon each other.—The rights of mankind, in a ftate of nature, ftill fub-fift in a fociety; they ought to fubfift; they ought to be abridged in none, farther than is abfolutely neceffary for the prefervation of fociety. It is in vain, it is nonfenfe to fay, that the fafety of fociety can fubfift in, can be advanced or preferved only by the ruin of the innocent widow, of the harm-lefs infant, and of thoufands yet unborn.

How then does the learned Gentleman attempt to palliate the force of this principle? *He owns the principle, and he fays, if any man will convince him that this claufe can deprive any one innocent perfon, either of his natural or legal rights, he will be*

VOL. I.   R   *againft*

againſt it himſelf. But, ſays he, no man has a right to any pro-
perty, but by the laws of the ſociety under which he lives; and the
laws of his country give no right to the child till the death of the
parent. Sir, the Gentleman has made but two miſtakes in
this argument; but they are unluckily ſuch as overturn the
whole.—Fọr firſt, every man may learn from his own breaſt,
that by the laws of nature, all mankind ought to ſucceed to
their anceſtors; they are entitled to expect it by the order of
all things, and as a kind of retribution from their parents,
for their being the authors of their exiſtence, which, without
any inheritance, is a ſtate of the utmoſt wretchedneſs.—And
as to the laws of this country, the very law which we are now
about to repeal, has created this property in the child, and the
child is actually veſted in this right, by the very laws of the
ſociety in which we live. The fine reaſonings of *Puffendorff*, or
Grotius, have therefore nothing to do in this queſtion. The
Gentleman ſupports his argument by authorities, which, putting the caſe as it really ſtands, all rather make againſt him :
he applies the reaſonings of *Puffendorff* and *Grotius* upon any
other caſe to this caſe, which totally and fundamentally differs,
from that upon which they argued.

Cicero too is brought in to ſupport this cruel opinion : a letter
of his to *Brutus* is quoted upon us, in which he juſtifies the
ſevcrities uſed to *Lepidus* and his poſterity. But I dare venture
to ſay, there is not one Gentleman in this Houſe, who knows
any thing of *Cicero*, or of his writings, who does not know,
that this very letter, which is to be put upon us as an irreſiſtible
authority, is no authority at all; for it is generally, if not
univerſally allowed to be a ſpurious lettter, not wrote by *Cicero*,
but wrote for *Cicero*, many hundred years after *Cicero* was departed out of this world. And, in truth, had he wrote this,
letter, it would have had very little weight with me, *Cicero*
was, indeed, a great orator ; he made long and fine ſpeeches ;
he is thought to have been greatly learned in the laws of his
country; but he was a notorious time-ferver, a thorough man

of

of party, and, with all that, a *coward.* Would it be any wonder then, when *Lepidus* was ruined, if he, in his familiar cor-· refpondence, had expreffed himfelf with bitternefs againft *Lepidus* and all that belonged to him ? Would it be any wonder, if fuch a man had rejoiced and exulted in the misfortune of his adverfary; or if his fears had carried him even to wifh deftruction and extirpation to a family, whofe recovery might have proved the ruin of him and his ! But, after all this, *Cicero* is an author who fhould be quoted with fome care ; for, whether from thefe reafons, or any other, as his public conduct was a fcene of contradictions, fo he contradicts himfelf in his writings too. Of this, I recollect an inftance to the very point : In his book *De Natura Deorum*, he pofitively fays, *that no man could bear to live in a country, where the fon and the grandfon fhould be punifhed for the crimes of their grandfather and father.* If, therefore, I fhould allow the Honourable Gentleman, that his letter to *Brutus* was (as it is not) a *genuine* letter, which would be the beft authority ? *Cicero,* in a familiar letter, in an unguarded, heated, fearful ftate ? Or *Cicero* in his ftudy, writing upon the moft ferious fubject, and upon the exprefs fubject; and ufing the utmoft care, and the utmoft reflection, to deliver down a fyftem of religion or morality to future ages ?

The learned Gentleman then goes on to inform us, that the laws of *Greece* bore hard upon the innocent; and that the children of *Themiftocles* were difinherited and banifhed for the crimes of their father. Firft, as to this, there is no example upon earth will ever weigh with a reafonable man to do that which is, in itfelf, either cruel or unjuft. And next, as to the laws of *Greece,* the Gentleman means, and muft mean chiefly, the laws of the *Athenians*; for of the laws of the other *Grecian* ftates we know but little ; and as to thefe laws of the *Athenians,* they have been univerfally confidered, in all ages, as the moft fevere and unjuft that ever any people ever lived under, excepting thofe of their neighbours, the *Macedonians*

nians

rians and the *Perfians*, who extirpated whole families for the crime of one fingle offender. But even here, as to *Themiflocles*, the learned Gentleman is again miftaken; for the children of *Themiflocles* were not banifhed for their father's crime. *The-miflocles* was accufed of a mifprifion of treafon, in not divulging what he knew of the confpiracy of *Paufanius* againft the Greeks in favour of the *Perfians*. Whether he was guilty of this crime or not, did never appear; for he was never tried for it. He fled, his children fled to him, and fo became *participes crimines*. They abandoned their own country, and were therefore pu-nifhed for their own fault; they retired to *Perfia*, and made themfelves fubject to another State, where they obtained dif-tinguifhed privileges and great eftates. *Plutarch* particularly tells us this, and that their defcendants particularly enjoyed thefe privileges in *Magnefia* which they received of *Xerxes*, even in his own time, which was near fix hundred years after.

I now come to fpeak of our ancient and modern Conftitu-tion, with which the Honourable Gentleman fays this claufe is perfectly confiftent. Perhaps I may be thought too venturous, when I conteft this point with a Gentleman fo eminent in his profeffion; but, Sir, I think I am well founded in main-taining the contrary. As to our Conftitution, we feldom hear it talked of with common fenfe. You may find, in what men commonly call our Conftitution, arguments and examples for any thing you will. Nothing is fo vague and unfettled as our Conftitution was for many centuries. If a man ftands up for the prerogative, he may quote you powerful precedents from the reigns of Richard the IId, and other Princes like him: another man, to enforce popular and romantic projects of re-formation, may quote upon you things equally extravagant on another fide, by turning his eye upon our hiftories in times when popular fury has overborne this Government. For my own part, therefore, I never knew how to afcertain the Conftitution of this Country in any degree, but in two periods; the *Saxon* times before the Conqueft; the prefent *Æra* fince the

the Revolution. The intervening fpace between thefe two was all confufion ; a *chaos* of contradi&ions in the regulations of this State ; an eternal ftruggle for uncertain power between the *Barons* and the Crown, the Crown and the people, or the people againft both.

Lord Perceval, May 3, 1744.

MEN will always be more governed by their paffions than their reafon ; and it is fo difficult to forefee and determine what is moft for the public good, that men are apt to determine that to be the moft for the public good, which beft fuits with their own private views and paffions. This is the caufe, that where the people have too great a fhare of the Government in their hands, the peace of the State muft always be difturbed with parties and factions : and as the vulgar, great as well as fmall, have generally very little forefight, and are violent in the purfuit of every paffion, this always, at laft, furnifhes the leader of fome party, or faction, with means to overturn the conftitution of their Government, and to ufurp to himfelf a fole and arbitrary power.

I could demonftrate this theorem, Sir, from obfervations upon the hiftory of almoft all the Commonwealths that ever had a being, and are now no more ; but as the Roman Hiftory is beft known, and moft adapted to this purpofe, I fhall confine my obfervations to this hiftory alone. After the expulfion of their Kings, and the eftablifhment of a republican form of government, the people got, it is true, immediately, a very great fhare in the government, by the law that introduced an appeal to the people ; for which the chief promoter got the name of *Publicola.* By this, and by the election of their annual Magiftrates, the people had, I fay, a very great fhare of the government : but for many years it was in appearance only ; for the Senate and chief *Patricians,* even after the Tribunes of the people were inftituted, had fo much influence among the people, that they preferved in their own hands the whole of the Adminiftration, by getting the people to chufe

R 3   fuch such Magistrates as they directed, and to make such decrees upon appeals as they thought proper and just : but the people, spirited up by popular leaders, were every day aiming at getting more and more power into their hands ; and by the same means the influence of the Senate and the chief *Patricians*, grew every day less and less.   The first conquest the people made upon the Senate, was that of obtaining the establishment of the Tribunes, with most extraordinary powers : and the next they made was, the obtaining a law for the allowing of marriages between Patricians and Plebeians. About the same time, they got introduced the custom of chusing Military Tribunes in the place of Consuls, because the *Patricians* would not allow that any *Plebeian* could be chosen a Consul, whereas a Plebeian might be chosen a Military Tribune ; and by means of this difpute, the Commonwealth came to be governed for many years by Military Tribunes instead of Consuls ; though such was the modesty of the people, that for above fifty years after this sort of magistracy was first introduced, no Plebeian could get himself chosen a Military Tribune.   But the greatest conquest which the People of Rome ever obtained over the Senate and *Patricians*, was the law for rendering a *Plebeian* capable of being chosen a Consul ; for from that time the influence of the Senate diminished very fast, and the people began to grow every day more licentious.

Thus, Sir, a way being opened for popular leaders, whether *Patrician* or *Plebeian*, to arrive at the chief dignities and magistracies of the State, and the people having got almost entirely into their own hands the conferring of those honours, and repeating them as often as they pleafed, a popular leader at last put an end to the liberties of the people for a time ; and soon after him, another popular leader put an end to them for ever. When I say this, every Gentleman must suppose, I mean *Caius Marius*, and *Julius Cæfar,* names well known to those who are versed in the Roman History. *Marius*, though of mean extraction, even among the Plebeians, raifed himself to such

favour

favour among the people of Rome, by his fuccefs in war, and by patronizing every popular law propofed, that he was chofen Conful for *three years fucceffively*, which enabled him to continue himfelf by force or corruption in the fame high office for three years more, in fpite of all that the Nobles of Rome could do againft him. I fay Nobles, Sir; for by admitting *Plebeians* into all high offices, the diftinction between *Patricians* and *Plebeians* had by this time begun to be forgot, and the diftinction that came in its place, was that of the *Nobles* and the *People*. It is true, the *Nobles*, by the help of *Sylla's* army, got the better of *Marius*, and drove him into exile in Africa; but the very next year, *Sylla* being gone with his army into Greece, againft *Mithridates*, *Marius* returned, and joining with *Cinna*, after a terrible flaughter of the Nobles, he feized upon the city and government by an armed force, which his party held by the fame means after his death, till *Sylla* returned with his army from Afia; and after feveral victories, deftroyed all the heads of that party, and reftored what was called the party of the Nobles, referving, however, to himfelf a dictatorial power.

Did thefe misfortunes, Sir, render the people of *Rome* more wife? Did they from thence learn not to aim at more power than they knew how to make ufe of, or not to put more confidence in their pretended *patriots* than they deferved? No, Sir, prefently after *Sylla's* death, *Julius Cæfar*, though he was of noble extraction, put himfelf at the head of the popular party, and patronized every propofition that tended to increafe the power of the people: becaufe from the experience of what happened in *Sylla's* time, he faw, that that was the only party that would fupport him in, as well as raife him to arbitrary power. By patronizing *Agrarian*, and fuch other laws, he recommended himfelf to great favour amongft the people; and as he knew that military glory and a good army were neceffary to raife him to the higheft pinnacle of power, he made ufe of that favour for obtaining the government of *Tranfalpine Gaul*; to which he got, by the fame favour, the province of *Cifalpine Gaul* after-

R 4

wards added; though every wife man at Rome faw, that it was dangerous to join thefe two commands together; becaufe the firft furnifhed him of courfe with a great army, and the fecond with an eafy accefs to Rome itfelf, in a condition to feize upon the government of his country : but the populace could not fee this danger, nor could they penetrate ifto his defign of involving his country in a war with the Gauls, or of defiring to continue for feveral years in the command of thofe two provinces : whereas his defign in both, was perceived by the Senate and great men at Rome. They faw, that by involving his country in war, his defign was to recommend himfelf to the populace by his military glory; and that by defiring to continue long in the fame command, he defigned to model his army, fo as to make it the army of *Julius Cæfar*, and not the army of the Commonwealth of Rome.

All this, I fay, Sir, was forefeen by the Senate and great men of Rome; but they neither could recall him, nor call him to an account for unneceffarily involving his country in a war, without the confent of the people : and they were fo blinded by his military exploits, and the favour he had formerly gained among them, that it was not poffible to make them fee the danger, or confent to recall a General, who was every day fending them accounts of victories gained againft their ancient and moft formidable enemies. There he ftaid, there he fought fuccefsfully, till he made the army his own; and then, inftead of difmiffing his army, as was required by the Senate, he marched with it to Rome, and conquered his country. So blind were the people to their own intereft, fo ready to affift their favourite, in overturning the liberties of their country, that the Tribunes they had chofen declared againft the Senate, and having fled from Rome, took fhelter in the camp of *Cæfar*. So it was, Sir, in the Commonwealth of Rome; fo it will be in all Commonwealths where the people are vefted with too much power. They are extravagant in their favours, as well as refentments, which makes it eafy for a favourite to obtain

fo

fo much power from them, or fuch a long poffeffion of power, as enables him to ftrip them of all manner of power whatfo- ever : therefore, in every free State, it is abfolutely neceffary, for the prefervation of its freedom, to have a Senate or Affembly of Nobles, or Chief Magiftrates, vefted with a power to give a check to the extravagancies of the people.

Right Hon. Henry Pelham, Feb. 12, 1744.

I HAVE been charged with giving birth to fedition in Ame- rica. They have fpoken their fentiments with freedom againft this unhappy Act, and that freedom has become their crime. Sorry I am to hear the liberty of fpeech in this Houfe, im- puted as a crime. But the imputation fhall not difcourage me. It is a liberty I mean to exercife. No Gentleman ought to be afraid to exercife it. It is a liberty by which the Gentleman (Mr. Grenville) who calumniates it, might have profited. He ought to have defifted from his project. The Gentleman tells us America is obftinate; America is almoft in open rebellion. I rejoice that America has refifted. Three millions of people, fo dead to all the feelings of liberty, as voluntarily to fubmit to be flaves, would have been fit inftruments to make flaves of the reft. I come not here armed at all points, with law cafes and Acts of Parliament, with the Statute Book doubled down in dogs-ears, to defend the caufe of liberty : if I had, I myfelf would have cited the two cafes of Chefter and Durham. I would have cited them to have fhewn, that even under any arbitrary reigns, Parliaments were afhamed of taxing a people without their confent, and allowed them Reprefentatives. Why did the Gentleman confine himfelf to Chefter and Durham ? He might have taken a higher example in Wales ; Wales that never was taxed by Parliament till it was incorporated. I would not debate a particular point of law with the Gentleman : I know his abilities. I have been obliged to his diligent re- fearches. But, for the defence of liberty upon a general prin- ciple, upon a conftitutional principle, it is a ground on which

I ftand

I ftand firm; on which I dare meet any man. The Gentleman tells us of many that are taxed, and are not reprefented. The India Company, Merchants, Stock-holders, Manufacturers. Surely many of thefe are reprefented in other capacities, as owners of land, or as freemen of boroughs. It is a misfortune that more are not actually reprefented. But they are all inhabitants, and as fuch are virtually reprefented. Many have it in their option to be actually reprefented. They have connections with thofe that elect, and they have influence over them. The Gentleman mentioned the Stock-holders: I hope he does not reckon the debts of the nation as a part of the national eftate. Since the acceffion of King William, many Minifters, fome of great, others of more moderate abilities, have taken the lead of Government.

When I had the honour to ferve his Majefty, there were not wanting fome, to propofe to me to burn my fingers with an American Stamp Act. With the enemy at their back, with our bayonets at their breafts, in the day of their diftrefs, perhaps the Americans would have fubmitted to the impofition; but it would have been taking an ungenerous and unjuft advantage. The Gentleman boafts of his bounties to America! Are not thefe bounties intended finally for the benefit of this kingdom? If they are not, he has mifapplied the national treafures. I am no Courtier of America, I ftand up for this kingdom. I maintain that the Parliament has a right to bind, to reftrain *America*. Our legiflative power over America is fovereign and fupreme. When it ceafes to be fovereign and fupreme, I would advife every Gentleman to fell his lands, if he can, and embark for that country. When two countries are connected together, like England and her Colonies, without being incorporated, the one muft neceffarily govern; the greater muft rule the lefs; but fo rule it, as not to contradict the fundamental principles that are common to both.

If the Gentleman does not underftand the difference between *internal* and *external* taxes, I cannot help it; but there is a plain diftinction

diftinction between taxes levied for the purpofes of raifing a revenue, and duties impofed for the regulation of trade, for the accommodation of the fubject ; although in the confequences, fome revenue might incidentally arife from the latter.

The Gentleman afks, when were the Colonies emancipated ? But I defire to know, when they were made flaves ? But I dwell not upon words. When I had the honour of ferving his Majefty, I availed myfelf of the means of information which I derived from my office : I fpeak, therefore, from knowledge. My materials were good. I was at pains to collect, to digeft, to confider them ; and I will be bold to affirm, that the profits to Great-Britain from the trade of the Colonies, through all its branches, is two millions a year. This is the fund that carried you triumphantly through the laft war. The eftates that were rented at two thoufand pounds a year, threefcore years ago, are at three thoufand pounds at prefent. Thofe eftates fold then from fifteen to eighteen years purchafe ; the fame may be now fold for thirty. You owe this to *America*. This is the price that America pays you for her protection. And fhall a miferable *Financier* come with a boaft, that he can fetch a pepper-corn into the Exchequer, to the lofs of millions to the nation ? I dare not fay how much higher thefe profits may be augmented. Omitting the immenfe increafe of people by natural propagation in the Northern Colonies, and the migration from every part of Europe, I am convinced the whole commercial fyftem of *America* may be altered to advantage. You have prohibited where you ought to have encouraged, and you have encouraged where you ought to have prohibited. Improper reftraints have been laid on the Continent in favour of the Iflands. You have but two nations to trade with in America. Would you had *twenty!* Let Acts of Parliament in confequence of Treaties remain ; but let not an Englifh Minifter become a Cuftom-Houfe Officer for Spain, or for any foreign power. Much is wrong, much may be amended for the general good of the whole.

Does

Does the Gentleman complain that he has been mifreprefented in the public prints ? It is a common misfortune. In
the Spanifh affair of the laft war, I was abufed in all the news-
papers, for having advifed his Majefty to violate the law of
nations refpecting Spain. The abufe was induftrioufly circulated even in hand-bills. If Adminiftration did not propagate
the abufe, *Adminiftration never contradicted it.* I will not fay
what advice I did give to the King. My advice is in writing
figned by myfelf, in the poffeffion of the Crown. But I will
fay what advice I did not give the King : I did not advife him
to violate any of the laws of nations.

As to the report of the Gentleman's preventing, in fome
way, the trade for bullion with the Spaniards, it was fpoken of
fo confidently, that I own I am one of thofe that did believe it
to be true.

The Gentleman muft not wonder he was not contradicted,
when, as the Minifter, he afferted the right of Parliament to
tax *America.* I know not how it is, but there is a modefty in
this Houfe which does not chufe to contradict a Minifter. I
wifh Gentlemen would get the better of this modefty. If they
do not, perhaps, the collective body may begin to abate of its
refpect for the reprefentative. Lord *Bacon* had told me, that a
great queftion would not fail of being agitated at one time or
another. I was willing to agitate that at the proper feafon,
the *German* war; my *German* war they called it. Every Seffions I called out, has any body any objections to the German
war ? Nobody would object to it ; one Gentleman only objected, fince removed to the Upper Houfe by fucceffion to an
ancient Barony, (meaning *Lord Le Defpencer,* formerly *Sir
. Francis Dafhwood)* he told me, " he did not like a *German
" war."* I honoured the man for it, and was forry when he
was turned out of his poft.

A great deal has been faid out of doors, of the power, of
the ftrength of *America.* It is a topic that ought to be cau-
tioufly meddled with. In a good caufe, on a found bottom,
the

the force of this country can crufh America to atoms. I know the valour of your troops. I know the fkill of your Officers. There is not a company of foot that has ferved in America, out of which you may not pick a man of fufficient knowledge and experience, to make a Governor of a colony there. But on this ground, on the Stamp-Aƈt, when fo many here will think it a crying injuftice, I am one who will lift up my hands againft it.

In fuch a caufe your fuccefs would be hazardous.—America, if fhe fell, would fall like a ftrong man. She would embrace the pillars of the State, and pull down the Conftitution along with her. Is this your boafted peace? Not to fheath the fword in its fcabbard, but to fheath it in the bowels of your country-men? Will you quarrel with yourfelves, now the whole Houfe of Bourbon is united againft you? While France difturbs your fifheries in Newfoundland, embarraffes your trade to Africa, and with-holds from your fubjeƈts in Canada their property ftipulated by Treaty; while the ranfom for *Manillas* is denied by Spain, and its gallant conqueror bafely traduced into a mean plunderer, a Gentleman (Colonel Draper) whofe noble and generous fpirit would do honour to the proudeft grandee of the country. The Americans have not aƈted in all things with prudence and temper. They have been wronged. They have been driven to madnefs by injuftice. Will you punifh them for the madnefs you have occafioned? Rather let prudence and temper come firft from this fide. I will undertake for America that fhe will follow the example. There are two lines in a ballad of *Prior*'s, of a man's behaviour to his wife, fo applica-ble to you and your Colonies, that I cannot help repeating them:

‘ Be to her faults a little blind,
‘ Be to her virtues very kind.’

Mr. Pitt, Dec. 17, 1765.

I here in my place, as a reprefentative of the nation, require and demand a full and impartial inquiry into the caufes of the mifcarriage of the northern army, in an expedition from Canada.

It is a great national object. The crifis of the time emphatically requires it. The exiftence of the Britifh Empire depends upon the exertions of the military, and the beft foundation for public fpirit is public juftice. In addition to the natural animation, which, as Britons, the army poffefs, place before their eyes that fecondary fpring and comptroller of human actions, reward and punifhment. Let the firft and moft glorious reward, the honeft applaufe of the country, be obtained by a fcrutiny into truth, for thofe who deferve it: on the contrary, if there has been delinquency, let the fpirit of *Manlius* prefide in the punifhment.

" The hand of fate is over us, and heaven

" Exacts feverity from all our thoughts."

If there has been difobedience; if unauthorized by circumftances, if *uncompelled by orders*, (for I will never fhrink from that plea) a General has rafhly advanced upon an enemy, and engaged againft infurmountable odds, the difcipline of the ftate fhould ftrike, though it were a favourite fon.

" *I, Lictor, deliga ad palum.*"

Thefe, Sir, are the means to excite true ambition in your leaders, thefe are the means to keep them in due reftraint; this was the fyftem of the glorious Patriot (Lord Chatham) whofe obfequies ye now celebrate; and, could his afhes awaken, they would burft their cerements to fupport it.

As for myfelf, if I am guilty, I fear I am deeply guilty: an army loft! the fanguine expectation of the kingdom difappointed! a foreign war caufed, or the commencement of it accelerated! an effufion of as brave blood as ever run in Britifh veins fhed! and the fevereft family diftreffes combined with public calamity! If this mafs of miferies be, indeed, the confequence of my mifconduct, vain will be the extenuation I can

plead

plead of my perfonal fufferings, fatigue and hardfhip, laborious
days and fleeplefs nights, ill health and trying fituations; poor
and infufficient will be fuch atonement in the judgment of my
country, or perhaps in the eyes of God—yet, with this dreadful alternative in view, I provoke a trial—give me inquiry—
I put the interefts that hang moft emphatically by the heart-
ftrings of man—my fortune—my honour—my head—I had
almoft faid my falvation, upon the teft.

But, Sir, it is a confolation to me to think that I fhall be,
even in furmife, the only culprit—Whatever fate may attend
the General who led the army to Saratoga, their behaviour at
that memorable fpot muft entitle them to the thanks of their
country. Sir, it was a calamitous, it was an awful, but it
was an honourable hour—during the fufpence of the anfwer
from the General of the enemy, to the refufal made by me of
complying with the ignominious conditions he had propofed,
the countenance of the troops beggars defcription—a patient
fortitude, a fort of ftern refignation, that no pencil nor language can reach, fat on every brow. I am confident every
breaft was prepared to devote its laft drop of blood, rather
than fuffer a precedent to ftand upon the Britifh annals of an
ignoble furrender.

Sir, an important fubject of enquiry ftill remains. The
tranfactions at Cambridge, and the caufe of the detention of
troops. If I there have been guilty, let me there alfo be the
only fufferer.

Sir, there is a famous ftory in ancient hiftory that bears fome
analogy to my circumftances; and when allufions tend to excite men's minds to exertions of virtue or policy, I fhall never
think them pedantic or mifplaced. The event I mean happened in an age when Roman virtue was at its height. It was
that wherein *Manlius* devoted his fon, and the firft *Decius* devoted himfelf. A Roman army, fhut up by the Samnites at
Caudium, were obliged to furrender their arms, and to fubmit
to the more ignominious condition of paffing under the yoke
of

of the enemy. The Conful who had commanded them, propofed in the Senate, to break the treaty whereby the army was
loft to the State, and to make him in perfon the expiation, by
fending him bound to the enemy to fuffer death at their hands.
In one point of view the prefent cafe extremely differs from
the example; becaufe, by the Treaty of Saratoga, the army
was faved to the State. It is the non-compliance with public
faith that alone can lofe it—and here the parallel will hold; if
I have been inftrumental to the lofs of thofe brave troops *since*
the Treaty, I am as culpable as if I had loft them *by* the Treaty,
and ought to be the facrifice to redeem them. Sir, this reference may appear vain-glorious. It may be doubted, whether
there exifts in thefe times, public fpirit ferioufly to emulate fuch'
examples. I perhaps fhould find myfelf unequal; but others
who are moft ready to judge me fo, muft at leaft give credit to
one motive for ftating the parallel—*That I am too confcious of*
innocence to apprehend there is the leaft rifk of being expofed to the
trial.

General Burgoyne, May 26, 1778.

You have now two wars before you, of which you muft
chufe one, for both you *cannot* fupport; the war againft America has hitherto been carrried on againft her alone, unaffifted
by any ally whatever; notwithftanding fhe ftood alone, you
have been obliged uniformly to increafe your exertions, and to
pufh your efforts in the end to the extent of your power,
without being able to bring it to any iffue: you have exerted
all your force hitherto without effect, and you cannot now
divide a force found already inadequate to its object: my opinion is for withdrawing your forces from America entirely,
for a defenfive war you never can think of there of any
fort: a defenfive war would ruin this nation at any time, and
in any circumftances; offenfive war is pointed out as proper
for this country; our fituation points it out, and the fpirit of
the nation impels us to *attack* rather than *defence :* attack

France

France then, for fhe is your objeét: the nature of the wars is
quite different; the war againft America is againft your own
countrymen, you have ftopped me from faying againft your fellow fubjeéts; that againft France is againft your inveterate enemy
and rival : every blow you ftrike in America is againft yourfelves; it is againft all idea of·reconciliation, and againft your
own intereft, though you fhould be able, as you never will, to
force them to fubmit: every ftroke againft France is of advantage to you; the more you lower the fcale in which France
lays in the balance, the more your own rifes, and the more
the Americans will be detached from her as ufelefs to them:
even your victories over America are in favour of France, from
what they muft coft you in men and money; your victories
over France will be felt by her ally; America muft be conquered in France, France never can be conquered in America.
The war of the Americans is a war of *paffion*; it is of fuch a
nature as to be fupported by the moft powerful virtues, love of
liberty and of their country; and at the· fame time by thofe
paffions in the human heart which give courage, ftrength, and
perfeverance to man; the fpirit of revenge for the injuries you
have done them, of retaliation for the hardfhips you have inflicted on them, and of oppofition to the unjuft powers you
have exercifed over them; every thing combines to animate
them to this war, and fuch a war is without end: for whatever
obftinacy enthufiafm ever infpired man with, you will now find
it in America; no matter what gives birth to that enthufiafm,
whether the name of religion or of liberty, the effects are the
fame; it infpires a fpirit that is unconquerable and folicitous to
undergo difficulty, danger, and hardfhip: and as long as there
is a man in America, a being formed fuch as we are, you will
have him prefent himfelf againft you in the field. The war of
France is a war of another fort; the war of France is a war
of intereft it : was her intereft firft induced her to engage in it,
and it is by that intereft that fhe will meafure its continuance:
turn your face at once againft her, attack her wherever fhe is

expofed,

expofed, crufh her commerce wherever you can, make her feel heavy and immediate diftrefs throughout the nation, the people will foon cry out to their government: whilft the advantages fhe promifes herfelf are remote and uncertain, inflict prefent evils and diftreffes upon her fubjects, the people will become difcontented and clamourous, fhe will find it a bad bargain having entered into this bufinefs, and you will force her to defert an ally that brings fo much trouble, and diftrefs, and misfortune, the advantages of whofe alliance may never take effect; or if they fhould be fubject always to difturbance from this country, which it always ought to be, and which I know you are able to give if you once get your hands clear of America. What is become of the antient fpirit of this nation? Where is that national fpirit that ever did honour to this country ? Have the prefent Minifters fpent that too with almoft the laft fhilling of your money? Are they not afhamed of the temporizing conduct they have ufed towards France? Her correfpondence with America has been clandefine, compare that with their conduct towards Holland fome time ago—but it is the characteriftic of little minds to exact in little things, whilft they fhrink from their rights in great ones.—The conduct of France is called clandefine; look back but a year ago to a letter from one of your Secretaries of State to Holland, " it is with " furprife and indignation" your conduct is feen—in fomething done by a petty Governor of an ifland—while they affect to call the meafures of France clandefine : this is the way that Minifters fupport the character of the nation, and the national honour and glory: but look again how that fame Holland is fpoke of to-day, even in your correfpondence with her your littlenefs appears,

> Pauper & exul uterque,
> Projecit ampullas, & fefquipedalia verba.

From this you may judge of your fituation, from this you may know what a ftate you are reduced to : how will the

French

French party in Holland exult over you and grow ſtrong; ſhe will never continue your ally when you meanly crouch to France, and do not dare to ſtir in your defence : but it is no-thing extraordinary that ſhe ſhould not, whilſt you keep the Mi-niſters you have; no power in Europe is blind ; there is none blind enough to ally itſelf with weakneſs, and become partner in bankruptcy ; there is no one blind enough to ally themſelves to obſtinacy, abſurdity, and imbecility.

Mr. Fox, Nov. 26, 1778.

THERE is not in the whole hiſtory of this country, a period that reſembles the preſent, except the reign of the unfortunate Henry the VIth. His family, like that of his preſent Majeſty, did not claim the Crown as their hereditary right ; it was by revolutions they both obtained it. Henry was an amiable and pious Prince, ſo is his preſent Majeſty : Henry was the ſon of the moſt renowned Monarch that ever ſat upon the Throne; George was the grandſon of a Hero ; Henry loſt all his father's conqueſts, and all his hereditary provinces in France : George has already ſeen the conqueſts of his grandfather wreſted from him in the Weſt-Indies, and his hereditary provinces of Ame-rica erected into an empire, that diſclaimed all connection.

His Majeſty ſet out in life with the brighteſt proſpects that a young man could have wiſhed for : poſſeſſed of immenſe do-minions, and the warmeſt affections of his people, his acceſſion to the Crown was completely flattering both to himſelf and his ſubjects. How ſadly is the ſcene reverſed ! his empire diſ-membered, his councils diſtracted, and his people falling off in their affection for his perſon. I only ſpeak within doors the language that is held without : the people are beginning to murmur, and their patience is not unlimited : they will at laſt do themſelves juſtice ; there certainly will be inſurrections : and though it is impoſſible that the calamities that will attend them can be juſtified, or compenſated by any good that can be obtained by them, yet they certainly will take place.

S 2   It

It cannot be a secret to this House, that the present Sovereign's claim to the Throne of this country was founded only
upon the delinquency of the Stuart family; a circumstance that
ought never to be out of his Majesty's recollection. It was true,
indeed, that the unfortunate race of that name, was universally
detested in this country, and therefore his Majesty had little to
fear from their pretensions: but he should ever remember, that
it was the conduct of wicked and ignorant Ministers that excited
that detestation for them. If there should be at this day one of
that unfortunate House remaining, what a scope for upbraid-
ings and remonstrance could he not find in the present reign!
Could he not say, " You have banished my ancestor from the
" Throne, and barred the Sceptre from all his progeny for the
" misconduct of his Ministers; and yet the Ministers of the pre-
" sent reign, are ten times more wicked and more ignorant than
." those were; and whilst you all agree in giving to your pre-
" sent Sovereign the title of best of Princes, his Ministers have
" rendered his reign beyond any degree of comparison, the most
" infamous that ever disgraced this nation." The Minister,
though with such a load of national censure and national calamity on his head, has the hardiness to boast of his innocence;
but it is not a conscious rectitude of mind that could excuse a
Minister from criminality. What he calls innocence may be
another name for ignorance, and ignorance in a Minister is
a crime of the first magnitude. But the wide ruin that the
counsels of Administration have spread through this great empire, and the miserable state to which they have reduced it in
the short space in which the present Parliament have been sitting, is so far beyond the natural effects of mere ignorance,
that I cannot help adopting the opinion of an Honourable Friend.
(Mr. J. Townshend) that there is treachery at the bottom of
the national councils. His Lordship (Lord North) may flatter himself as much as he pleases in the protection of a majority,
or in the security of the law; but when a nation is reduced to
such a state of wretchedness and distraction that the laws can

afford

afford the people no relief, they will give a Minister who has caufed the evil but little protection. What the law of the land could not do, the law of nature would accomplifh; the people would inevitably take up arms, and the firft chara{\`e}ters in the kingdom would be feen in their ranks !

Mr. Fox, Nov. 25, 1779.

THE neceffity of my faying fomething upon the prefent oc-cafion, is fo obvious to the Houfe, that no apology will, I hope, be expected from me in troubling them even at fo late an hour, (two o'clock in the morning.) I fhall not enter much into a detail, or minute defence, of the particulars of the Eaft-India Bill before you, becaufe few particular objections have been made. The oppofition to it confifting only in general reafonings, of little application fome, and fome totally diftant from the point in queftion.

This Bill has been combated through its paft ftages upon va-rious principles; but to this moment the Houfe has not heard it canvaffed upon its own intrinfic merits. The debate this night has turned chiefly upon two points—*violation of charter,* and *increafe of influence*; and upon both thefe points I fhall fay a few words.

The Honourable Gentleman, who opened the debate, (Mr. Powys) firft demands my attention, not indeed for the wif-dom of the obfervations which fell from him this night, acute and judicious though he is upon moft occafions) but from the natural weight of all fuch characters in this country, the aggre-gate of whom fhould, in my opinion, always decide upon pub-lic meafures: but his ingenuity was never, in my opinion, exerted more ineffectually, upon more miftaken principles, and more inconfiftent with the common tenor of his conduct, than in this debate.

The Honourable Gentleman charges me with abandoning that caufe, which, he fays, in terms of flattery, I had once fo fuccefsfully afferted. I tell him, in reply, that if he were

S 3

to fearch the hiftory of my life, he would find that the period of it, in which I ftruggled moft for the real, fubftantial
caufe of Liberty, is this very moment that I am addreffing
you. Freedom, according to my conception of it, confifts in
the fafe and facred poffeffion of a man's property, governed by
laws defined and certain ; with many perfonal privileges, natural, civil, and religious, which he cannot furrender without ruin
to himfelf; and of which to be deprived by any other power, is
defpotifm. This Bill, inftead of fubverting, is deftined to fta-
bilitate thefe principles ; inftead of narrowing the bafis of freedom, it tends to enlarge it ; inftead of fuppreffing, its object is
to infufe and circulate the fpirit of Liberty.

What is the moft odious fpecies of tyranny? Precifely that
which this Bill is meant to annihilate. That a handful of men,
free themfelves, fhould execute the moft bafe and abominable
defpotifm over millions of their fellow-creatures ; that innocence fhould be the victim of oppreffion ; that induftry fhould
toil for rapine ; that the harmlefs labourer fhould fweat, not for
his own benefit, but for the luxury and rapacity of tyrannic depredation. In a word, that thirty millions of men, gifted by
Providence with the ordinary endowments of humanity, fhould
groan under a fyftem of defpotifm, unmatched in all the hiftories of the world.

What is the end of all government? Certainly the happinefs
of the governed.—Others may hold other opinions ; but this is
mine, and I proclaim it. What are we to think of a government, whofe good fortune is fuppofed to fpring from the calamities of its fubjects, whofe aggrandifement grows out of the
miferies of mankind? This is the kind of government exercifed
under the Eaft-India Company upon the natives of Indoftan ;
and the fubverfion of that infamous government, is the main
object of the Bill in queftion. But in the progrefs of accom-
plifhing this end, it is objected that the Charter of the Company fhould not be violated ; and upon this point, Sir, I fhall
deliver my opinion without difguife. A Charter is a truft to
one

one or more perfons for fome given benefit, If this truft be
abufed, if the benefit be not obtained, and that its failure arifes
from palpable guilt, or (what in this cafe is full as bad) from
palpable ignorance or mifmanagement, will any man gravely
fay, that truft fhould not be refumed' and delivered to other
hands; more efpecially in the cafe of the Eaft-India Company,
whofe manner of executing this truft, whofe laxity and languor
produced, and tend to produce, confequences diametrically oppofite to the ends of confiding that truft, and of the inftitution
for which it was granted?—I beg of Gentlemen to be aware
of the lengths to which their arguments upon the intangibility
of this Charter may be carried. Every fyllable virtually im-
peaches the eftablifhment by which we fit in this Houfe, in
the enjoyment of this freedom, and of every other bleffing
of our government. Thefe kind of arguments are batteries
againft the main pillar of the Britifh Conftitution. Some
men are confiftent with their own private opinions, and difcover the inheritance of family maxims, when they queftion
the principles of the Revolution; but I have no fcruple in
fubfcribing to the articles of that creed which produced it.
Sovereigns are facred, and reverence·is due to every King:
yet, with all my attachments to the perfon of a firft Magiftrate,
had I lived in the reign of James the Second, I fhould moft
certainly have contributed my efforts, and borne part in thofe
illuftrious ftruggles which vindicated an empire from hereditary
fervitude, and recorded this valuable doctrine, *that truft abufed*
was revocable.

No man will tell me, that a truft to a company of merchants, ftands upon the folemn and fanctified ground by which
a truft is committed to a Monarch; and I am at a lofs to reconcile the conduct of men who approve that refumption of
violated truft, which refcued and re-eftablifhed our unparalleled and admirable Conftitution with a thoufand valuable improvements and advantages at the Revolution, and who, at
this moment, rife up the champions of the Eaft-India Com-

pany's

pany's Charter, although the incapacity and incompetence of that Company to a due and adequate difcharge of the truft depofited in them by that Charter, are themes of ridicule and contempt to all the world : and although, in confequence of their mifmanagement, connivance, and imbecillity, combined with the wickednefs of their fervants, the very name of an Englifhman is detefted, even to a proverb, through all Afia, and the national character is become degraded and difhonoured. To refcue that name from odium, and redeem this character from difgrace, are fome of the objects of the prefent Bill ; and Gentlemen fhould indeed gravely weigh their oppofition to a meafure which, with a thoufand other points not lefs valuable, aims at the attainment of thefe objects.

Thofe who condemn the prefent Bill as a violation of the chartered rights of the Eaft-India Company, condemn, on the the fame ground, I fay again, the Revolution, as a violation of the chartered rights of King James II. He, with as much reafon, might have claimed the property of dominion ; but what was the language of the people ? No, you have no property in dominion; dominion was vefted in you, as it is in every Chief Magiftrate, for the benefit of the community to be governed ; it was a facred truft delegated by compact ; you have abufed the truft ; you have exercifed dominion for the purpofes of vexation and tyranny—not of comfort, protection, and good order ; and we therefore refume the power which was originally ours : we recur to the firft principles of all government, the will of the many ; and it is our will that you fhall no longer abufe your dominion. The cafe is the fame with the Eaft-India Company's government over a territory, as it has been faid by Mr. Burke, of 280,000 fquare miles in extent, nearly equal to all Chriftian Europe, and containing 30,000,000 of the human race. It matters not whether dominion arifes from conqueft or from compact. Conqueft gives no right to the conqueror to be a tyrant ; and it is no violation of right to abolifh the authority which is mifufed.

I   Having

Having faid fo much upon the general matter of the Bill, I muft beg leave to make a few obfervations upon the remarks of particular Gentlemen; and firft of the learned Gentleman over-againft me (Mr. Dundas.) The learned Gentleman has made a long, and, as he always does, an able fpeech; yet, tranflated into plain Englifh, and difrobed of the dexterous ambiguity in which it has been inveloped, what does it amount to? To an eftablifhment of the principles upon which this Bill is founded, and an indirect confeffion of its neceffity. He allows the fran-gibility of Charters, when abfolute occafion requires it; and admits that the Charter of the Company fhould not prevent the adoption of a proper plan for the future government of India, if a proper plan can be atchieved upon no other terms. The firft of thefe admiffions feems agreeable to the civil maxims of the learned Gentleman's life, fo far as a maxim can be traced in a political character, fo various and flexible: and to deny the fecond of thefe conceffions was impoffible, even for the learned Gentleman, with a ftaring reafon * upon your table to confront him if he attempted it. The learned Gentleman's Bill, and the Bill before you, are grounded upon the fame bottom, of abufe of truft, male-adminiftration, debility, and incapacity in the Company and their fervants; but the difference in the remedy is this: the learned Gentleman's Bill opens a door to an influence a hundred times more danger-ous than any that can be imputed to this Bill, and depofits in one man an arbitrary power over millions, not in England, where the evil of this corrupt Miniftry could not be felt, but in the Eaft-Indies, the fcene of every mifchief, fraud, and violence. The learned Gentleman's Bill afforded the moft extenfive latitude for malverfation; the Bill before you guards againft it with all imaginable precaution. Every line in both the Bills which I have had the honour to intro-duce, prefumes the poffibility of bad Adminiftration, for every

* Mr. Dundas's Bill, brought in laft year.

word

word breathes fufpicion. This bill fuppofes that men are but
men; it confides in no integrity, it trufts no character;
it inculcates the wifdom of a jealoufy of power, and an-
nexes refponfibility not only to every *action*, but even to the
inaction of thofe who are to difpenfe it. The neceffity of
thefe provifions muft be evident, when it is known that
the different misfortunes of the Company refulted not more
from what the fervants *did*, than from what the mafters
did *not*.

To the probable effects of the learned Gentleman's Bill and
this, I beg to call the attention of the Houfe. Allowing, for
argument's fake, to the Governor General of India, under the
firft-named Bill, the moft unlimited and fuperior ablilities,
with foundnefs of heart and integrity the moft unqueftionable;
what good confequences could be reafonably expected from his
extraordinary, extravagant, and unconftitutional power, under
the tenure by which he held it? Were his projects the moft
enlarged, his fyftems the moft wife and excellent which human fkill could advife; what fair hope could be entertained of
their eventual fuccefs, when, perhaps, before he could enter
upon the execution of any meafure, he may be recalled in confequence of one of thofe changes in the Adminiftrations of this
country, which have been fo frequent for a few years, and
which fome good men wifh to fee every year? Exactly the fame
reafons which banifh all rational hope of benefit from an Indian
Adminiftration under the Bill of the learned Gentleman, juftify
the duration of the propofed commiffion. If the difpenfers of
the plan of governing India, (a place from which the anfwer of
a letter cannot be expected in lefs than twelve months) have
not greater ftability in their fituations than a Britifh Miniftry—
adieu to all hopes of rendering our Eaftern territories of any
real advantage to this country; adieu to every expectation of
purging or purifying the Indian fyftem, of reform, of improvement, of reviving confidence, of regulating the trade upon
its proper principles, of reftoring tranquillity, of re-eftablifh-

ing

ing the natives in comfort, and of fecuring the perpetuity of thefe bleffings, by the cordial reconcilement of the Indians with their former tyrants upon fixed terms of amity, friendfhip, and fellowfhip. I will leave the Houfe and the kingdom to judge which is beft calculated to accomplifh thofe falutary ends; the Bill of the learned Gentleman, which leaves all to the difcretion of one man, or the Bill before you which depends upon the duty of feveral men, who are in a ftate of daily account to this Houfe, of hourly account to the Minifters of the Crown, of occafional account to the Proprietors of Eaft-India ftock, and who are allowed fufficient time to practife their plans, unaffected by every political fluctuation.

But the learned Gentleman wifhes the appointment of an Indian Secretary of State in preference to thefe Commiffioners: in all the learned Gentleman's ideas on the government of India, the notion of a new Secretary of State for the Indian department fprings up, and feems to be cherifhed with the fondnefs of confanguinity * ; but that fcheme ftrikes me as liable to a thoufand times more objections than the plan in agitation. Nay, the learned Gentleman had rather, it feems, the affairs of India were blended with the bufinefs of the office which I have the honour to hold. His good difpofition towards me upon all occafions cannot be doubted, and his fincerity in this opinion is unqueftionable. I beg the Houfe to attend to the reafon which the learned Gentleman gives for this preference, and to fee the plights to which men, even of his underftanding, are reduced, who *muft* oppofe. He laughs at the refponfibility of the Commiffioners to this Houfe, who, in his judgment, will find means of foothing, and foftening, and meliorating the

---

* Mr. Dundas's Bill was to have appointed a Secretary of State for the Indian department, and to have made the Governor General defpotic in India. If the Earl of Shelburne had continued in power, it was underftood that Mr. Dundas was to be the Indian Secretary. Mr. Fox here alluded to this anecdote.

Members

Members into an oblivion of their male-adminiftration. What opinion has the learned Gentleman of a Secretary of State? Does he think *him* fo inert, fo inactive, fo incapable a creature, that with all this vaunted patronage of the feven in his own hands, the fame means of foothing, and foftening, and meliorating are thrown away upon him. The learned Gentleman has been for fome years converfant with Minifters; but his experience has taught him, it feems, to confider Secretaries not only untainted and immaculate, but innocent, harmlefs, and incapable. In his time, Secretaries were all purity—with every power of corruption in their hands; but fo inflexibly attached to rigid rectitude, that no temptation could feduce them to ufe that power for the purpofe of corupting, or, to ufe his own words, for foothing, or foftening, or meliorating. The learned Gentleman has formed his opinion of the fimplicity and inaction of Secretaries, from that golden age of political probity, when his own friends were in power, and when himfelf was every thing but a Minifter. This erroneous humanity of opinion arifes in the learned Gentleman's unfufpecting, unfullied nature, as well as in a commerce with only the beft and pureft Minifters of this country, which has given him fo favourable an impreffion of a Secretary of State, that he thinks this patronage, fo dangerous in the hands of feven Commiffioners, perfectly fafe in *his* hands. I leave to the learned Gentleman that pleafure which his mind muft feel under the conviction with which he certainly gives this opinion; but I fubmit to every man who hears me, what would be the probable comments of the other fide of the Houfe, had I propofed either the erection of an Indian Secretary, or the annexation of the Indian bufinefs to the office which I hold.

In the affemblage of the learned Gentleman's objections, there is one ftill more curious than thofe I have mentioned. He diflikes this Bill, becaufe it eftablifhes an *imperium in imperio.* In the courfe of oppofition to this meafure, we have been fami-

liarized

liarized to hear certain fentiments and particular words in this
Houfe—but directed, in reality, to *other* places. Taking it,
therefore, for granted, that the learned Gentleman has not fo
defpicable an idea of the good fenfe of the Members, as to expect any more attention within thefe walls to fuch a dogma,
than has been fhewn to the favourite phrafe of his Hon. Friend
near him, (Mr. William Pitt) who calls a Bill which backs this
finking Company with the credit of the State, a *confifcation* of
their *property*, I would wifh to afk the learned Gentleman, if
he really holds the underftanding, even of the multitude, in
fuch contempt, as to imagine this fpecies of argument can have
the very flighteft effect? The multitude know the fallacy of it
as well as the learned Gentleman himfelf. They know that a
diffolution of the Eaft-India Company has been wifhed for fcores
of years, by many good people in this country, for the *very*
reafon that it was an *imperium in imperio*. Yet the learned
Gentleman, with infinite gravity of face, tells you he diflikes
this Bill, becaufes it eftablifhes this novel and odious principle.
Even a glance of this Bill, compared with the prefent conftitution of the Company, manifefts the futility of this objection,
and proves that the Company is, in its prefent form, a thoufand
times more an *imperium in imperio* than the propofed Commiffioners. The worft fpecies of Government is that which can
run counter to all the ends of its inftitution with impunity.
Such exactly was the Eaft-India Company. No man can fay,
that the Directors and Proprietors have not, in a thoufand inftances, merited fevere infliction; yet who did ever think of a
legal punifhment for either body? Now the great feature of
this Bill is to render the Commiffioners amenable, and to punifh
them upon delinquency.

The learned Gentleman prides himfelf that his Bill did not
meddle with the commerce of the Company; and another Gentleman, after acknowledging the folly of leaving the government in the hands of the Company, propofes to feparate the
commerce entirely from the dominion, and leave the former fafe

and

and untouched to the Company itfelf. I beg leave to appeal to every Gentleman converfant in the Company's affairs, whether this meafure is, in the nature of things, practicable at this moment. That the feparation of the commerce from the government of the Eaft may be ultimately brought about, I doubt not; but when Gentlemen reflect upon the immediate ftate of the Company's affairs, when they reflect that their government was carried on for the fake of their commerce, that both have been blended together for fuch a feries of years; when they review the peculiar, perplexed, and involved ftate of the eaftern territories, their diffimilitude to every fyftem in this part of the globe, and confider the deep and laborious deliberation with which every ftep for the eftablifhment of a falutary plan of government, in the room of the prefent odious one, muft be taken —the utter impoffibility of inftantly detaching the governing power from interference with the commercial body, will be clear and indubitable.

A Gentleman has afked, why not choofe the Commiffioners out of the body of Directors; and why not leave the choice of the Affiftant Directors in the Court of Proprietors? That is to fay, why not do that which would infallibly undo all you are aiming at? I mean no general difparagement when I fay, that the body of the Directors have given memorable proofs, that they are not the fort of people to whom any man can look for the fuccefs or falvation of India. Amongft them there are, without doubt, fome individuals, refpectable both for their knowledge and integrity; but I put it to the candour of Gentlemen, whether they are the fpecies of men whofe wifdom, energy, and diligence, would give any promife of emancipating the Eaft-India concerns from their prefent difafters and difgraces. Indeed, both queftions may be anfwered in two words. Why not choofe the Directors, *who have ruined the Company?* Why not leave the power of election in the Proprietors, *who have thwarted every good attempted by the Directors?*

The

. The laſt point adverted to by the learned Gentleman relates to *influence*; and upon his remarks, combined with what fell from ſome others upon the ſame ſubject, I beg leave to make a few obſervations. Much of my life has been employed to diminiſh the inordinate influence of the Crown. In common, with others, I ſucceeded, and I glory in it. To ſupport that kind of influence which I formerly ſubverted, is a deed of which I ſhall never deſerve to be accuſed. The affirmation with which I firſt introduced this plan, I now repeat: I re-aſſert that this Bill as little augments the influence of the Crown, as any meaſure which can be deviſed for the government of India, that preſents the ſlighteſt promiſe of ſolid ſuccefs, and that it tends to increaſe it in a far leſs degree than the Bill propoſed by the learned Gentleman. The very genius of influence conſiſts in hope or fear; fear of loſing what we have, or hope of gaining more. Make theſe Commiſſioners removeable at will, and you ſet all the little paſſions of human nature afloat. If benefit can be derived from the Bill, you had better burn it than make the duration ſhort of the time neceſſary to accompliſh the plans it is deſtined for. *That* conſideration pointed out the expediency of a fixed period; and in that reſpect it accords with the principle of the learned Gentleman's Bill; with this ſuperior advantage, that inſtead of leaving the Commiſſioners liable to all the influence which ſprings from the appointment of a Governor-General, removeable at *pleaſure*, this Bill inveſts them with the power for *the time ſpecified*, upon the ſame tenure that Britiſh Judges hold their ſtation, removeable upon delinquency, puniſhable upon guilt, but fearleſs of power if they diſcharge their truſt; liable to no ſeducement, and with full time and authority to execute their functions for the common good of the country, and for their own glory. I beg of the Houſe to attend to this difference, and then judge upon the point of increaſing the influence of the Crown, contraſted with the learned Gentleman's Bill.

The

The ftate of accufations againft me upon this fubject of in-fluence, is truly curious. The learned Gentleman, (Mr. Dundas) in ftrains of emphafis, declares, that this Bill diminifhes the influence of the Crown beyond all former attempts; and calls upon thofe who formerly voted with him in fupport of that influence, againft our efforts to reduce it, and who now fit near me, to join him now in oppofing my attempts to diminifh that darling influence. He tells them, I *out-herod Herod*; that I am out-doing all my former out-doings; and proclaims me as the mercilefs and infatiate enemy of the influence of the Crown.

Down fits the learned Gentleman, and up ftarts an Hon. Gentleman, with a charge againft me, upon the fame fubject, of a nature the direct reverfe. I have fought under your banner, cries the Hon. Gentleman, (Mr. Martin) againft that fell giant the influence of the Crown; I have bled in that battle which you commanded, and have a claim upon the rights of foldierfhip. You have conquered through us; and now that victory is in your arms, you turn traitor to our caufe, and carry over your powers to the enemy. The fierceft of your former combatants in the caufe of influence, falls far fhort of you at this moment; your attempts in re-erecting this monfter, exceed all the exertions of your former foes. This night you will make the influence of the Crown a coloffus, that fhall beftride the land, and crufh every impediment. I impeach you for treachery to your ancient principles—come, come, and divide with us!

This Hon. Gentleman, after a thruft or two at the Coalition, fits down: and whilft the Houfe is perplexing itfelf to reconcile thefe wide differences, the Right Hon. Gentleman over the way (Mr. W. Pitt) confounds all paft contradictions, by combining, in his own perfon, thefe extravagant extremes. He acknowledges that he has digefted a paradox; and a paradox well he might call it, for never did a groffer one puzzle the intellects of a public affembly. By a miraculous kind of difcernment

ment

ment he has found out, that the Bill both *increaſes* and *diminiſhes* the influence of the Crown.

The Bill diminiſhes the influence of the Crown, ſays one: - you are wrong, ſays a ſecond, it increaſes it: you are both right, ſays a third, for it both increaſes and diminiſhes the influence of the Crown. Now, as moſt Members have one or other of theſe opinions upon the ſubject, the Hon. Gentleman can ſafely join with all parties upon this point; but few, I truſt, will be found to join him.

Thus, Sir, is this Bill combated, and thus am I accuſed. The nature and ſubſtance of theſe objections, I conſtrue as the ſtrongeſt comment upon the excellence of the Bill. If a more rational oppoſition *could* be made to it, no doubt it would. The truth is, it increaſes the influence of the Crown and the influence of party as little as poſſible ; and if the reform of India, or any other matter, is to be poſtponed until a ſcheme be de- viſed, againſt which ingenuity, or ignorance, or caprice, ſhall not raiſe objections, the affairs of human life muſt ſtand ſtill.

I beg the Houſe will attend a little to the manner in which the progreſs of this Bill has been retarded, eſpecially by the Right Hon. Gentleman (Mr. Pitt.) Firſt, the Members were not all in town, and time was deſired upon that account. Next, the finances of the Eaſt-India Company were miſ-ſtated by me, and time was deſired to prove that. The time came, the proofs exhibited, Counſel heard, and yet the iſſue was, that my former ſtatement, inſtead of being controverted, became more eſta- bliſhed by the very proofs which were brought to overturn it. The Hon. Gentleman has miſrepreſented me to-night again : he has an evident pleaſure in it, which indeed I cannot prevent ; but I can prevent this Houſe and this country from believing him. He prefers the authority of his own conception (eager enough in all conſcience to miſunderſtand me) of what I ſaid to my own repeated declarations of my own meaning. He ſuppoſes a miſtake becauſe he wiſhes it. I never did ſay the Company were abſolute bankrupts to the amount of the debt, but I faid there was immediate neceffity of paying that given fum, without any immediate means of providing for it. The account of the Company's circumftances, prefented laft week, furnifhed matter of triumph to the Hon. Gentleman for the full fpace of *three hours*; that is to fay, whilft Counfel were at the Bar. I made no objection to the account but this *trifling* one —that 12,000,000 l. were ftated which ought not to appear at all there, and which were placed there only for delufion and fallacy. I never objected to the arithmetic of the account. The fums, I doubt not, were accurately caft up even to a figure: yet the Houfe will recollect, that the Hon. Gentleman, about this very hour of that debate, endeavoured to protract the bufinefs to the next day, upon affuring the Houfe that the Company would then fupport their ftatement. I refufed to accede, becaufe I knew the matter to be mere fhifting, and manœuvering for a vote, and that the Company *could not* fupport their ftatement. Was I right? The Houfe fees whether I was: the Houfe fees the finance poft is now totally abandoned, and for the beft reafon in the world, becaufe it is no longer tenable. But the Hon. Gentleman is indeed a man of refources; he now gives me a challenge, and I beg the Houfe to remark, that I accept his challenge, and that I prophefy he will no more meet me upon this than upon the former points.

But there is no limit to a youthful and vigorous fancy.—The Right Hon. Gentleman juft now, in very ferious terms, and with all his habitual gravity, engages, if the Houfe will join in oppofing us to-night, that he will digeft and methodife a plan, the outline of which he has already conceived. · He has nothing *new* to offer; but juftly confiding in the fertility of his own imagination, and the future exercife of his faculties, he promifes that he *will* bring a plan, *provided* the majority of this Houfe will join him to-night. Now, if ever an idea was thrown out to pick up a ftray vote or two in the heel of a debate, by a device, the idea given a while ago by the Hon. Gentleman is precifely fuch: but if I can augur rightly from the complexion

of

6

of the Houfe, his prefent will have exactly the fame fuccefs with all his paft ftratagems to oppofe this Bill *.

His learned Friend, (Mr. Dundas) with fingular placidnefs, without fmile or fneer, has faid, " as this meafure was probably decided upon fome time fince, the Eaft-India Company, *who could not expect fuch a blow*, ought to have been informed of the intended project. The Company was evidently unaware of this attack, and, in fairnefs, fhould have been apprifed of it." Does the learned Gentleman imagine men are in their fober fenfes, who liften to fuch cavilling and quibbling oppofition? The Company unaware of this attack! The learned Gentleman's own labours, independent of any other intimation, had been an ample warning to the Company to be prepared. Every man in the kingdom, who reads a newfpaper, expected fome-thing; and the only wonder with the nation was, how it could be fo long delayed. The Reports of the Committees alarmed the Public fo much, for the honour of the country, and for the falvation of the Company, that all eyes were upon Eaft-India affairs. This fort of obfervation had indeed much better come from any other man in this Houfe, than from that identical Gentleman.

If thefe were not fufficient to roufe the attention and diligence of the Company, his Majefty's Speech at the commencement and conclufion of the late Seffion of Parliament, gave them note of preparation in the moft plain and decifive terms. In his opening fpeech, his Majefty thus fpeaks to Parliament upon the fubject of India:——

" The regulation of a vaft territory in Afia, opens a large field for your wifdom, prudence, and forefight: I truft that you will be able to form fome fundamental laws which may make their connection with Great-Britain a bleffing to India ; and that you will take therein proper meafures to give all foreign

* He was right; for the Miniftry had an acceffion of five votes this night, above the former divifion.

nations,

nations, in matters of foreign commerce, an entire and perfect confidence in the probity, punctuality, and good order of our government. You may be affured that whatever depends upon me, fhall be executed with a fteadinefs, which can alone preferve that part of my dominions, or the commerce which arifes from it."

The learned Gentleman, who knows more of the difpofitions of the Cabinet at that time than I do, can better tell whether any meafure of this nature was then intended. The words are very wide, and feem to portend at leaft fomething very important; but whether any thing fimilar to this meafure was meant, as this paffage feems to imply, or not, is indifferent to the point in queftion. This is clear from it, that it gives a very ceremonious warning to the Eaft-India Company; enough furely to expofe the weaknefs and futility of the learned Gentleman's remark. The changes and circumftances of the Cabinet, in the courfe of the laft feffion, can be the only excufe for the delay of fome decifive meafure with regard to India: and if in addition to all thefe, any thing more is requifite to confirm the notoriety of Parliament's being to enter upon the bufinefs, the following paragraph of the King's clofing Speech, laft July, completes the mafs of evidence againft the learned Gentleman.

His Majefty, after intimating a belief that he fhall be obliged to call his Parliament together earlier than ufual, thus fpeaks :—

" The confideration of the affairs of the Eaft-Indies will require to be refumed as early as poffible, and to be purfued with a ferious and unremiting attention." Superadd to all this, the part of the King's opening fpeech this year upon India ; and if the whole do not conftitute fufficient teftimony that the Company had full notice, nothing can.

Yet, notwithftanding all this, the learned Gentleman accufes us of *furprifing* the Company ; and his Right Honourable Friend, in hopes his propofal of another Bill may have weight

in

in the divifion—repeats the hacknied charge of *precipitation*, and forces the argument for delay in a taunt, " that we wifh to " get rid of our torments, by fending this Bill to the other " Houfe." The Honourable Gentleman's talents are fplendid and various ; but I affure him, that all his efforts, for the laft eight days, have not given me a fingle torment. Were I to chufe a fpecies of oppofition to infure a minifterial tranquillity, it would be the kind of oppofition which this Bill has received, in which every thing brought to confute, has tended to confirm, and in which the arguments adduced to expofe the weaknefs, have furnifhed materials to eftablifh the wifdom of the meafure : fo impoffible is it, without fomething of a tolerable caufe, even for the Right Honourable Gentleman's abilities to have effect, though his genius may make a flourifhing and fuperior figure in the attempt.

Before I proceed to the other parts of the debate, I wifh to fay one word upon a remark of the learned Gentleman : he fays, that the claufe relative to the zemindars was fuggefted by his obfervations. God forbid I fhould detract from the merit, or diminifh the defert of any man. Undoubtedly that excellent part of the Regulation Bill derives from the learned Gentleman ; and if he were in this Houfe when I introduced the fubject of India, he would have known that I did him full and complete juftice upon that point.

My Noble Friend (Lord John Cavendifh) has faid, this Bill does not arife from the poverty of the Company, but that liberal policy and national honour demanded it. Upon the laft day this Bill was debated, I confined myfelf chiefly to the demonftration of the fallacy and impofture of that notable fchedule prefented by the Eaft-India Company ; and having proved its falfehood, I can now with the greater fafety declare, that if every fhilling of that fictitious property was real and forth coming, a Bill of this nature was not therefore the lefs neceffary. I thought we were fully underftood upon this point, from the opening fpeech in this bufinefs, which did not fo degrade the

T 3 meafure

meafure as to fay it originated in the poverty of the Company, which, as my Noble Friend rightly remarks, was the fmalleft reafon to its adoption, and which opinion is not, as the Right Honourable Gentleman infinuates, " fhifting," but recognifing and recording the true grounds of the Bill. If any mifunderstanding then has hitherto taken place upon this head, it will, I truft, ceafe henceforth; and fo odious a libel upon 'this country will not pafs current, as that fordid motives only induced the government of England to *that* which we were bound to do, as politicians, as Chriftians, and as men, by every confideration which makes a nation refpeſtable, great, and glorious !

Having vindicated the Bill from this afperfion, and founded it upon that bafis which every honeft and fenfible man in England muft approve, I may be allowed to fay that fome regard may be had even to the mean and mercenary upon this fubject (a portion of whom we have here, in common with all other countries.) Will fuch men endure with temper a conftant drain upon this kingdom, for the fake of this monopolizing Corporation? Will thofe, for inftance, who clamour againft a twopenny tax, afford, with good humour, million after million to the Eaft-India Company? The Sinking Fund is at this moment a million the worfe for the deficiencies of the Company, and as the Noble Lord (Lord John) fays, an extent muft in three weeks arreft their property, if Parliament does not interpofe or enable them to difcharge a part of their debt to the Crown. Let thofe, therefore, who think the commerce ought to be inftantly feparated from the dominion, (were that at this time poffible) and who think it ought to be left wholly in the prefent hands, reflect, that the formation of a vigorous fyftem of government for India is not more incumbent upon us, than the eftablifhment of the eaftern trade upon fuch principles of folidity and fitnefs, as fhall give fome juft hopes that the public may be fpeedily relieved from the

monftrous

monftrous preffure of conftantly fupporting the indigence of the Company.

I have fpoke of myfelf very often in the courfe of what I have faid this night, and muft fpeak ftill more frequently in the courfe of what I have to fay: the Houfe will fee this aukward talk is rendered indifpenfable, infinitely more having been faid concerning *me*, during the debate, than concerning the queftion, which is the proper fubject of agitation. The Right Honourable Gentleman (Mr. Pitt) fays, that nothing ever happened to give him an impreffion of my character, or to prevent a mutual confidence. He fays rightly; there have been interchanges of civility, and amicable habits between us, in which I truft I have given him no caufe to complain. But after pronouncing a brilliant eulogy upon me and my capacity to ferve the country, the Honourable Gentleman confiders me at the fame time the moft dangerous man in the kingdom, (Mr. Pitt faid acrofs the Houfe, " *dangerous only* " *from this meafure.*" To which Mr. Fox inftantly made this reply) I call upon the Houfe to attend to the Honourable Gentleman; he thinks me dangerous *only from this meafure*, and confeffes, that *hitherto* he has feen nothing in my conduct to obliterate his good opinion. Compare this with his oppofition during the laft and the prefent feffion. Let every man reflect, that up to this moment the Honourable Gentleman deemed me worthy of confidence, and competent to my fituation in the State. I thank him for the *fupport* he has afforded to the Minifter he thus efteemed, and fhall not prefs the advantage he gives me, farther than leaving to himfelf to reconcile his practice and his doctrine in the beft manner he can.

The Honourable Gentleman could not for one night pafs by the *Coalition*, yet I think he might have chofen a fitter time to exprefs his indignation againft the Noble Lord (Lord North) than the prefent moment. An attack upon the Noble Lord in his prefence would bear a more liberal colour; and the

caufe

cause of his abfence now through indifpofition, would furely rather difarm than irritate a generous enemy. There are diftinctions in hatred, and the direft foes upon fuch occafions moderate their averfion. The Coalition is, however, a fruitful topic, and the power of traducing it, which the weakeft and meaneft creatures in the country enjoy and exercife, is of courfe equally vefted in men of rank and parts, though every man of parts and rank would not be apt to participate the privilege. Upon the Coalition, the Honourable Gentleman is welcome to employ his ingenuity, but upon another fubject alluded to him, I fhall beg leave to advife, nay even to inftruct him.

In what fyftem of ethics will the Honourable Gentleman find the precept taught of ripping up old fores, and revivng animofities among individuals, of which the parties themfelves retain no memory? This kind of practice may incur a much worfe charge than weaknefs of underftanding, and fubject a man to much greater imputations than are commonly applied to political miftakes or party violence. The foundnefs of the heart may be liable to fufpicion, and the moral character be in danger of fuffe ing by it, in the opinion of mankind. To cover the heats, and obliterate the fenfe of former quarrels between two perfons, is a very diftinguifhed virtue : to renew the fubject of *fuch* differences, and attempt the revival of *fuch* difputes, deferves a name which I could give it, if that Hon. Gentleman had not forgotten himfelf, and fallen into fome fuch deviation. He values himfelf, I doubt not, too much, again to make a fimilar flip, and muft even feel thankful to me for the counfel I thus take the liberty to give him.

An Honourable Gentleman under the gallery, (Mr. Martin) to whom an abufe of the Coalition feems a fort of luxury, wifhes that a ftarling were at the right hand of the chair to cry out difgraceful Coalition ! Sir, upon this fubject I fhall fay but few words :

The calamitous fituation of this country required an Adminiftration whofe ftability could give it a tone of firmnefs with foreign

foreign nations, and promife fome hope of reftoring the faded
glories of the country. Such an Adminiftration could not be
formed without *fome* junction of parties; and if former differences were to be an infurmountable barrier to union, no
chance of falvation remained for the country, as it is well
known, that four public men could not be found, who had
not, at one time or other, taken oppofite fides in politics. The
great caufe of difference between us and the Noble Lord in
the blue ribband no longer exifted; his perfonal character ftood
high; and thinking it fafer to truft him than thofe who had
before deceived us, we preferred to unite with the Noble Lord.
A fimilar junction, in 1757, againft which a fimilar clamour
was raifed, faved the empire from ruin, and raifed it above
the rivalfhip of all its enemies. The country, when we came
into office, bore not a very aufpicious complexion; yet, Sir, I
do not defpair of feeing it once again refume its confequence
in the fcale of nations, and make as fplendid a figure as ever.
Thofe who have afferted the impoffibility of our agreeing with
the Noble Lord and his friends, were falfe prophets; for events
have belied their augury. We have differed like men, and
like men we have agreed.

A body of the beft and honefteft men in this Houfe, who
ferve their country without any other reward than the glory of
the difinterefted difcharge of their public duty, approved that
junction, and fanctify the meafure by their cordial fupport.

Such, Sir, is this Coalition, which the ftate of the country
rendered indifpenfable; and for which the hiftory of every
country records a thoufand precedents, yet to this the term difgraceful is applied. Is it not extraordinary, then, that Gentlemen fhould be under fuch fpells of falfe delufion, as not to
fee, that if calling it difgraceful makes it fo, thefe epithets operate with equal force againft themfelves. If the *coalition* be
difgraceful, what is the *anti-coalition?* When I fee the Right
Honourable Gentleman (Mr. Pitt) furrounded by the early objects of his political, nay his hereditary hatred, and hear him
revile

revile the Coalition, I am loft in the aftonifhment how men
can be fo blind to their own fituation, as to attempt to wound
us in this particular point, poffeffed as we are of the power of
returning. the fame blow, with the vulnerable part ftaring us
directly in the face. If the Honourable Gentleman under the
gallery wifhes that a ftarling were perched upon the right-hand
of the chair, I tell him, that the wifh is juft as reafonable, to
have another ftarling upon the left-hand of the chair, to chirp
up *coalition* againft *coalition*, and fo harmonize their mutual difgrace, if difgrace there be.   -

With the fame confiftency, an Honourable Gentleman calls
us *deferters——us!* a few cold and difaffected members fall off,
then turn about, and, to palliate their own defection, call the
body of the army *deferters! We* have not deferted; here we
are a firm phalanx. Deferted indeed we have been in the moment of difafter, but never dejected, and feldom complaining.
Some of thofe who rofe upon our wreck, and who eagerly
grafped that power which we had the labour of erecting, now
call us deferters. We retort the term with juft indignation.
Yet whilft they prefume we have the attributes of men, they
would expect us to have the obduracy of favages. They would
have our refentments infatiate, our rancour eternal. In our
opinion, an oblivion of ufelefs animofity is much more noble;
and in that, the conduct of our accufers goes hand in hand
with us. But I beg the Houfe, and I wifh the world to obferve, that although, like them, we have abandoned our enmi-
ties, we have not, like them, relinquifhed our friendfhips:
but there are a fet of men, who, from the mere vanity of
having confequence as decifive voters, object to all ftable Government; thefe men hate to fee an Adminiftration fo fixed,
as not to be moveable by their vote. They affume their dignity on the mere negative merit of not accepting places, and
in the pride of this felf-denial, and the vanity of fancied independence, they object to every fyftem that has a folid bafis,
becaufe their confequence is unfelt: Of fuch men I cannot be
                                                              the

the panegyrift, and I am forry that fome fuch men are among
the moft eftimable in the Houfe.

An Honourable Gentleman advifes me for the future, not to
mention the name of the Marquis of Rockingham, who, he
fays, would never countenance a Bill of this kind. This is
indeed, impofing hard conditions upon thofe, who have willingly
fuffered a fort of political martyrdom in the caufe of that Noble
Lord's principles, thofe who furrendered pomp and power,
rather than remain where his principles ceafed to be fafhiona-
ble, and were withering into contempt. I venerate the name
of that Noble Marquis, and fhall ever mention it with love
and reverence; but at no period of my life with more confidence than at this moment, when I fay, that his foul fpeaks in
every line of the Bill before you; for his foul fpeaks in every
meafure of virtue, wifdom, humane policy, general juftice,
and national honour. The name of the Noble Lord who enjoys his fortune has been mentioned in this debate, and will be
mentioned again by me; I will tell the Honourable Gentleman,
that this Noble Lord, (Earl Fitzwilliam) though not the iffue
of his loins, inherits, with his property, the principles of that
Noble Marquis in all their purity and foundnefs; and is as incapable as that Noble Marquis himfelf, or as any man on earth,
of countenancing any act which either immediately or ultimately
tended to the prejudice of his country, or the injury of the
Conftitution. I have had the honour of knowing the Noble
Earl from an early age. I have obferved the motives of his
actions: I am endeared to him by every tie of kindred fenti-
ment, and of mutual principle. A character more dignified
and exalted exifts not in the empire; a mind more firmly attached to the Conftitution of his country: he is, what the nation would defire in the heir of Lord Rockingham, the only
compenfation we could have for his lofs.

An Honourable Gentleman (Mr. T. Pitt) at the other fide,
has ufed violent terms againft this Bill, and the movers of it.
Sir, I tell that Honourable Gentleman (looking directly in the
face

face of Mr. T. Pitt) that the movers of this Bill are not to
be brow-beaten by ftudied gefture, nor frightened by tremulous
tones, folemn phrafes, or hard epithets. To arguments they
are ready to reply; but all the notice they can take of affertions, is to mark to the Houfe, that they are *only* affertions.
The Honourable Gentleman again repeats his favourite language of our having *feized upon the Government*; his Majefty
changed his Miniftry laft April, in confequence of a vote of
this Houfe; his Majefty did the fame twelve months before, in
confequence of a vote of this Houfe. His Majefty, in fo
doing, followed the example of his predeceffors; and his fucceffors will, I doubt not, follow the example of his Majefty.
The votes of Parliament have always decided upon the duration of Miniftry, and always will, I truft. It is the nature of
our Conftitution, and thofe who diflike it, had better attempt
to alter it. The Honourable Gentleman called the change in
1782 a glorious one; this in 1783 a difgraceful one. Why?
for a very obvious, though a very bad reafon. The Honourable
Gentleman affifted in effecting the firft, and ftrenuoufly laboured to prevent the fecond. The firft battle he fought with
us; the fecond againft us, and we vanquifhed him. In 1782
his friends were *out*, and would be *in*. In 1783 his friends
were *in*, nor *would* go out. Thus having done without him
what we once did with him, the Houfe fees his motive. It is
human nature certainly; but certainly not the better part of
human nature. He fays he is no party man, and he abhors a
fyftematic oppofition. I have always acknowledged myfelf to
be a party man; I have always acted with a party in whofe
principles I have confidence; and if I had fuch an opinion of
any Miniftry as the Gentleman profeffes to have of us, I would
purfue their overthrow by a fyftematic oppofition. I have
done fo more than once, and I think that in fucceeding I faved
my country. Once the Right Honourable Gentleman, as I
have faid, was with me, and our conduct was fair, manly,
conftitutional, and honourable. The next time he was againft
me,

me, and our conduct was violent and unconstitutional, it was
treasonable; and yet the means were in both instances the same,
the means were the votes of this House.

A game of a two-fold quality is playing by the other side of
the House upon this occasion, to which I hope the House, and
I hope the kingdom, will attend. They are endeavouring to
injure us through two channels at the same time, through a
certain great quarter, and through the People. They are attempting to alarm the first, by asserting that this Bill increases
the influence of Ministry *against* the Crown; and rousing the
People, under an idea that it increases the influence of the
Crown *against them*. That they will fail in both I doubt not.
In the great quarter I trust they are well understood, and the
princely mind of that high person is a security against their de-
vices: they are running swiftly to take off whatever little im-
position might have been put upon any part, even of the multitude. And I wish to rescue the character of the public understanding from the contemptuous implication, that it is capable
of being gulled by such artifices. I feel for my country's honour when I say, that Englishmen, free themselves, and fond
of giving freedom to others, disdain these stratagems, and
are equally above the sillinefs of crediting the revilers of this
act, as above the baseness of confederating or making common
cause with those who would support a system which has difhonoured this country, and which keeps thirty millions of the
human race in wretchednefs. I make allowances for the hair-
brained headstrong delusions of folly and ignorance, and the
effects of design. To such evils every meature is liable, and
every man must expect a portion of the consequence. But for
the serious and grave determinations of the public judgment
I have the highest value, I ever had, and ever shall have. If
it be a weaknefs, I confefs it, that to lose the good opinion of
even the meaneft man, gives me some pain; and whatever
triumph my enemies can derive from such a frame of mind,
they are welcome to. I do not, after the example of the

Honourable

Honourable Gentleman who began this debate, (Mr. Powys) hold the opinion of Conftituents in difparagement. The clear and decided opinion of the more reafonable and refpect-able fhould, in my opinion, weigh the Member upon the fame principle that, I think, with the voice of the nation fhould prevail in this Houfe, and in every other place. But when the Reprefentative yields to the Conftituent, it fhould indeed be by the majority of the reafonable and refpectable, and not, as we fhall fee in a day or two, fome of the honefteft men in England voting againft the moft popular tax was ever introduced into this Houfe, in direct oppofition to their own conviction, and *not* upon the opinion of either the more refpectable or rea-fonable clafs of their Conftituents.

My noble friend, (Lord John) with his characteriftic fpirit, has faid, that *we* never fought power by cabal or intrigue, or undherhand operations; and this he faid in reply to an Honour-able Gentleman, (Mr. T. Pitt) whofe conduct demonftrates, that he thinks *thofe* the fureft path for his friends. This bill, as a ground of contention, is farcical: this bill, if it admitted it, would be combated upon its intrinfic qualities, and not by abufing the coalition, or raifing a clamour about influence; but why don't the Gantlemen fpeak out fairly, as we do, and then let the world judge between us? Our love and loyalty to the Sovereign are as ardent and firm as their own. Yet the broad bafis of public character, upon which we received, is the principle by which we hope to retain this power; convinced that the fureft road to the favour of the Prince, is by ferving him with zeal and fidelity; that the fafeft path to popularity, is by reducing the burden, and reftoring the glory of the na-tion. Let thofe (looking at Mr. Jenkinfon) who aim at office by *other* means, by infcrutable and myfterious methods, fpeak out; or, if they will not, let the world know it is becaufe their arts will not bear examination, and that their fafety confifts in their obfcurity. *Our* principles are well known; and I

fhould

fhould prefer to perifh with them, rather than profper with any other.

The Honourable Gentleman under the gallery (Mr. Martin) alfo fays, he diflikes fyftematic oppofition. Whether perpetually rifing up with peevifh, capricious objeCtions to every thing propofed by us, deferve that name or not, I leave the Gentleman himfelf to determine, and leave the Houfe to refleCt upon that kind of conduCt which condemns the theory of its own conftant praCtice; but I meet the Gentleman direCtly upon the principle of the term. He diflikes fyftematic oppofition; now I like it. A fyftematic oppofition to a dangerous Government is, in my opinion, a noble employment for the brighteft faculties; 'and if the Honourable Gentleman thinks our Adminiftration a bad one, he is right to contribute to its downfal. Oppofition is natural in fuch a political fyftem as ours; it has fubfifted in all fuch Governments; and perhaps it is neceffary. But to thofe who oppofe it, it is extremely effential that their manner of conduCting it incur not a fufpicion of their motives. If they appear to oppofe from difappointment, from mortification, from pique, from whim, the people will be againft them. If they oppofe from public principle, from love of their country rather than hatred to Adminiftration, from evident conviCtion of the badnefs of meafures, and a full perfuafion that in their refiftance to men, they are aiming at the public welfare, the People will be with them. We oppofed upon *thefe* principles, and the People were with us; if we are oppofed upon *other* principles, they will not be againft us. Much labour has been employed to infufe a prejudice upon the prefent fubjeCt; and I have the fatisfaCtion to believe that the labour has been fruitlefs; (making a reafonable exception for the miftakes of the uninformed, the firft impreffions of novelty, and the natural refult of deliberate malice) we defire to be tried by the teft of this Bill, and rifk our charaCter upon the iffue: confiding thoroughly in the good fenfe, the juftice, and the fpirit of Englifhmen. Not lofty founds, nor felected epithets,

thets, nor paffionate declamation in this Houfe, nor all the fordid efforts of interefted men out of this Houfe, (of men whofe
acts in the Eaft have branded the Britifh name, and whofe ill-
gotten opulence, working through a thoufand channels to delude
and debauch the public underftanding) can faften odium upon
this meafure, or draw an obloquy upon the authors of it.   We
have been tried in the caufe of the public ; and until we defert
that caufe, we are affured of public confidence and protection.

The Honourable Gentleman (Mr. Powys) has fuppofed for
me a foliloquy, and has put into my mouth fome things which
I do not think are likely to be attributed to me : he infinuates
that I was incited by avarice, or ambition, or party fpirit.   I
have failings in common with every human being, befide my
own peculiar faults : but of avarice I have indeed held myfelf
guiltlefs.   My abufe has been, for many years, even the profeffion of feveral people ; it was their traffic, their livelihood ;
yet until this moment, I knew not that avarice was in the cata-
logue of the fins imputed to me.   Ambition I confefs I have,
but not ambition upon a narrow bottom, or built upon paltry
principles.   If, from the devotion of my life to political objects, if from the direction of my induftry to the attainment of
fome knowledge of the Conftitution, and the true interefts of
the Britifh empire, the ambition of taking no mean part in
thofe acts that elevate nations, and make a people happy, be
criminal, that ambition I acknowledge.   And as to party
fpirit—that I feel it, that I have ever been under its impulfe,
and that I ever fhall, is what I proclaim to the world.   That
I am one of a party, a party never known to facrifice the interefts, or barter the liberties of the nation for mercenary purpofes, for perfonal emolument or honours ; a party linked together upon principles which comprehend whatever is dear
and moft precious to free men, and effential to a free Conftitution, is my pride and my boaft.

The Honourable Gentleman has given me one affertion,
which it is my pride to make : he fays that I am connected
with

with a number of the firſt families in the country. Yes, Sir,
I have a peculiar glory that a body of men, renowned for their
anceſtry, important for their poſſeſſions, diſtinguiſhed for their
perſonal worth, with all that is valuable to men at ſtake, hereditary fortunes and hereditary honours, deem me worthy of
their confidence. With ſuch men I am ſomething—without
them, nothing. My reliance is upon their good opinion; and
in that reſpect, perhaps, I am fortunate. Although I have a
juſt confidence in my own integrity, yet as I am but man,
perhaps it is well that I have no choice but between my own
eternal diſgrace and a faithful diſcharge of my public duty;
whilſt theſe kind of men are overſeers of my conduct, whilſt
men, whoſe uprightneſs of heart and ſpotleſs honour are even
proverbial in the country, (looking at Lord John Cavendiſh)
are the vigils of my deeds, it is a pledge to the public for the
purity and rectitude of my conduct. The proſperity and honour of the country are blended with the proſperity and honour
of theſe illuſtrious perſons. They have ſo much at ſtake, that
if the country falls, they fall with it; and to countenance any
thing againſt its intereſt, would be a ſuicide upon themſelves.
The good opinion and protection of theſe men is a ſecurity
to the nation for my behaviour, becauſe, if I loſe them, I loſe
my all.

Having ſaid ſo much upon the extraneous ſubjects introduced
by the Hon. Gentleman into the debate, I ſhall proceed to
make ſome obſervations upon the buſineſs in queſtion. When
the learned Gentleman brought in his Bill laſt year, the Houſe
ſaw its frightful features with juſt horror; but a very good method was adopted to ſoften the terrors of the extravagant power
that Bill veſted in the Governor-General. The name of a Noble Lord (Lord Cornwallis) was ſent forth at the ſame time,
whoſe great character lent a grace to a propoſition, which, def-
titute of ſuch an advantage, could not be liſtened to for one
moment. Now, Sir, obſerve how differently we have acted
upon the ſame occaſion.

Vol. I. U Earl

Earl Fitzwilliam has been fpoken of here this day in thofe terms of admiration with which his name is always mentioned. Take notice, however, that we did not avail ourfelves of the fame of his virtue and abilities in paffing this Bill through the Houfe.

If fuch a thing were to have taken place as the inftitution of an Indian Secretaryfhip, (according to the fuggeftions of fome Gentlemen) this Noble Lord would certainly have been the very perfon whom, for my part, I fhould have advifed his Majefty to inveft with that office. Yet, although his erect mind and fpotlefs honour would have held forth to the public the fulleft confidence of a faithful execution of its duties, the objections in regard to influence upon a removeable Officer, are tenfold in comparifon with the prefent fcheme. The Houfe muft now fee, that with all the benefits we might derive from that Noble Lord's character—that although his name would have imparted a fanctity, an ornament, and an honour to the Bill, we ufhered it in without that ceremony, to ftand or fall by its own intrinfic merits, neither fhielding it under the reputation, nor gracing it under the mantle, of any man's virtue. Our merit will be more in this, when the names of thofe are known whom we mean to propofe to this Houfe, to execute this commiffion. (Name them, faid Mr. Arden, acrofs the Houfe.) I will not—I will not name them; the Bill fhall ftand or fall by its own merits, without aid or injury from their character. An Hon. Gentleman has faid thefe Commiffioners will be made up of our " adherents and creatures." Sir, there is nothing more eafy than to ufe difparaging terms; yet I fhould have thought the name of Earl Fitzwilliam would have given a fair prefumption, that the colleagues we fhall recommend to this Houfe for the co-execution of this bufinefs with that Noble Lord, will not be of a defcription to merit thefe unhandfome epithets. I affure the Hon. Gentleman they are not. I affure him they are not men whofe faculties of corrupting, or whofe corruptibility, will give any alarm to this Houfe, or to this country: they are men whofe whose private and public characters stand high and untainted; who are not likely to countenance depredation, or participate the spoils of rapacity. They are not men to screen delinquency, or to pollute the service by disgraceful appointments. Would such men as Earl Fitzwilliam suffer unbecoming appointments to be made? Is Earl Fitzwilliam a man likely to do the dirty work of a Minister? If they, for instance, were to nominate a Paul Benfield to go to India in the Supreme Council, would Earl Fitzwilliam subscribe to his appointment? This is the benefit of having a commission of high honour, chary of reputation, noble and pure in their sentiments, who are superior to the little jobs and traffic of political intrigue.

But this Bill, Sir, presumes not upon the probity of the men; it looks to the future possibility of dissimilar successors, and to the morality of the present Commissioners, who are merely human, and therefore not incapable of alteration. Under all the caution of this Bill, with the responsibility it imposes, I will take upon me to say, that if the aggregate body of this Board, determined to use all its power for the purpose of corruption, this House, and the people at large, would have less to dread from them, in the way of influence, than from a few Asiatics who will probably be displaced in consequence of this arrangement; some of whom will return to this country with a million, some with seven hundred thousand, some with five, beside the three or four hundred thousand of others, who are cut off in their career by the hand of fate. An inundation of such wealth is far more dangerous, than any influence that is likely to spring from a plan of Government so constituted as this proposed— whether the operation of such a mass of wealth be considered in its probable effects, upon the principles of the Members of this House, or the manners of the people at large, more especially when a reflection that Orientalists are in general the most exemplary class of people in their morals, and in their deportment the most moderate, and corresponding with the distinction of their high birth and family, furnishes a very reasonable presump-

tion,

tion, that the expenditure of their money will be much about as honourable as its acquirement.

. I fhall now, Sir, conclude my fpeech with a few words upon the opinion of the Right Hon. Gentleman (Mr. Pitt.) He fays, " he will flake his character upon the danger of this Bill." I meet him in his own phrafe, and oppofe him, character to character: I rifk my all upon the excellence of this Bill; I rifk upon it whatever is moft dear to me, whatever men moft value, the character of integrity, of talents, of honour, of prefent reputation and future fame; thefe, and whatever elfe is precious to me, I ftake upon the conftitutional fafety, the enlarged policy, the equity, and the wifdom of this meafure; and have no fear in faying, (whatever may be the fate of its authors) that this Bill will produce to this country every blefling of commerce and revenue; and that by extending a generous and humane Government over thofe millions whom the infcrutable deftinations of Providence have placed under us in the remoteft regions of the earth, it will confecrate the name of England amongft the nobleft of nations.

Mr. Fox, Dec. 1, 1783.

I HAVE ventured to confider ourfelves as re-affembled this .day, after the neceffary adjournment of the feafon, under his Majefty's folemn promife, that we fhould not be interrupted in our deliberations on the affairs of the Eaft-Indies, and the fupport of the public credit, by any prorogation or diffolution of the Parliament: for, if his Majefty's Anfwer to our late Addrefs means any thing fhort of that, his Minifters, who have advifed and perufed it, have not only abufed his Royal confidence, but grofsly deceived and infulted this Houfe. For the Anfwer in acknowledging the urgency of thofe objects, mentioned in the Addrefs, as reafons againft diffolving, and likewife the expediency of proceeding on them with vigilance, moft undoubtedly conveys, that the Houfe will be permitted not merely to meet, but to meet for the furtherance of thofe objects. On the

day

day the Anfwer was read in this Houfe, there were no refponfible Minifters prefent; but as they are here now, the Houfe is entitled to know, in the moft explicit and unequivocal terms, previous to the difcuffion of any queftion of India, whether they
are to underftand, that they are met again freely, independently,
and with ultimate effect to deliberate on the affairs of India, and
the other great confiderations that preffes upon them; or whether they are only tenants at the will of the new Minifter, to be
fent back to their conftituents as delinquents, unlefs they fhall
recede from every principle of conftitutional policy, to which
they are folemnly and publicly pledged, and fhall agree to regifter any edict upon the fubject which the new Treafury Bench
may dictate to them, however repugnant to their former opinions? For if that fhould be their fyftem, I, for one, would not
give up a moment of my time to deliberation which muft be
fruitlefs, and which could end in the final execution of no permanent fyftem of Government in Afia or Europe; if Minifters
meet us only by way of experiment, to try our opinions with
the rod of diffolution hung over our heads as the fcourge of difobedience, determined, inftead of retiring on a difappointment,
ftill to diftract and difturb a Government which they cannot
guide, and to gain over a future Parliament, by the arts of
cabal and corruption, which the virtue of the prefent has refifted, it will become us to know, not from the Minifters, but
from the Throne itfelf, whether this country is to be governed
by men whom the Houfe of Commons can confide in, or whether we, the people of England's Reprefentatives, are to be the
fport and foot-ball of any junto that may hope to rule over us
by an unfeen and unexplorable principle of Government, utterly
unknown to the Conftitution? This is the great queftion to
which every public-fpirited Citizen of this country fhould direct
his view. A queftion that goes very wide of the policy to be
adopted concerning India, about which very wife and very honeft men, not only might, but have and did materially differ,
The total removal of all the executive fervants of the Crown,

U 3 while

while they are in the full enjoyment of the confidence of that
Houfe, and indeed without any other vifible or avowed caufe of
removal, than becaufe they do enjoy that confidence, and the
appointment of others in their room, without any other apparent ground of feledion than becaufe they enjoyed it not, is, in
my mind, a moft alarming and portentous attack on the public
freedom; becaufe, though no outward form of the Government
· is relaxed or violated by it, fo as inftantly to fupply the conftitutional remedy of oppofition, the whole fpirit and energy of
the Government is annihilated by it. That the prerogative of
chufing Minifters belongs to, and ought to belong to his Majefty, and let no man hope to hear from me a fingle expreffion
that ftrikes at the juft independence of the Crown; but as all
its prerogatives, like our own privileges, are but trufts for the
people, and as none of them can be abufed but by the agency
of others, I perfuade myfelf that they will look to thofe, who,
in an evil hour, have given the Crown the moft refponfible
advice on the fubject alluded to, by accepting of all the pofts
of executive power, merely as it fhould feem, becaufe the voice
of the people's Reprefentatives in this Houfe has been recently,
repeatedly, and loudly lifted up againft them. I ventured to
exprefs my aftonifhment on a former day, when the Firft Lord
of the Treafury was not in his place, that when the affairs of
India were the firft and moft important objects of the King's
Government, he could venture to take upon him the conduct
of that Government in a Houfe of Commons, adverfe to all his
ideas and principles on the fubject, and the majority of which
he had on the fame fubject loaded with the moft opprobrious
epithets; an expreffion he thought himfelf at liberty to ufe, becaufe after a great and refpectable majority had affented to the
Bill upon the fecond reading, and in the Committee, the Right
Hon. Gentleman did ftill, on the third reading, confider the
friends of it collectively as fupporting a defperate faction, in an
attempt to maintain themfelves in power at the expence of the
moft facred chartered rights of individuals, and the moft valu-
.able

able interefts of the public, with many other galling expreffions.
My objection to this language, as I explained it when I firft
ftated it, is not fo much becaufe it was unparliamentary or unprecedented, though I thought it fufficiently fo: it was not an
arraignment of the Right Hon. Gentleman for ufing it, fince
on moft contefted public meafures the fame fort of language
was but too frequent from both fides of the Houfe ; but I did,
as we may all remember, exprefs my utter aftonifhment, which
I again exprefs, (for it grows on me every inftant) that the
Right Hon. Gentleman fhould hope to continue one day the
Minifter in a Houfe of Commons, while that majority, whofe
principles of government he has thus fo recently reprobated,
continues to fubfift: that was, and continues to be my obfervation ; and I am not afraid to truft the juftice and propriety of it
to the good fenfe, the dignity, and the memory of the Houfe.
If the Right Hon. Gentleman retains his own opinions, and if
the Houfe likewife retains its own, is it not evident, that he
came into office without the moft diftant profpect of ferving
the public ? Is it not evident, that he has brought on a ftruggle
between executive and legiflative authority, at a time when
they are pointing with equal vigour, unity, and effect, to the
common interefts of the nation ? Is it not palpable, that inftead
of giving ftability, dignity, and authority to the Government of
his country, at a time when its affairs are falling into ruin in
every part of the world from the want of them, he has crippled
and enervated all its operations, ftirred dangerous queftions between the Prerogatives of the Crown and the Privileges of the
People, and wafted the important hours of deliberation in this
Houfe, in bringing things back to the very condition they were
in originally, when he ftepped forth to difturb them. Can the
Right Hon. Gentleman, or any body for him, explain to the
Houfe why the Crown, by its Anfwer to our Addrefs, fhould
promife not to difturb our proceedings, yet fhould at the fame
moment change the whole executive authority of Government,
and place it in the hands of perfons adverfe to every principle

U 4   they

they had pledged themfelves to adopt, on the very meafure they were defired to proceed upon? Is it not plain to the meaneft underftanding, that it ftruck a palfy into every member of executive power, which could not, and ought not to have any energy or ftrength, when deprived of that vital fpirit of popular government, which could only circulate life and heat through the medium of the people's Reprefentatives in this Houfe?

I truft, that whenever the Crown of England removes its Minifters, enjoying the full confidence of the Commons, and chufe fo ftrange and inaufpicious an hour for that removal, as when upheld by that confidence they were planning great and neceffary fyftems of Government, and when it not only chofe that feafon for removing them, but put into their room perfons whofe principles on the fame objects the people's Reprefentatives had recently rejected and condemned, I hope, whatever may be our differences on other fubjects, that we fhall be unanimous in confidering that moment as a great and alarming crifis, in which the freedom of the Government is to be decided on for ever: and that though we fhould proceed like prudent and virtuous men, with forefight and moderation, taking care not to touch any of the forms of the Government, yet that we fhould convince the Crown by our conduct, that the wifeft and ableft individual, who fhall ever venture to ftand upon fecret influence againft the confidence of this Houfe, will find, that his abilities, whatever they may be, or whatever they may be fancied, inftead of being a fupport and protection to him, will only be like the convulfions of a ftrong man in the agonies of difeafe, which exhauft the vital fpirit fafter than the fainter ftruggles of weaknefs, and bring on death the fooner.

Such, in a few hours, I truft will be the fate of the Right Hon. Gentleman at the head of the prefent Government: indeed he never compared, in his own mind, his firft appearances in this Houfe, when under the banners of a Right Hon. Gentleman, he fupported the genuine caufe of liberty, with his prefent melancholy ridiculous fituation in it, than he was drawn

into

Into an involuntary parody of the fcene of Hamlet and his mother in the clofet :

> Look here upon this picture, and on this:
> See what a grace was feated in this youth,
> His father's fire—the foul of Pitt himfelf,
> A tongue like his to foften or command,
> A ftation like the Genius of England
> New lighted on this top of Freedom's hill;
> A combination and a form indeed,
> Where every god did feem to fet his feal
> To give his country earneft of a Patriot,

Look you now what follows;

> Dark, fecret influence, like a mildew'd ear,
> Blafting this public virtue: Has he eyes!
> Could he this bright affembly leave to pleafe,
> To batten on that bench!

The Right Hon. Gentleman may profit the lefs from thefe
obfervations, from believing that I feek them, and that I have
a pleafure in making them : if he thinks fo, I can affure him
upon my honour, that he is miftaken ; fo very much miftaken,
that the inconveniencies which the country fuffer at this moment, from the want of a fettled Government, are greatly
heightened to my feelings from the reflection, that they are increafed by his unguided ambition. Our fathers were friends,
and I was taught from my infancy to reverence the name of
Pitt; an original partiality, which inftead of being diminifhed,
was ftrongly confirmed by an acquaintance with the Right Hon.
Gentleman himfelf, which I was cultivating with pleafure, when
he was taken from his profeffion into a different fcene. Let
him not think that I am the lefs his friend, or the mean envier
of his talents, becaufe they have been too much the topic of panegyric here already, and both I and the public are now reap-
ing

ing the bitter fruits of thefe intemperate praifes. " It is
good (faid Jeremiah) for a man to bear the yoke in his youth;"
and if the Right Hon. Gentleman had attended to this maxim,
he would not at fo early a period have declared againft a fubordinate fituation, but would have lent the aid of his faculties
to carry on the affairs of this country, which wanted nothing
but ftability to render them glorious, inftead of fetting up at
once for himfelf to be the firft; becaufe he had too haftily declared againft being fubordinate, and doing it under circumftances, which could not but for a time at leaft (the fpirit of the
Houfe would take care it fhould not be long) difturb and diftract all the operations of Government, and difappoint the moft
folid interefts of the public.

How very different has been the progrefs of my Hon. Friend
that fits near me, who was not hatched at once into a Minifter
by the heat of his own ambition, but who, as it was good for
him to do in the words of the Prophet, " bore the yoke in his
youth," paffed through the fubordinate offices, and matured his
talents in long and laborious oppofitions; arriving, by the natural progrefs of his powerful mind, to a fuperiority of political
wifdom and comprehenfion, which this Houfe had long with delight and fatisfaction acknowledged. To pluck fuch a man
from the Councils of his country in the hour of her diftreffes,
while he enjoyed the full confidence of the Houfe, to give effect
to vigorous plans for her interefts, and to throw every thing
into confufion by the introduction of other men, introduced, as
it fhould feem, for no other purpofe than to beget that confufion,
is an evil that, if we cannot rectify, we may at leaft have leave
to lament: thefe evils are, however, imputed, by the Right
Hon. Gentleman and his colleagues, to another fource—to the
Bill for the regulation of the Eaft Indies, from the mifchiefs of
which they had ftepped forth to fave the country—a language
moft indecent in this Houfe of Commons, which thought it
their duty to the public to pafs it by a majority of above an
hundred; but which was, however, to be taken to be deftructive

7 •   and

and dangerous, notwithſtanding that authority, becauſe it had
been diſapproved by a majority of eighteen votes in the Lords,
ſome of whom I reverence as conſcientious and independent
opinions; but the majority of which ſmall majority voted upon
principles, which the forms of the Houſe will not permit me to
allude to, farther than to ſay, that individual Noblemen are not
always Gentlemen.

Mr. Erſkine, Jan. 12, 1784.

AFTER the teſtimony of ſo many honourable and independent
Gentlemen who have, with one voice, acknowledged, that the
Reſolution before you, for removing the preſent Miniſtry, is, in
the preſent caſe, abſolutely unwarrantable, I riſe with peculiar
ſatisfaction and peculiar advantage; and I muſt therefore be allowed to augur well of the event of this night's Debate. Sir,
I rejoice to ſee the moderation and temper which has ſhewn itſelf on this day; I rejoice that we meet the queſtion fairly, and
that it is not brought forward as that was, upon which this Reſolution is to be founded, and of which it is ſaid to be nothing
more than a mere corollary.—The former, important as it was,
not only to the intereſts, but to the perſonal honour of his Majeſty's preſent Miniſters, was brought before us ſuddenly and
unexpectedly at five o'clock in the morning, when every man's
faculties for ſpeaking, for hearing, and for judging properly,
were exhauſted by a previous Debate of more than twelve hours,
and when a very conſiderable part of the Houſe had departed,
under the firm and very natural perſuaſion that no more queftions of conſequence were likely to be introduced. The preſent queſtion, as it is brought forward at a better hour, and
with a better temper, ſo will it be decided upon, I truſt, with a
better and clearer judgment; and I aſſure you, Sir, I ſhall attempt ſo far to follow the example of thoſe before me, and of
the Right Hon. Gentleman himſelf, (Mr. Fox) as to ſuffer nothing perſonal, nothing indecent, nothing heated, nothing unbecoming

becoming the critical and awful hour in which I fpeak, to efcape out of my lips.

Sir, the firft thing I have to obferve is clearly and diftinctly this; that allowing, for argument's fake, actual credit for every report without doors, and every infinuation that has been made here, the prefent refolution is neverthelefs utterly without foundation.

What, Sir, is the utmoft that reports have ever faid? That my Lord Temple has indifcreetly, wantonly, and, if you will, unconftitutionally reported his Majefty's private opinion on the fubject of the India Bill, and that in the Houfe of Lords that Bill has been by this. means thrown out. But, Sir, is my Lord Temple a Minifter? Your refolution fays his Majefty's prefent Minifters : Lords of the Bedchamber are no Minifters; whom, therefore, are thofe men that your refolution means to flander? I call on the Noble Lord to amend his Motion, and to name in it the names of every Minifter of his Majefty, on whofe character he means that this ftigma fhould alight. Sir, I defy any man even to infinuate that any one of his Majefty's Cabinet has ever had the leaft fhare of that fecret influence upon which this Motion is founded, and for which it is to turn them out of Office. Sir, they are not even accufed; they have a right to be accufed, and they will deny every part of the imputation. The throwing out of the India Bill was a matter previous to their appointment, in which they had no concern, and for which they can fhare no blame, even if I allow, for argument's fake, that blame is due any where.

His Majefty's prefent Minifters have, I affert, been conftitutionally chofen by him who has the fole right to chufe them; and by this refolution they are by this Houfe inftantly turned out.

Sir, is it therefore for their incapacity and infufficiency that you overthrow them? (The Houfe having cried hear! hear!) Mr. Dundas faid, then, Sir, I infift that their incapacity and infufficiency fhall be named in the Motion as the ground upon which

which you at once deny them your confidence. Let this Houfe judge and know upon what ground they give their vote. Let me tell you, Sir, our Conftituents will afk to know, the People of England muft and will know, why Minifters named by his Majefty are inftantly turned out by the Houfe of Commons; turned out, I fay, before they are tried, and condemned before they are accufed.

Sir, if this refolution means any thing, it is in the nature and fpirit of an addrefs, requefting the King to appoint a whole new fet of Minifters. I am forced, therefore, to view it in this light, fince it is in effect pointed at his Majefty, and muft, probably, be followed up by an addrefs in the fame tenor, and to the fame purport.

I beg, therefore, the Houfe will go with me in confidering how the Royal mind muft feel, and what fort of language his Majefty muft hold to himfelf upon fuch an addrefs.

" You fend me back the Minifters I have juft chofen; have I not then the right to chufe my Minifters? Certainly yes, you fay. But what crimes have they committed? What is it they have fo foon perpetrated? Certainly not one act of their Adminiftration is yet paffed. Are they, therefore, without the confidence of the Houfe of Commons? Are they men fo unpopular, fo incapable, fo infufficient, that you will not bear with them even for a moment? Is the Minifter who devotes himfelf to the Houfe of Commons, particularly, fo unpopular and fo incapable? I had chofen him, I had fingled him out as a man, of talents the moft aftonifhing, of integrity the moft uncorrupt, of a reputation the moft extraordinary. I had fondly imagined him the favourite of the Houfe of Commons; I had been taught to fancy, that in celebrating his name, all my People joined in one anthem of praife.

" Is it for this, therefore, that the Houfe of Commons thus inftantly condemns him? Is it on account of his fair fame and unexampled reputation, that I am defired to withdraw my public confidence from fuch a perfon as this? It follows,

no

no doubt, therefore, that you wifh me to fubftitute charaéters
as oppofite as poffible to this. You wifh me then to name
fome man or men in whom I can place no confidence; fome
man or men whom my People execrate, and in whom I myfelf,
in perfeét union with my People, cannot confide. If fuch
men are to be my only choice, if unpopularity, hatred, and
diftruft, are to be the qualifications and the great charaéteriftics
that form a Miniftor in thefe days, it would be matter of the
fincereft joy to me, if the Houfe of Commons would permit
me to wave my choice; let the Houfe of Commons name
their Minifter; let them fearch out perfons fuited to their purpofes, only let me not be forced to play the farce of naming
to them men whom they have fingled out, whom my confcience condemns on public grounds, and whom my People
tell me they do not approve."—Such would be the natural
anfwer of a King, allowing him to be a man of feeling, and
a man of honour, like ourfelves, on fuch an unheard-of Addrefs as this; juft this neceffarily muft be his private fentiments
and foliloquy on the occafion. Therefore, fays he, I would
befeech the Houfe of Commons at once to name the men in
whom alone they are determined to confide. Already we know
- their names. Let us bring in a Bill, naming the Right Hon.
Gentleman and the Noble Lord exclufive Minifters of this
country for a terms of years; for that is precifely the fpirit
and meaning, that, Sir, is the plain Englifh of this refolution,
except indeed that by the prefent Motion, the Houfe of Lords
is exempted from any fhare in the nomination; whereas, if it
was a Bill, it would not be the Houfe of Commons alone that
would name the Minifter of this country.

Sir, we have been told by the Right Honourable Gentleman,
that this is a great conftitutional queftion, and not a queftion
who fhall be Minifter. I meet the Houfe on that ground, and
I beg leave to requeft no more favour than this, viz. that
every man who thinks with the Right Honourable Gentleman,
that this is not a queftion who fhall be Minifter, will vote

with

with him, and I am content that all the reft fhould vote with me. Nay, Sir, if there is any man in this Houfe who in his confcience does not think, that this refolution ferves to name the Right Honourable Gentleman and his colleague, the Mi- nifters and the only Minifters of this country, I am content that all fuch perfons, to a man, fhould vote againft me. I feel on this ground very fure of finding myfelf to-night in a moft refpectable majority indeed.

Sir, I have no perfonal objections or diflike to the Noble Lord or the Right Honourable Gentleman; it is upon clear conftitutional grounds that I refift this vote, and I call upon the independent part of the Houfe that they will ftand forth and maintain the character, the moderation, for thus I will venture to fay they will moft effectually maintain the true con- fequence of this Britifh Houfe of Commons. Let the Houfe look well to its conduct this night, for this night it is about to decide what is the Conftitution of this country. The af- fumption of power and privileges which did not belong to it, has once proved the overthrow of this Conftitution; we are verging towards the fame precipice again, we are claiming to ourfelves the right of appointing Minifters, we are difclaiming the nomination of his Majefty, without caufe and without trial: let us confider this queftion, I fay, without favour or affection, for we are this night deciding on the Conftitution.

Mr. Henry Dundas, Jan. 16, 1784.

THERE are feveral perfons, ufeful and deferving members of fociety, who are unfortunately, at this time, deprived of the happinefs and comfort of enjoying their hereditary poffeffions. Thofe unhappy men have fuffered from the active part which their anceftors or themfelves have taken in a late alarming re- bellion, that had convulfed the empire, and nearly overthrown the prefent Royal Family; but thofe feuds and animofities are now entirely done away, and I can with truth and juftice af- firm, that his prefent Majefty has not in his dominions a more brave

brave and loyal people than thofe who poffefs the mountains of
the north. They have frequently given the moft diftinguifhed
and memorable proofs of their prowefs—their affection to their
country—and their loyalty to the beft of Sovereigns, by ex-
pending their treafures, and often pouring forth their blood for
the defence and glory of Great-Britain.

Surely, therefore, that people who have called forth their
military 'fkill for the honour of their countrymen, who have
often repelled the enemy, who have often added new luftre to
our former glorious atchievements, merit at leaft fome fmall
degree of acknowledgment and gratitude from their fellow-
fubjects.—Their caufe of former mifunderftanding is now no
more; and as they have made themfelves illuftrious in the field,
they claim the protection of the Britifh Adminiftration in the
Cabinet. I need hardly mention, that the people I allude to
are thofe hardy fons of Britain, who inhabited the mountains
in the Highlands of Scotland; a race of men to whom an illuftrious Statefman, in a former war, has paid the higheft tri-
bute of applaufe for their military prowefs.

I am proud to have been the firft who called forth thofe refources from the bleak wilds and mountainous parts of the
North, as they have been the means of reftoring peace and
tranquillity to our dominions, when moft other refources had
been applied in vain. I, like the illuftrious ftatefman to whom
I allude, am not too partial to this or that part of the country,
but freely confefs, that I am ftimulated from motives of juftice and humanity, to make a propofition, which has for its
ultimate object, the reftoration of property to the real proprietors, and giving peace and happinefs to fome individuals
who merit well of fociety. The illuftrious perfon to whom I
allude, is the late Earl of Chatham, a name glorious in the
annals of Great-Britain, and who has fpoken of the hardy fons
of the North in terms of the moft expreffive panegyric. " I
" am not," faid he, " attached to one part of the country
" more than to another. I am above all *local* prejudices. It

" is

" is a matter of indifference to me, whether a man was rocked
" in his cradle on this or on the other fide of the *Tweed*. I
" fought for *merit* where I could find it, aad I found it in the
" mountains of the *North*. Thofe hardy fons anfwered the
" emergency of the times, and I have the honour to boaft
" of being the firft who called their powers forth into action.
" They were in a manner profcribed and forgotten, till I
" emancipated them from their bondage, and helped to wipe
" away the odium which was illiberally fixed upon them. No
" fooner had they taken the field in the fervice of their coun-
" try, than they turned the tide of war, and our manly ex-
" ertions were crowned with fuccefs. They fought our
" battles,—they bled freely in the fame caufe,—and gave the
" enemy to underftand, that Britifh valour was not to be con-
" quered without a fuperior degree of perfonal courage and
" bravery. Their fidelity could only be equalled by their in-
" trepidity, which has fignalized their own and their country's
" renown all over the world."

Thefe were the fentiments of that great Minifter, who had
fhaken the dominions of the French Monarch to the center.
I confefs, I am as free from national prejudices as the much-
efteemed Earl; and adopt the prefent propofition from motives
of found policy. I am not attached to one part of the country
more than to another, and would be happy to embrace an opportunity of fhewing my impartiality. The unfortunate perfons, whofe cafe I now fubmit to Parliament, have been deprived of their eftates for near forty years. I do not call to
queftion the national expediency which has impelled the Legiflature to enact thofe laws that have operated fo rigidly againft
them; but if, by an alteration of the times, and an alteration
of opinion, motives of humanity could be adopted, it would,
I am convinced, be worthy of a Britifh Parliament, to alleviate
the diftreffes of their fellow-creatures, by reftoring to them
thofe poffeffions which they once had a right to enjoy. Their
paft atonement demands it as an act of juftice: their future con-

duct, if we may judge from their paft fervices to the ftate, will make it an act of national wifdom. They have already fuffered fufficiently for the part they have taken in the late rebellion in 1745. They have been profcribed—they have been forced into exile—they have frequently been reduced to the moft deplorable dilemma—in fhort, they have laboured under every fpecies of misfortune and affliction.—Inftead of comfortably enjoying their own lands and poffeffions—inftead of paffing their time in the fweet fociety of their wives and children—inftead of enjoying thofe bleffings which God had in a former period beftowed upon them, they are—excruciating thought!—doomed to a variety of the moft complicated difafters, and forced to feek that afylum and happinefs in a foreign land, which are denied them at their native homes.

I am happy to think that my propofition has been frequently in the contemplation of feveral Adminiftrations. I have often mentioned it to the Noble Lord in the blue ribbon, when he was Minifter of the country; and I can affure the Committee, that, to the honour of his Lordfhip be it faid, he has often entered into the fubject with the greateft warmth and tendernefs; and has on all thofe occafions acted as a man of honour, integrity, and univerfal philanthropy. In juftice to the late Adminiftration, it is proper to mention, that they intended to bring forward a propofition of a fimilar nature. But the different Adminiftrations of this country have of late been fo fluctuating, that it has been impoffible for them to profecute any fuch defign with effect. However, I can now congratulate the People on the occafion, when the prefent Miniftry will have it in their power to alleviate the diftreffes of thofe unfortunate perfons, by reftoring to them their eftates and property.

The immortal Earl of Chatham was the firft man, after the late unfortunate rebellion, that called thofe men forth from obfcurity. He intended to have rewarded them in a fimilar manner, as appears from the encomiums which he beftowed on them fome years ago on a queftion relative to the Stamp-act,

when

when he had an opportunity of doing juftice to the merit of
the Highlanders. This defign, however, was fruftrated; but
it gives me fingular felicity to think, that what was fo happily
begun, under the adminiftration of that illuftrious perfonage,
will be completed under that of his fon; for I am fully perfuaded, that none will object to a meafure which is pregnant
with the moft happy confequences.

Mr. Dundas, Aug. 2, 1784.

END of VOL. I.

www.ingramcontent.com/pod-product-compliance
Lightning Source LLC
Chambersburg PA
CBHW021214270326
41929CB00010B/1121